Future of Business and Fi

The Future of Business and Finance book series features professional works aimed at defining, describing and charting the future trends in these fields. The focus is mainly on strategic directions, technological advances, challenges and solutions which may affect the way we do business tomorrow, including the future of sustainability and governance practices. Mainly written by practitioners, consultants and academic thinkers, the books are intended to spark and inform further discussions and developments.

More information about this series at https://link.springer.com/bookseries/16360

Carlos Lassala · Samuel Ribeiro-Navarrete
Editors

Financing Startups

Understanding Strategic Risks, Funding Sources, and the Impact of Emerging Technologies

 Springer

Cátedra Excelencia y Desarrollo
en Emprendimiento:
De Estudiante a Empresario
DACSA
GROUP
VNIVERSITAT
ID VALENCIA
Facultat ᴅᴇ Economia

Editors
Carlos Lassala
University of Valencia
Valencia, Spain

Samuel Ribeiro-Navarrete
Société Générale
Valencia, Spain

ISSN 2662-2467   ISSN 2662-2475   (electronic)
Future of Business and Finance
ISBN 978-3-030-94060-7   ISBN 978-3-030-94058-4   (eBook)
https://doi.org/10.1007/978-3-030-94058-4

This Springer imprint is published by the registered company Springer Nature Switzerland AG
The registered company address is: Gewerbestrasse 11, 6330 Cham, Switzerland

Foreword

The current information age in which we find ourselves, also known as the digital age, is characterized by technological development by leaps and bounds. These advances are undoubtedly driving the speed at which information and ideas are transmitted. This new era has been accompanied with new technologies and economic growth that have expanded human possibilities to previously unimaginable limits and have totally transformed our lifestyle and the way we interact with our environment. This has brought with it both positive and negative aspects. In an era characterized by abrupt and rapid changes and in the face of global challenges such as climate change, poverty, unemployment, inequality, and lack of education, innovation is becoming increasingly essential to correct the errors and problems of a system that is still far from perfect.

Although ideas can arise at any time, it has been shown that there are certain situations that help to enhance creativity. In addition, great ideas can come from anyone, anywhere, and, therefore, it is important to create and understand mechanisms that reward innovation and help direct individual efforts towards common interests. In the past, it was common for ideas with a high level of innovation and potential for impact to be buried for lack of support. Today, thanks to technological development and the emergence of new business models, this problem is becoming a thing of the past. Based on these reflections, there is no doubt that the proliferation of entrepreneurial activity is a current issue with a very significant impact. From a more detailed point of view, we find the growing popularity of *startups*, whose success is based on their ability to enable an effective transformation of knowledge, generating a high added value to the society.

The objective of this book is to address the financing of the entrepreneurial process as a necessary element to build a solid business fabric, based on the exploitation of new opportunities. The book is structured into two parts. The first takes as a reference the scarcity of financing in the entrepreneurial process and analyzes the different sources of investment available to entrepreneurs depending on the stage of the project. In the second, innovation is linked to the financing of *startups* through the *impact of emerging technologies* and *fintech services* and the support of artificial intelligence. The book concludes with an analysis of the concept of *decentralized finance* (DeFi), as an idea that is changing the financial world, giving rise to new paradigms.

From the Dacsa Group, we fervently support initiatives such as the creation of this book, which reflects the effort in the collection and transmission of valuable knowledge for the society.

Dacsa Group   Araceli Císcar
Valencia, Spain

Contents

Part I
Investment Cycles

Financing Rounds with Private Capital

Dolores Botella-Carrubi, Ana Maqueda-Llongo,
and Alejandro Valero-Moya

1   Introduction

A start-up is an emerging technology-based company whose main problem throughout its development may be a lack of financing. This is because, unlike more traditional business models, these types of companies operate in new and disruptive markets that carry a high risk for the banking sector.

These types of companies need to financially cover any technological development and the market launch until they are able to generate their own resources. However, the lack of indicators and traction in the earliest stages of the business means that these companies do not find bank support and are forced to seek other types of financing, both public and private, and the aim of this chapter is to analyse the characteristics of the latter.

In addition to an in-depth knowledge of all sources of private financing and at what point in a company's life one or the other is appropriate, the preparation for companies to cope with this type of financing will also be discussed in detail.

D. Botella-Carrubi (✉)
Universitat Politècnica de València, Valencia, Spain
e-mail: dbotella@omp.upv.es

A. Maqueda-Llongo
Demium Startups, Valencia, Spain

A. Valero-Moya
Think Bigger Capital, Valencia, Spain

2   At What Point Should a Company Consider Seeking Private Finance?

The amount of capital a start-up needs and the timing of raising it will depend on the initial equity capital that the co-founders have, as well as the nature of the business. Equity capital is the money that the co-founders contribute at the time of incorporation of the company to start the business. But it is not only at the start of the business when a start-up may need external financing, but also during the course of the company's life and its different stages. All of this must be linked to the strategy and milestones that each company has set.

Today, there are a multitude of companies with different business models, some more capital-intensive than others. These companies, in turn, have management teams with different management styles. The growth perspective of a business changes depending on whether we are talking about a traditional business model, for example, a manufacturer and retailer of shoes, or whether the analysis refers to a digital native brand, companies that are created in the online world and their marketing is carried out through their own electronic channels. These businesses have a strong brand identity and a defined community.

Not all businesses have the same needs or interests. This difference is greater when you have a traditional business that sells and invoices shortly after setting up their business and growth is expected as its turnover increases. Therefore, growth occurs organically according to the resources generated by the company itself. However, for business models where the scalability component is fundamental, i.e., where the same resources are used to achieve greater income, entrepreneurs or business people resort to obtaining external, public, private or combined resources to boost growth and design strategies for financial leverage.

In summary, each company will have to analyse the ideal and appropriate moment to seek external financing based on its objectives, and this will require careful planning and preparation.

3   Phases of an Investment Round

When companies launch themselves into the market in search of financing, they must have previously defined a target volume of funds. This volume falls under the term financing or investment round and comes from an Anglo-Saxon nomenclature that arises from the need for entrepreneurs to obtain capital to finance their companies.

This fundraising can be carried out in different settings, individually, where only the entrepreneur and the investor participate, or in one of the most common spaces, the investment forums. These forums consist of rounds in which entrepreneurs show investors the strengths and innovations of their companies. This is a process in which the company gets one or several investors to invest a certain amount of money at a certain time in exchange for a percentage of the company's share capital or a loan, thus acquiring the status of shareholder or stakeholder.

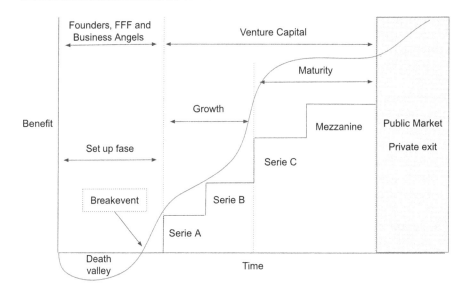

Fig. 1 Development of investment rounds

Closing a successful financing round can take between 3 and 6 months, depending on the experience and contacts of the CEO or other co-founders, as well as the development of the company. For this reason, it is essential to start working on planning in good time, especially if the company does not have sufficient resources or liquid assets in the medium term.

Start-ups have a predefined life cycle that begins in the development phase of the idea (ideation) and where, generally, there is no availability of funds, and ends with the sale of the company, both public and private, or exponential international growth. Obviously, this is without taking into account the fact that 80% of start-ups fail to develop the business model and, therefore, end up being closed by the shareholders.

However, depending on the business model and the stage of the life cycle in which the start-up finds itself, its financial needs will be different. Each phase involves a stage of business development and is associated with financial requirements that are backed by specialized investors in each of these stages. This is shown in Fig. 1.

Each of the phases is described below:

Initial Phase: Pre-Seed Development of the idea with the entrepreneurs' own money or that of friends and family. This is a stage of market research and analysis, competitor analysis, product-market fit and development of the MVP (minimum viable product). The MVP consists of a first version of the product or service without its full functionalities, but which allows validation with the clients of whether the product or service solves the problem that the entrepreneurs had detected in the analysis phase, as well as gathering the necessary information from the clients to finish designing the product or service according to the needs of the market. This phase ends with the validation of the business model and the creation of the necessary team to carry it out.

Early Stage: Seed/Early Stage It is now possible to measure the business and its main variables with more precise numbers. And in many cases, the company begins to make itself known, through the media and its own customers.

Growth Phase: Growth This is one of the most critical phases of a start-up's life cycle. As a general rule, the company is at the break-even point with an appropriate cost structure and is competitive in the market.

Expansion Phase: Growth The benchmark for this phase can be geographical expansion or new products/services offered. Only companies that have achieved a good product-market fit are those that manage to reach this stage.

Sale: Exit It is quite possible that many of the companies that reach the expansion phase will remain in it, enjoying a well-functioning and profitable business. However, there will be many other companies whose objective is to sell the business, either to a potential competitor, to other large companies in the sector or to large private equity funds.

To advance in each of these phases, the company will reach certain milestones, which will help to increase the company's valuation in each round. However, the start-up sector is a sector in which the buying and selling of shares is not regulated. Therefore, supply and demand ultimately determine the price of a company. If the financial planning of the round has been well executed, the share price negotiation may be tilted in favour of the company. Conversely, if the planning has been poorly carried out, it is possible that the market will work against the company, and they will have to reduce the share price in order to raise the same amount of funds.

3.1 Planning and Preparation

The search for all types of financing requires good preparation and planning, and some reference manuals such as Gladstone and Gladstone (2002) can give a more professional view in order to invest as little time as possible in the search and closing of a financing round, as well as to obtain it in the most favourable conditions for the company.

Despite the fact that financial resources and the number of investments continue to grow, there is still more supply of projects to invest in than resources to invest in them. This is why companies need to be very well prepared before starting the search for investment and thus attract the interest of investors before their competitors do.

To this end, there is a good deal of research that needs to be carried out in advance. Some of this is outlined below:

Market and Competition Research By knowing the size of the market in which you operate, you will know what potential market share you can acquire and what resources you need to achieve it, as well as what the current weaknesses of your business are and how you can capitalise on them to distinguish yourself from others.

Financial Model Fundamental document for the planning of the financing strategy. This model is made in a spreadsheet and must contain an exhaustive, historical and future financial analysis of the main variables of the business, as well as the balance sheet, the income statement and the cash flow, the control of the latter being the most important factor. The aim is to know the exact financing needs for the short, medium and long term, depending on the objectives and milestones to be achieved. With this study, the possible future investment rounds are planned for a period of 3–5 years, depending on how far ahead the forecasts are being made. Therefore, this document sets out the company's investment strategy, which will undoubtedly be linked to the company's financial strategy.

Based on the data available, it is difficult to predict the future in a fast-growing business, although it is true that similar and comparable business models can be sought, albeit in other sectors or other markets. The design of the financial model requires the use of a large number of comparative resources to try to achieve realistic approximations.

Caution is one of the fundamental considerations here; therefore, the financial model must be based on the financial reality of the company in order to translate the set strategy into numbers in the future. Thus, there must be consistency with the information transmitted to the investor in the different meetings held, in relation to the current reality of the company and what the future numbers reflect in the spreadsheet. Ambitious financial planning will often generate uncertainty for the investor. Therefore, working with different scenarios depending on the growth of the company is the best option to generate a climate of trust with future shareholders. It may seem obvious, but a financial model does not remain stagnant over time, but needs to be updated according to the company's current situation and the sector in which it operates.

Once the growth variables have been set, the volume of funding required can be defined. On a prudent basis, taking into account an entrepreneur's optimism about the reality of his/her own business, it is advisable to increase the projected financing needs by 20%. The amount of financing needed should at least cover the company's objectives for the next 12–18 months. However, the amount of funding required must be in line with the valuation that will be set for the company, in order not to overly dilute the founding partners' stake at the beginning and in the following phases.

Other Investment Documents
In addition to the financial model derived from the economic-financial analysis of the company, the following documentation are required in order to start the investment search:

1. One Pager or Executive Summary Short version of the company's presentation, which should be no longer than one sheet of paper on both sides.

2. Investor's Deck Support document of the entrepreneur in relation to the investor, the main objective of which is to capture the investor's attention.

3. Business Plan Extended version of the company description, business model and strategy.

4. Cap Table A document that breaks down the company's share capital among the different shareholders and their respective percentages. It is important that the fully diluted version is shown, as this will take into account not only the shares that have been put into circulation through the various capital increases, but also those that will be issued if stock option plans are implemented with employees or if convertible loans are capitalised.

5. Partners Agreement Private document reflecting the agreements adopted for the proper functioning of the relationship between the partners and the company.

6. Other Legal Documentation The company must have available the deeds of incorporation and other capital increases, the convertible notes or the letter of intent (term sheet or LOI) depending on the format of the investment round. The latter two are the documents where the investor shows its interest in investing in the project and the terms of its entry are set out. Once signed, the investment is finalised through the transfer of funds. However, it is important to stress that neither of these are binding.

In more advanced rounds it will be necessary to have a confidentiality agreement (NDA) to ensure that information shared with investors cannot be disclosed to third parties, especially prior to conducting due diligence.

The preparation of all these documents is essential, but it does not mean that the company should not be in possession of any other relevant information that may be requested by an investor in case it needs to carry out a due diligence prior to making its investment.

3.2   Research

Having discussed the investment phases in the life cycle of a start-up, as well as analysing the supporting documentation to support the business in the search for funding, this section explains how to approach the process of finding investors.

The search for investment begins with drawing up a list of potential investors to contact, according to the sectors and stages in which they invest. These lists can be taken from public sources or investment platforms. It is advisable to start with as extensive a list as possible and add to it as the investment round progresses.

After drawing up the list, each of these investors must be screened, both to find out whether they are in the investment phase and also to find out their criteria (rounds, average ticket, sectors with synergies, etc.). Knowing which companies the investor has in its portfolio is essential for designing the strategy with each investor, as well as knowing the companies in its portfolio in case it is already a partner of the competition and to be able to obtain references, so as to avoid having partners who may become conflictive or generate friction in future sales.

3.3   Commercial Process

The search for financing is a process in which the company tries to show its best image in order to attract investors. Therefore, once the company has drawn up a list of potential investors, the first contacts are made.

There are different ways to establish contact with potential investors, such as investment forums, business angel networks or directly through LinkedIn. But possibly one of the most effective is referral, thanks to the fact that other investors or acquaintances in the professional environment can put the entrepreneur in contact with the investors of interest.

It is very important that the company documents the results of each meeting. There are many investors to be dealt with and a lot of information to be gathered.

For a better monitoring of the process it is very useful to use an IRM (investors relationship management) and measure it as a conversion funnel, similar to the one used for customer acquisition.

In this funnel, investors can be placed according to the degree of progress in the process and the degree of interest where they can be classified if there has been interest in the first contact, through the sending of more information to continue analysing the investment opportunity until the final moment of receiving the funds and signing the investment agreement. In this way, you can quickly find out how close or far you are from concluding the financing round.

3.4   Negotiation and Closing

It is possible that the investment round may be delayed and this may jeopardise the liquidity of the company. Therefore, any leverage around the project that may favour the closing of the round should be taken into account. Some examples could be a lead investor, i.e., a benchmark investor who is one of the first to invest a significant amount in the project, which could generate a FOMO (fear of missing out) effect. Showing several months of positive development in the business is another variable that motivates investors. It is also valued to take advantage of the good news of the sector to create expectation.

It is necessary to be prepared for all possible questions that the investor may have or to know how to defend to the hilt all the points of the shareholders' agreement, valuation of the company or other critical points in order to show confidence and conviction. If there is any point of tension with the investor due to neither of the parties giving in on some points, it is also positive to draw some red lines, up to

which the entrepreneur could give in to the investor if he/she is very interested in the
investor's entry into the company.

In the book *How to close funding rounds successfully* by Feld and Mendelson
(2017), special mention is made of the most common negotiation techniques in
venture capital.

3.5 Due Diligence and Auditing

The due diligence (DD) process consists of an exhaustive analysis of the main
employment, commercial and legal aspects of the company to ensure that there are
no potential risks that could influence the business a posteriori and that it would be
impossible to be warned of with the previously mentioned documentation. Therefore, in this process, special emphasis is placed on all contractual obligations of the
company.

At certain stages of the start-up and depending on the type of investor, normally
from VC funds (venture capital) onwards (depending on the amount invested), it is
common to ask the entrepreneur to undergo a due diligence process or request an
external audit of the start-up by a firm of recognised prestige. Both of these will
provide veracity of the start-up's operations and financial accounts, as well as
facilitating knowledge of other possible contracts that may entail a significant
payment obligation.

Unlike a DD, an audit process is based on the opinion of an external and
independent professional on the company's financial statements in accordance
with generally accepted accounting principles. Some companies are obliged to go
through an audit process. However, in companies that do not yet meet these
requirements but are involved in large investment rounds, it gives investors a certain
degree of security that the process has been carried out on a voluntary basis,
provided that an unqualified report is obtained, i.e. that no non-compliances are
detected.

3.6 Post Closing

Depending on the country in which the capital increase takes place, there are a
number of legal obligations, such as the capital increase must be approved by the
general meeting of shareholders, notarised and registered in the commercial registry.
There is an obligation to inform the shareholders arising from the shareholders'
agreement. A regular information channel with the shareholders will benefit the
relationship with the shareholders and even in the follow-on in future rounds.

3.6.1 Post-confirmation of Investment Compliance Procedure

After the closing of transactions, where the company has new shareholders, it is
necessary to follow a strict protocol for the storage of documentation. Such information is highly sensitive for all purposes. Therefore, it must be meticulously recorded.

It should be kept under lock and key and only accessible to the team responsible for updating and maintaining it.

When designing and setting up the documentation system and the information to be included in the registers, it should be borne in mind that this varies according to the stage and legal form of the company receiving the investment. In this respect, companies where the shareholding structure is much more complex or where there is an obligation to be audited, will be subject to much stricter requirements than newly created companies.

Once the investor's commitment has been obtained, appropriate traceability of the origin of the funds must be generated, as well as knowledge of the ultimate beneficiaries behind the entities making the investments.

In this respect, by virtue of the Law on the Prevention of Money Laundering and Terrorist Financing, it is customary for investors to complete a KYC (Know your customer), a basic document specifying the investor's key data (address, name, main activity, etc.) which will later be used to draw up the legal information and obtain proof of the origin of the funds.

The KYC contains the following information:

- Customer statements and risk factors, relating to the sector of business and commercial activity or countries in which they operate, as well as whether they have held past or present public office or are involved in criminal activities.
- General information concerning the customer depending on whether the customer is a natural or legal person: name and surname or company name, legal status, date of birth or incorporation, nationality, tax domicile for communication purposes and identification document (type, number, country of issue, expiry date).
- Origin of funds and banking entities. Last beneficial owners (only for institutions), specifying the investors with more than 25% of the shares of the investing company.
- The tax owner (for entities only). This case is specific to those investors who have several holding structures. Where the natural person who has effective control may be behind several interlinked companies.

The registration of the investor's documents is essential to provide a record of the company's analysis. In this way, the finance or compliance department can ensure that the benchmark investor did and does meet all the criteria for acceptance of the transaction. The documents that should be included in the investor's register are as follows:

For a natural person:

- Passport or national identity card.
- Tax identification card.
- Document accrediting the legal origin of the funds. For this purpose, it is usual to have the latest tax return filed.

- Bank certificate issued by the bank showing the account number from which the payment is made.

For a legal person:

- Memorandum of association.
- Articles of association, shareholders' agreement and bylaws.
- List of the directors of the company.
- Passport or national identity card of the representatives or signatories.
- Deed accrediting the power of attorney by which the signatory acts.
- Tax identification card.
- Activity of the investor, providing: (a) latest annual accounts or (b) latest annual taxes filed.
- Bank certificate issued by the bank showing the account number from which the payment is made.

All documentation must be updated at the time of modification or expiry of the documents in order to keep the file complete and up to date.

Once all this information has been collected, we must include the documents evidencing the closing of the transaction, adherence to the shareholders' agreement, convertible notes and any other additional document generated and signed by the investor in the process.

3.6.2 Documentation to Be Received by the Investor upon Completion of the Transaction

After the collection of the investor's information, the assessment of suitability and the registration of the capital increase transaction with the notary, the investor becomes a stakeholder or shareholder in the company and obtains political power within it.

Therefore, once the transaction has been registered, it is essential to send investors a summary of the content of the transaction which sets out the final outcome of it. The documentation to which investors will have access will be as follows:

- Copy of the public document specifying the holdings or shares that have been given to each investor and the economic counterpart of the transaction. In this way, existing and new shareholders know the status of the company's assets.
- Cap table. Once the investment has been made, the old shareholders will reduce their percentage to accommodate the new shareholders, which is known as dilution, so the percentage distribution of the invested company will change. Both new and old shareholders will receive this table with the shareholding situation of the company after the capital increase.

4   Types of Funding Round

Having analysed all the qualitative and quantitative aspects, this section focuses on the typology of financing rounds. In the world of start-ups, it is identified by a set of acronyms and concepts derived from Anglo-Saxon terminology.

These small private financing windows for unlisted companies can range from contributions from non-professional investors of no more than 50 euros to investments of several 100 million euros led by large investment funds.

In order to try to narrow down the ranges of such operations, there is a nomenclature based on three main aspects:

- Amount invested.
- Valuation of the company.
- Purpose of the investment.

In any case, this is an inefficient measurement system that fluctuates depending on the regions or markets where the company operates. Based on the calculations in the annual report issued by Pitchbook (2020) in certain phases the amount of investment and valuation in the same stage, for example, pre-seed, can be up to 4 times higher in the American market versus the European market.

This means that if a pre-seed start-up in Europe gets a million euros, a start-up in the same stage but in the United States would get a larger injection of capital to tackle the same 'stage'.

There are standards for defining each of the phases, which are outlined below and summarised in Fig. 1 and Table 1.

Table 1 Phases and characteristics of the investment stages

Investment phase	Investment	Characteristics
Pre-seed	5–500 thousand euros	– Validation of the business model – Configuration of the promoter team – Problem-solution – Stage with the greatest risk/return potential
Seed	500 thousand euros to 2 million euros	– Recurring sales – Validation phase – Organic month-on-month increase in sales – First signs of the power of scalability
Series A	2–10 million euros	– Scalability – Expansion – Phase where profit generation begins
Series B	10–20 million euros	– Leadership in a given market – Preparation for aggressive expansion and positioning as a benchmark in the sector – Growth with maximum liquidity – Pre-IPO phase

Pre-seed The initial phase of the project where a quick validation of the minimum viable product is sought in order to know the potential that the solution proposed to the market may have. Phase where the first customers who are willing to pay for an unfinished product enter.

Seed The seed stage is one of the most dangerous stages in business development. It is common for many planning mistakes to be made at this stage, leading to excessive dilution mainly due to financial planning that is misaligned with real cash flow needs and the development of the business. In the seed stage, the company is perfecting the product and starts to see recurring revenues, which confirms that there is a need in the market.

Series A The start of the series (A, B, C) marks the beginning of the scalability and consolidation of the business model. In the company's first series, the main focus is on scaling the business to maximise profits and broaden the range of markets in which it operates.

Series B After business consolidation (stabilisation of revenues, stable margins) it is common for companies to seek a series B and C to consolidate the revaluation of the company and adjust its value prior to an IPO (Initial public offering) or aggressive expansion and growth in pursuit of market or sector leadership.

The dilution of existing investors in each of the financing rounds is between 10 and 20% depending on the stage and business plan. Excessive dilution in each of these rounds could lead to an excessive loss of control by the founding team.

5 Types of Private Financing

For each of the financing phases described above, there are alternatives to turn to in the search for private financing. However, each of them has different characteristics when it comes to investing in start-ups, whether due to the stage the start-up is in, the amount of money to be contributed or the strategy when it comes to entering or exiting the investee's capital. The following list shows the types of financing according to investment capacity, from the lowest to the highest capacity:

- *Incubators and accelerators*: Are the most suitable to use in the pre-seed phase. When the company is still in the MVP or launch development phase, starting to validate its business model and obtaining its first metrics.
- *Business Angels (BA)*: A business angel, also known as smart money, is a private individual investor who invests his or her own capital, but has knowledge and experience in start-up investment. In addition, they usually have an important network of contacts, either through their own professional experience or by belonging to business angel networks. This is why they are usually beneficial for the development of the company. The investment that a business angel can

provide depends a lot on the person, ranging from pre-seed to growth rounds. They can be found on the main start-up investment platforms, investment forums of BA networks or business schools, as well as being mentioned in the news as participants in the main investment rounds of the ecosystem. Fund finders usually have access to most of them. However, the fees are often prohibitive in the early stages of a start-up's life.

- *Equity crowdfunding*: is the financing of a project by multiple investors through collective investment platforms, i.e. a project can be jointly financed by many investors without the need for them to invest a large amount of money. This allows less qualified investors to experiment with other investments and, in turn, these investors will take part of the company's share capital. The projects to be invested in are previously filtered by the platforms and support the whole investment process.

- *VC*: Venture Capital. VC funds, for the most part, start investing in the growth phase. When the start-up needs a large injection of capital to scale the business. They may cover the round in its entirety or invest with other specialised investors. They do not get involved in the business in the same way as a business angel, but they usually demand a seat on the board of directors to exercise a supervisory role. In addition, as VC managers have to thoroughly justify all investments to their investors, they put the start-up through a due diligence process.

- *Venture Debt Funds or Convertible Equity Loans*: This is another financing tool with the difference that most of the loan is repaid at maturity (between 3 and 5 years depending on the development of the business) and a small part is converted into shares in the company. They carry with them above-market interest rates resulting from higher risk-taking. They participate in rounds in which there is already a business angel or a benchmark VC with the aim of not assuming the main risk of the investment and taking a minority stake. Even so, they usually seek a seat on the board of directors to support the development of the business.

- *Family Office*: are high net worth families seeking to diversify their investments by investing in start-ups. Traditionally, the main business of family offices has always been the holding and exploitation of real estate assets, mainly because of the high profitability and tax benefits. However, following the tax reforms after the 2008 crisis, many family offices have found great potential for growth in the start-up sector, which in turn allows them to obtain large tax capital gains.

- *Public funds linked to private funds*: Public money invested by private venture capital managers, among other things, for the promotion and development of R&D, digitalisation and start-ups. It all leads to the use of mixed investment funds for further support.

6   Venture Capital Financing Formats

The final decision to be made is the format in which the capital inflow into the company will be structured. Within the start-up ecosystem, there is a wide range of solutions for financing start-ups. The main ones are detailed below:

6.1   Capital Increase

A capital increase refers to an increase in a company's shares or holdings as a result of the entry of new capital into the company.

This capital increase is not only intended to grant shares to new investors, but can also be a new distribution of shares among existing shareholders who have decided to increase their presence in the company.

One of the main disadvantages of designing a structured financing round entirely through a capital increase is that the availability of funds is released at the moment when the partners become, to all intents and purposes, shareholders in the company's share capital.

It is, therefore, common to carry out a combination of different types of financing so as not to compromise the company's liquidity if external factors affect the marketing of the new shares to be issued.

This type of operation is formalised by means of an investment commitment between the parties and a capital increase subscription contract to be accepted by all existing investors.

6.2   Convertible Note

Convertible notes are the second most common instrument used to raise funds for a start-up company. The concept of a convertible note is simply a loan between two entities, whether individuals or legal entities, which is entered into privately between the parties.

Another of the main uses of convertible notes is the possibility of setting a price range within which the final valuation of the company will be set. At certain stages of growth it may not be possible to fix an objective valuation based on metrics. This would, therefore, result in excessive dilution for shareholders.

This mechanism is structured on the basis of a cap and a floor, where the floor is the minimum valuation at which the loan will be converted in the event that the objective for which the convertible notes were designed is not achieved; it is usual to set the floor at the post money value of the last round so as not to harm existing partners. On the other hand, the cap is the maximum valuation at which the loan will convert. This happens when the company has achieved its targets and is raising more capital at a higher valuation. It is a mechanism that protects the investor who has taken a risk before the previous investors. The cap, unlike the floor, is a mechanism that protects current investors from over-dilution.

This type of loan has a series of specific conditions that greatly limit the lender's political rights, since it is a financial instrument that seeks to solve a company's short-term lack of liquidity, with the objective of ultimately executing a financing round.

It is, therefore, common to see convertible note contracts subject to a certain periodicity and the possibility of converting them into capital at the time the company deems appropriate, in accordance with the criteria set out in the contract. They usually contain a minimum interest rate that never materialises.

6.3   Venture Debt

Venture debt is another of the financing formats that is gaining momentum within the venture capital sector. It is essentially a financial product that is a hybrid between direct equity investment and a current loan. The operation is more similar to that of a loan, but with the peculiarity that the lender takes a minority stake in the form of equity in order to reduce the risk/reward of the operation. Unlike a standard loan, venture debt is divided into two transactions.

First, through an equity kicker, which is usually around 25% of the total loan, equity equivalent to that percentage of the loan is delivered to the lender. For example, for a venture debt of 1,000,000 euros and an equity kicker of 25%, 250,000 euros will be converted into equity at the valuation agreed between the investor and the company.

The second transaction is the signing of the loan. Despite having an equity kicker, this does not mean that the 250,000 euros referred to above no longer has to be repaid. On the contrary, the entire capital loaned by the venture debt must be repaid. This is one of the most common sticking points for entrepreneurs, as it can seem abusive. Not to be overlooked is the trend in the sector, where 80% of start-ups die before achieving profitability. This situation forces venture debt funds to cover this risk by taking shares. Otherwise, it would be impossible to undertake such transactions. It would become an operation more typical of a public entity that promotes entrepreneurship than of a fund, whose objective is to provide a return to its investors.

However, compared to other more traditional financial products, it is a more efficient method of financing for start-ups or companies seeking to increase their value quickly in the coming years where they will have to repay the loan money but will be paying it back with much higher income than they had at the point of origin. This financial product is not recommended for companies without high revaluation expectations as the interest and equity kicker can weigh heavily over the repayment period. Table 2 below shows an example of equity and venture debt financing of a company.

A start-up company is increasing its sales by an average of 20% month-on-month and is considering taking out a loan to accelerate sales and business development. Loan target 1,000,000 euros.

Table 2 Comparison of venture debt and equity

	Venture debt	Equity
Initial valuation of the company	5,000,000 euros	5,000,000 euros
Interest	7–12%	Na
Equity	25%	100%
Cost of the loan for 3 years	195,715 euros	0 euros
Valuation in 3 years' time	12,000,000 euros	12,000,000 euros
Cost of buying back the shares	500,000 euros	1,999,999 euros
Total cash outflow (interest + repurchase of units + repayment)	1,695,715 euros	1,999,999 euros

By the same criteria, it can be assumed that traditional (non-venture debt) loan financing may be a more efficient method of financing the company. However, the risk limits set by financial institutions prevent them from entering into operations of this type, mainly due to the inherent risk of the business.

On the other hand, venture debt tries to compensate for the excess risk with a portion of equity that will help it to achieve a return that is in balance with the risk assumed.

As has been shown above, the great danger of venture debt is not achieving a clear revaluation with the loan granted. In this case, both the equity provided and the loan repayment can strangle the business model financially.

6.4 Equity for Services

There are alternative forms of early-stage company financing that are not based on capital injections into the company. These forms of financing are based on paying for the cost of a given service with shares or equity in the company that is to receive the service.

This financing model is common when the objective of a financing round is highly focused on contracting or optimising a specific resource, such as technological development, marketing campaigns or other services.

The most common forms of equity for services are:

- *Tech for equity*: The aim is to subcontract technological development work that the company itself cannot take on.
- *Legal for equity*: On certain occasions, there are complex legal processes (sales of companies) that entail an unaffordable additional cost for the company.
- *Media for equity*: Campaigns in more traditional media tend to cost far more than the usual budgets of start-ups. Therefore, this type of financing is the bridge between the classic media of large companies and growing companies.

In the vast majority of cases, these financial instruments are executed through a private contract, the issuance of an invoice for the services and the capitalisation of this invoice in the company's share capital. Thanks to this operation and the intangibility of the business, it is possible to reduce the theoretical value of the services when the service provider understands the potential for revaluation of the work performed.

6.5 Crowdfunding

Crowdfunding was one of the most widely used financing instruments after the 2008 crisis because it gave access to anyone (professional and non-professional investors) to invest amounts from 50 euros. However, the professionalisation of the sector and the emergence of regulation have relegated this method of financing to the bottom of the list of most used financial products.

It is even common to think of crowdfunding as a financing instrument that is used once it has not been possible to close deals with other instruments.

Crowdfunding is one of the best instruments to finance engineering developments or physical products (not software). Physical products or products that will be sold directly to the end customer tend to attract much more attention from non-professional investors and can also be a useful financial instrument to achieve the first pre-sales.

An example would be the case of a crowdfunding aimed at financing the development of a new comb against hair loss and the development of software to make the user experience easier. An uncomplicated product with a good marketing positioning will get many more investors than a complex one.

The understanding of this method of financing is based on the syndication of a large number of retail investors to take a stake in a company. The main problem with this method of financing is the fragmentation of the investor base within the company.

This fragmentation generates a legal and supervisory burden that often slows down decision-making within the company. Spanish regulation, for example, sometimes requires the signature of all partners (regardless of their shareholding). Therefore, a fragmented cap table impedes agile decision-making.

6.6 IPO

IPOs (Initial public offerings) are forms of financing that companies undertake mainly to provide liquidity to investors who wish to buy or sell shares.

Once the maturity stage of the company has been reached, the investors who have accompanied the company in the growth phase have finished their journey within the company and are looking for liquidity windows to allow more conservative investors to enter.

Generally, investment banks are used as assistants in this type of operation, as it is these entities that have the contacts and investors for this first phase, known as book building.

As part of the service provided by banks, they are responsible for generating supply and demand in the first phase of the public offering, with the entity itself providing the necessary guarantees for the operation.

Although it is true that in more financially developed markets such as the American or the English market, it is common for start-ups to end up going public on a listed market to compete on equal terms with the rest of the operators. In this way, the 'startup' journey is usually over and the corporate journey begins, where the regulations themselves require the professionalisation of the different areas of the business.

7 Conclusions

As has been made clear throughout the chapter, there are a large number of variables that determine the feasibility or success of an efficient financing strategy.

This success lies primarily in planning, understanding and determining the needs of the company and the financing objective. Making the right decisions when it comes to financing the company will be of great benefit in the medium and long term. Therefore, it is necessary to know what tools the company has at its disposal to generate demand among investors and what the returns will be for them.

In turn, the strengths that are attractive to investors need to be identified, as well as which type of investors and which financial product is best suited to that type of investor.

At the end of the day, the positive conclusion of a financing round is measured when both the investor and the company are satisfied with the process, timing and mechanism for achieving the financing objective and profitability for both parties.

References

Carver, L. (2011). *Venture capital valuation: Case studies and methodology* (Vol. 631). Wiley.
Demaria, C. (2020). *Introduction to private equity, debt and real assets: From venture capital to LBO, senior to distressed debt, immaterial to fixed assets*. Wiley.
Feld, B., & Mendelson, J. (2017). *Venture deals: Be smarter than your lawyer and venture capitalist* (3rd ed.). Wiley.
Gladstone, D., & Gladstone, L. (2002). *Venture capital handbook: An entrepreneur's guide to raising venture capital*. FT Press.
López, J. (2019). *La farsa de las startups: la cara oculta del mito emprendedor*. Catarata.
Nesbitt, S. L. (2019). *Private debt: opportunities in corporate direct lending*. Wiley.
O'Malley, T., Walsh, J., & Watts, W. (2004). *Investment adviser's legal and compliance guide*. Wolters Kluwer.
Pitchbook. (2020). *Annual European VC valuations report*.

Angel Investing Startups

Edward Graham

1   Some Angel Investing Background

In the USA, an angel investor is 'qualified', with income and net worth requirements. But, with crowdfunding and other avenues of less-regulated digital funding (sometimes of over $1 million, by hundreds or thousands of 'investors'), and with the evolution of such platforms as GoFundMe or Kickstarter, the angel universe has expanded greatly in the early twenty-first century. Discussion here will focus on the traditional qualified angel investor.

In the USA, a qualified or accredited investor (affirmed by Matthew Frankel, CFP in https://www.fool.com/investing/2018/02/14/what-is-a-qualified-investor.aspx) must have individual, or joint, income of $200,000, or $300,000, 'during each of the previous two full calendar years, and a reasonable expectation of the same for the current year'. Security and Exchange Commission (SEC) guidelines further require an individual or joint (referencing both husband and wife) net worth of $1 million, excluding the primary residence.

In a simple search of 'total angel funding in the US per year', a wealth of information is provided. The Small Business Administration (SBA) estimates there are 'now over 250,000 active angel investors in the USA .... providing funding to about 30,000 firms per year.' The Angel Capital Association allows that the typical angel group averages just over 40 members, and invests around $2.4 million per year in just under ten deals. Such angel groups, providing funding to the universe of startups, exist worldwide.

E. Graham (✉)
University of North Carolina Wilmington, Wilmington, NC, USA
e-mail: edgraham@uncw.edu

© The Author(s), under exclusive license to Springer Nature Switzerland AG 2022   21
C. Lassala, S. Ribeiro-Navarrete (eds.), *Financing Startups*, Future of Business and Finance, https://doi.org/10.1007/978-3-030-94058-4_2

1.1 Additional Background and Unregistered Securities

The 'unregistered securities' often used to fund startups must be sold by firms or individuals that 'verify' the investor(s) 'eligibility'. But in this investor's experience, that affirmation is rarely pursued. Informally, but practiced by angel groups across the USA, an investor's qualification will be plainly visible to other angel investors, through an awareness of the investor's profession, family background, or other visible 'deals'. That visibility alone will suffice, in most cases, to affirm that person's accredited status.

Among several mid-Atlantic angel groups in the USA, eligibility to join an angel group is framed by a minimum individual income of $200,000 and a net worth of $2 million, though this author is unaware of any investor ever having to 'prove' their accreditation with past years' tax returns or an audited personal financial statement. The US regulations, however, seem to imply that such proof of qualification is required. The SEC wishes to protect the unsophisticated investor from the total losses that often attach to angel investments, such loss more easily borne by a relatively wealthy accredited investor.

1.2 GoFundMe, Kickstarter and SPACs

The SEC nonetheless has allowed the evolution of GoFundMe and Kickstarter, mentioned above, and special purpose acquisition companies or SPACs, (https://www.marketplace.org/2021/02/18/whats-a-spac-a-simple-guide-to-the-investment-trend/), with total deal values since the end of 2019 of over $100 billion. Those vehicles allow largely unfettered access to small risky startups without the regulatory oversight that attaches to angel investors and angel-investing groups, as with the one in which this author is a member.

Rather than being required to meet the criteria of an accredited investor, with assets of several million dollars and annual income in the low to mid-six figures (in dollar terms), these new platforms allow the 'average' investor with only a few thousand dollars (or even a few hundred, as with experiences portrayed in the daily press in early 2021) to participate. https://www.cnbc.com/2021/01/30/gamestop-reddit-and-robinhood-a-full-recap-of-the-historic-retail-trading-mania-on-wall-street.html.

1.3 GameStop, Reddit and Robinhood

The experience of GameStop, Reddit and Robinhood illustrate this trend: GameStop, 'a struggling brick-and-mortar video game retailer', finished January of 2021 at over 15-times its value early in the year. Its 'value' had been highlighted by members of Reddit, at reddit.com, who bet against the high published short interest of GameStop; they bought the stock, thus 'squeezing' the 'shorts'. The shorts, of course, were betting on a decline in the price of GameStop stock.

Recall that a short sale is a sale, by an individual or institutional investor, that is placed *before* that investor has taken delivery of the stock. With this sale, the investor is either hedging another investment that is highly correlated with the stock being sold short (thus effectively buying insurance against a decline in the highly correlated other investment) or is betting that the stock price will decline, planning a later purchase at a lower price. [These details on the character of a short sale are provided as 'the literature' suggests that many readers—even the best-credentialed—are unfamiliar with the nature of a short sale.]

Many of these traders squeezing the short-sellers used the Robinhood trading platform. No special investor accreditation requirements were attached to Reddit users using the Robinhood platform to buy GameStop. The rapid runup in GameStop's stock price led to the near insolvency of Robinhood, as it sought to clear trades of GameStop, whose value often moved over 50% daily. Recall that Redditt is simply a 'network of communities' online with each community sharing some interest, as the day-traders that pushed up the value (and down, with their later sales) of GameStop.

The experience of Redditt members, using Robinhood to invest in GameStop, is mentioned here as it underscores, frankly, much of the near chaos that can exist absent the guidelines framing angel investing. For the accredited (and 'sophisticated', according to the regulatory language in the USA) angel investor, much of the entire reasoning for the angel investor derives from a wish to avoid events such as those that unfolded surrounding GameStop in early 2021.

2   The Idea of Angel Investing Explored

Broadly considered, 'angel capital', or funds provided by angel investors, is the primary source of capital for firms in their earliest stages. While 'friends, family and other fools' may provide the very first monies invested in a startup, it is the angel investor, described above, that provides the first arms-length funding. This is a capital structure event—angel investors 'live' on the right-hand side of the balance sheet—occupying an equity-related account among the long-term accounts on that side of the balance sheet.

These angel investments are made before any public offering, like an initial public offering or IPO. The special purpose acquisition companies or SPACs, introduced above, may 1 day largely displace the angel investor, but the existence and role of the angel investor will, by their very nature, remain. SPACs circumnavigate the regulatory hindrances confronting a firm considering an IPO, but the angel investor commits resources earlier in the firm's 'journey'.

2.1   Angel Investors Across the USA

An angel investor is someone that often also provides special guidance, as with being a member of a firm's advisory committee or board of directors, along with funds, to small startups or individual entrepreneurs. https://www.investopedia.com/terms/a/angelinvestor.asp.

That funding and, commonly, guidance, encourages a new firm down a more productive path. While no precise set of institutional guidelines exists in the USA for 'angel investing', the markers that start this monograph—concerning the guidelines for a sophisticated or accredited investor—provide a general backdrop. It is this angel investor's experience that the angel investor acting alone, (as with a 'lone wolf') or along with an angel group, brings to a startup.

2.1.1 Angel Investors in the Carolinas: North and South Carolina

The state of North Carolina, on the mid-Atlantic coast of the USA, includes a number of these groups: The Carolina Angel Network, the Wilmington Investor Network and the Piedmont Angel Network come to mind. Each of these, and many others across the Carolinas (this term encompassing both North and South Carolina, states midway between Florida and New York) and across the USA (and around the world), exist to fill the 'funding gap for early stage startup businesses'. Direct and indirect membership in North Carolina angel groups alone exceeds 500 people. Across the USA, tens of thousands of investors loosely identify themselves as 'angel investors'.

2.1.2 An Angel Group Example

Founded in 2005, the Wilmington Investor Network (WIN) invests between $250,000 and $750,000 per year in various startups. WIN is headquartered in Wilmington, NC, a city of around 200,000 on the Mid-Atlantic coast of the USA. Relative to other angel groups across the USA, WIN is small—regularly investing less than $1 million per year in total—but long-lived; it has been around for over 15 years, and many of its current members are drawn from the original membership. Most of the firms considered by WIN, and which later present at the formal monthly WIN meetings (which migrated to ZOOM for the 12 or 14 months of COVID), are from North Carolina or the southeastern USA. There are between 12 and 20 active members. Investments are made by WIN, with funds invested by individuals.

There is a modest annual membership fee, paid by WIN members, for accounting work completed on behalf of WIN, and to cover the expenses of monthly meetings. Those meetings, abbreviated by COVID but back in session in the late spring of 2021, take place in office settings and typically include a light meal for the 90–120-min sessions. At those meetings, past investments are reviewed, and new firms—commonly with a 20–40 min PowerPoint presentation by one of the founders—present their business ideas and solicit both financial commitments from the angel group, and management insights as well.

This is typical of angel groups across the USA, and around the world; the new firms come to the groups seeking both money, and guidance. In fact, many angel groups will require a seat on the new firm's board of directors, if not some other role in management. The angel groups do not simply invest their resources, and then wish the new firm well! Angel groups are far more engaged with the new firms than is the norm among investors in the stock markets.

2.1.3   Angel Investment Experience

WIN invests in four to ten startups each year. Individual members choose the deals they wish to be a part of, and the investment is made through WIN, the angel group. Since its founding, many of the firms, into which WIN members invested, have exhausted their resources and gone out of business. Others have been absorbed by acquiring firms. The slim minority of WIN 'deals' that have provided a positive return to investors have generated exits representing returns of 2–12 times the initial investment. WIN's experience—with most firms breaking even or going out of business—is typical of angel groups across the USA. It is a highly risky universe in which the angel group exists.

Details concerning WIN's experience are proprietary, but it is widely known that WIN's investments in the biotech, financial and digital realms have met with mixed results. The need for angel investors to be 'qualified', as described in the opening remarks of this chapter, is underscored by WIN's experiences.

3   Extant Research

A substantial library of research reminds the reader of the critical importance of a firm's capital structure—of the manner with which the firm 'builds' the right-hand side of its balance sheet. It is the duty of any manager to gather resources, the sources of which are revealed by that 'right-hand side'. Once gathered, the firm manages those resources to generate cash flows to satisfy debt requirements and to reward the risk-taking equity holder. The equity holder near the front of the line is the angel investor.

3.1   The Academic

For the theoretical academic, in a frictionless world—the source of a firm's funding should not matter. If there are no taxes, or transaction costs, free flows of information, and borrowing costs shared by everyone, the configuration of a firm's balance sheet does not matter. The mathematical tenets of this premise hold simply that 'a company's capital structure is not a factor in its value'. (See *Investopedia*, and an article by James Chen in April of 2020.)

This theory has underpinned discussions of corporate finance in the decades since it was first developed in 1958. But with a relaxation of its varied assumptions, the theory—generously treated here—'evolves'. If the costs of debt, for example, become tax-deductible, then a firm operating in this theoretical world would employ only debt as a source of capital. That outcome is intuitive—if costs of equity, as with either dividends or capital gains—are *not* deductible against the firm's taxable income, then debt will—again, *theoretically*—become not just the primary source of funding for the firm, but the *only* source. This theory, of funding-irrelevance in a frictionless world, and of nothing- but-debt-funding in a world with corporate income taxes and deductible interest expenses, is developed in Modigliani and Miller (1958, 1963).

In a practical sense, and illustrated in an encyclopaedia of research since the seminal work by Modigliani and Miller (1958, 1963), the businessperson assembling their capital structure in the 'real world' depends upon a multitude of capital sources, and the angel investor is but one of the candidates for the funding needs of the firm early in its life cycle.

3.2   The Practitioner

As highlighted by Benjamin and Margulis (2000), the practitioner may select from various capital sources to meet their early, and continuing, funding needs. As with Exhibit 4.1 on page 61 of the Benjamin and Margulis text, *Angel Financing: How to Find and Invest in Private Equity*, those sources include research grants (popular since the 1990s in the varied biotech and other technology sectors), incubators, and sundry private and public development programmes. The latter have become especially prominent over the last two or three decades, as communities compete for new businesses. The recent experiences of New York City, and other major US communities, in trying to lure Amazon with its site selection for a second headquarters, come to mind.

Partnerships with universities are also common sources of intellectual and physical capital, if not direct funding. Duke University, in the southern USA, for example, provides new firms (which are often developed by members of the university faculty) with access to the skills of its faculty along with office and laboratory space. Schools like Duke, upon providing the imprimatur of its partnership along with human and physical capital, then take—typically—a 5–10% equity ownership. The presence of Duke, or other schools like MIT or UC Berkley, on the board of a startup often encourages angel investors to provide additional needed funding.

Other capital sources—not considered in detail here, but worthy of mention—include joint ventures, licensing deals (particularly popular with ideas requiring large scale manufacturing or distribution capacities), strategic alliances, and 'direct investing by financial institutions'.

For the firm with existing sales, and beyond the angel-funding stage, venture capital and traditional bank lending become practical, though banks will often require personal guarantees from the firm's founders to fulfil lending requests.

4   Angel Investing in the Twenty-First Century

Large private equity funds and family offices have grown in importance, as well, over the last few decades. 'Family offices' is a generic term and includes those groups managing the wealth of such well-known families as the Rockefellers or Carnegies in the USA, or lesser-known families with substantial wealth. Those funds, and family offices, exist alongside, or in concert with, angel investors. In fact, the 'currency', or capacity of an angel group to attract prospective firms in which to invest, will often be a function of the family offices, or high-net-worth individuals, that are members of the angel group. The varied angel 'networks' elicit interest from new business founders by developing reputations for being viable funding sources. The new businesses, in search of angel funding, after personal and family resources have been exhausted, turn to these networks for directions.

Word circulates in the startup communities of the likelihood of a given angel group providing needed funding, often as a function of the membership in that group of a well-heeled family office. Though the family office or wealthy individual may have the scale and capacity to enter the venture capital (or VC) realm, those offices and individuals often make angel-scale investments (of $1 million or less, typically) in the earliest stages of a new business.

Every experienced angel investor has witnessed extraordinary gains being earned by 'angels'. Ram Shriram https://www.venturegiants.com/the-angel-investors-behind-google/ comes to mind, his initial investment in Google of less than $250,000 now worth billions. Ram Shriram highlights a principal feature of successful angel investors: they are not only 'investors', as with an employee building a retirement account over several decades, they are also visionaries with talents to both deploy their initial investment and to guide the startup as it grows. Ram Shriram's focus on creativity and world-changing technologies underscore this feature of the successful angel investor; he has searched for and found 'team(s)' that provide 'different and unique solutions to existing problems' around the world.

4.1   In the USA

Qualified individuals across the USA have a broad menu of options as they become angel investors. From the largest financial communities in and around New York City, to the medical environs near Boston and in the Midwest, to the high-tech neighbourhoods in or near Silicon Valley and Seattle, a great many alternatives exist.

Benjamin and Margulis (2000) highlight some of the angel venues that have existed in the USA for two decades or more. Many of these organisations exist in concert with, and often with the support of, local and regional governments. The Atlanta Development Authority (3, p. 153) is such an entity that 'represents a partnership of the public and private sectors'. The Capital Network https://thecapitalnetwork.org/about/ in Boston is another such organisation. It is a non-profit organisation that serves to guide 'early stage entrepreneurs' as they 'raise seed capital'. Its membership includes Boston Harbor Angels, a group of investors who have partnered with the Wilmington Investor Network on several, primarily medical, startups. A multitude of other angel groups that invest alongside the Capital Network is listed on its home page.

That is the nature of angel investing in the USA. Many angel groups exist with a focus on a given area, as with Boston Harbor Angels in Massachusetts and the Angels Forum in California. Those groups, like most, will also entertain investments from other areas across the USA, and often internationally. But some groups, like the

North Carolina IDEA Fund, are 'committed to supporting entrepreneurial ambition' in a single location or area.

Angel funds across the USA, with hundreds listed on the internet, have met with varied success since their inception with family offices over 100 years ago. As the concept and regulation of angel funds have matured over the last two or three decades, a great many costly lessons have been learned by thousands of investors, and fortunes earned by a lucky few.

4.2   Across the World

Angel investing is hardly unique to the western side of the Atlantic. Europe has witnessed an explosive growth in the funding of startups over the last 20 or more years, with the time since the falling of the Berlin Wall being especially meaningful. Startups, particularly since the early 1990s, have portrayed remarkable success, generally with the assistance of angel investors. The fastest-growing firms in Poland, the Czech Republic, Germany, France, the UK and Spain, for example, have often had their initial growth funded by the European equivalent of the angel investor in the USA.

Recent remarks in the business press https://businessangelinstitute.org/blog/2021/04/15/angel-investments-in-figures/ suggest that the UK has the greatest number of 'angels' in Europe, but angel activity across the continent has grown greatly over the past 20 or 30 years.

Regulatory restrictions on those allowed to make high-risk angel investments vary by country, but Germany provides a good example. As in the USA, and detailed in 'Angel Funding Germany' https://www.angelfundinggermany.com/nl_NL/, angel groups in Germany, and across Europe, often focus on specific areas (as with AngelEngine in 'the Dusseldorf economic area and the neighboring countries'), or industries. Entrepreneurs are invited to request invitations to investors and opportunities to present their ideas to angel groups across the continent.

Monitored in a fashion similar to the guidelines that exist in the USA, German (and other European) startups are encouraged to solicit funding, and guidance, from qualified investors. The angel networks across the world provide a rich, and competitive, backdrop for startups as they pursue funding. This competition exists both among startups pursuing funding, and between angel groups as they compete for the best deals. The pricing or valuation of startups both before and after a given funding effort ('pre' and 'post' valuations, estimating startup value before funds are received, and after) is a centrepiece of the framing of funding 'rounds'. Most successful startups will engage angels for a series of equity and convertible debt rounds, with control and payout privileges depending on the startup, and the group to which it is making its 'pitch'.

5   Further Reading

A common theme, as this topic was examined online and with investors, was the similarity between angel, and venture capital (VC), funding. Though the two groups—angel investors and VCs—have much in common, they occupy different locations on the continuum of investors. Angels often fund ideas, where a startup has not generated its first sale. VCs, on the other hand, are viewed as 'knocking at the door' later on, as a firm engages in business, generates its first cash flows, and suffers growing pains.

The VC may be held in a harsher light, in this regard, than the angel investor. But the VC, coming *after* the angel, is presumed to have more money—and greater skills and industry contacts—to take the startup to the next level. But the shared characteristics, between the angel and the VC, are noteworthy. Both are willing to take great risk, and to offset that risk they are expecting far higher returns with this illiquid alternative investment, than is the norm for the traditional stock markets.

A rich and expansive research, begun decades ago, considers the angel investing topic. The '36 Best Angel Investing Books of All Time' are given in https://bookauthority.org/books/best-angel-investing-books. The texts highlight issues confronting both the investor and the entrepreneur. Those ideas are familiar to the readers of Benjamin and Margulis (2000) and Gompers and Lerner (1999). An overview of angel investing is given in Benjamin and Margulis (2000), and contrasts between angel investing and venture capital funding are reviewed in Gompers and Lerner (1999).

References

Benjamin, G., & Margulis, J. (2000). Angel investing: How to find and invest in private equity. In *A book in the Wiley Investment series*. Wiley.

Gompers, P., & Lerner, J. (1999). *The venture capital cycle*. MIT Press.

Modigliani, F., & Miller, M. H. (1958). The cost of capital, corporation finance and the theory of investment. *The American Economic Review, 48*, 261–297.

Modigliani, F., & Miller, M. H. (1963). Corporate income taxes and the cost of capital: A correction. *American Economic Review, 53*, 433–443.

Crowdfunding: Another Way of Financing My Business

Luis René Vásquez-Ordóñez, Carlos Lassala, and Samuel Ribeiro-Navarrete

1   What Is Crowdfunding?

Crowdfunding is regarded as a scalable, flexible and efficient source of financing. Its particular qualities make it a viable alternative to conventional financing methods. It is an ideal option for converting novel initiatives into projects and companies, especially for those ideas that face difficulties in obtaining financing due to their innovation-oriented nature (IMARC Group, 2020). Its popularity is largely justified by the problems that entrepreneurs encounter in seeking finance through conventional means. These difficulties cause many to seek direct support from the community (Kuppuswamy & Bayus, 2013).

This chapter gives a broad understanding of its operation, including its qualities as a financing alternative, its different models and the motivations that govern the behaviour of its participants. It also addresses the factors that determine the success of its campaigns and its potential to finance sustainable projects. Finally, we present conclusions and assess its future prospects as a potential financing alternative.

1.1   Crowdfunding: Basics Concepts

Crowdfunding can be defined as the process of raising capital for a charity campaign, a project or a new business through the relatively small contributions of a relatively large group of individuals over a set period of time. Although it is inspired by the concepts of micro-financing and crowdsourcing, it is classified in its own category,

L. R. Vásquez-Ordóñez (✉) · C. Lassala
University of Valencia, Valencia, Spain
e-mail: carlos.lassala@uv.es

S. Ribeiro-Navarrete
Polytechnic University of Valencia, Valencia, Spain
e-mail: samuel.ribeiro@sgcib.com

© The Author(s), under exclusive license to Springer Nature Switzerland AG 2022   31
C. Lassala, S. Ribeiro-Navarrete (eds.), *Financing Startups*, Future of Business and Finance, https://doi.org/10.1007/978-3-030-94058-4_3

and several Internet sites are devoted to it alone. A major reason for its success is that its model allows all types of promoters to obtain financing for all types of projects: with or without profit, large or small, and with social, ecological, artistic or cultural objectives, not only economic ones. Another reason is that it bypasses conventional financial intermediaries, as promoters can use the platforms very simply, via the Internet (Mollick, 2014).

The crowdfunding business model is made possible by technology. The opportunities offered by the Internet, through online platforms, provide its participants with new communication channels and a model that simplifies the capital-raising process (IMARC Group, 2020). In addition, it substantially exploits the potential of social bonds.

The operation of the crowdfunding model is relatively simple. The promoters of a project or a new business go to a platform specialised in crowdfunding. There, they publish a description of the project, using texts, images, videos etc., to provide detailed information about it (Koch & Siering, 2019). Potential funders (the crowd) can then see the available projects on the platform, analyse the information provided about them and decide which campaigns to support and how much money to contribute. Depending on the platform and its orientation, both funders and promoters can be individuals or organisations and professionals or non-professionals.

The information published by crowdfunding platforms usually includes the characteristics of the project. These characteristics are the size of the target amount, the amount raised so far, the amount remaining to reach the goal, the number of funders currently participating and the number of days within which the campaign hopes to succeed. The type and amount of information provided by the platform depend on its orientation and the crowdfunding model on which it is based. For example, in the debt-based model (crowdlending), the platforms also provide the interest rate offered and the terms and conditions under which the loan will be repaid.

1.2   Crowdfunding Attributes

The characteristics of crowdfunding demonstrate its attractiveness as a financing alternative. Its main quality is that it establishes a market that directly connects the funders with the promoters of projects. It thus eliminates the need for intermediaries such as banks or venture capitalists (Belleflamme et al., 2014). The only element absolutely required is the online platform, one of whose advantages over conventional media is much-reduced time and costs spent in bureaucratic processes (Fernandez-Blanco et al., 2020). Therefore, by using crowdfunding, project promoters can obtain funds relatively simply, efficiently and quickly.

One peculiar characteristic of crowdfunding is that it fits perfectly with the financing of innovative projects in their earliest stages (Leboeuf & Schwienbacher, 2018). It is considered a viable alternative for obtaining seed capital and starting new businesses. Its model allows all types of individuals to invest in projects, including contributors perhaps conventionally regarded as 'unqualified'. Thus, it makes it easier for promoters of relatively small and innovative projects to obtain capital to allow them to grow solid and well-established companies (Mollick, 2014).

Unlike traditional financing models, in which one or a few investors provide all the funds, in crowdfunding resources are obtained from a multitude of contributors, usually called 'the crowd'. This makes it possible to decentralise risks and distribute them among many investors, thus minimising possible individual losses. Significantly, also, contributors are often influenced by motivations other than economic ones. Crowdfunding allows the objectives of the project to be aligned with those of the contributors. These are often more complex objectives than mere economic benefit and can be as deep as ideals, interests or visions (Lehner, 2013). The evidence suggests that contributors may give more importance to the principles and values behind the project than to other factors related to their performance (Bento et al., 2019).

Finally, it is worth mentioning that funders often provide not only funding but also valuable information, support and prestige. This source of information is often referred to as the 'wisdom of the masses', and it offers several benefits. First, during the development of the campaign, feedback from funders allows promoters to obtain important information about the project, including new perspectives that bring more opportunities for action. Promoters can even allow funders to participate in the design of the products they will buy or invest in. Campaigns can also serve as a more effective type of market research than conventional methodologies: promoters gain valuable insight into the potential and acceptance of the project before investing additional time and resources in it (Mollick, 2014). On some platforms, campaigns allow you to sell the product before you produce it. In this way, the risk of low demand is considerably reduced (IMARC Group, 2020). Finally, in parallel to obtaining funding, crowdfunding campaigns publicise the project thanks to 'word of mouth' communication between promoters, funders and their social ties.

1.3   Crowdfunding Models

The literature identifies two crowdfunding funding mechanisms: (1) *the 'Keep it All' (KIA) model*, in which the promoter receives the funds raised regardless of whether the campaign reaches the target amount or not, and (2) *the 'All or Nothing' (AON) model*, in which the promoter receives the funds only if the campaign reaches the target amount (Cumming et al., 2020). The performance of a campaign can depend on which model is chosen. This will be explored in depth in Sect. 2.4.

Additionally, there are four main models classified according to the objectives of the funders (Sajardo, 2016):

- *Donation-based*: In this model, contributors provide funds for purely philanthropic purposes. They care only about the cause they support and receive nothing tangible in return.
- *Reward-based*: In this model, contributors provide funds and in return receive tangible non-monetary rewards.

- *Based on investment or equity*: In this model, financiers receive rights to future profits in much the same way as when buying shares in the conventional investment system. The primary motivation of the contributors is to receive an economic remuneration for their investment through the distribution of profits. Due to its complexity and its growing popularity, it is subjected to very high levels of regulation (Sajardo, 2016). Likewise, any new crowdfunding model based on rights to future profits, stock acquisition plans or other types of equity-based investments must also be subject to strict regulations (Mollick, 2014).
- *Based on loans or crowdlending*: In this model, the contributors provide funds as a loan, generally obtaining a return on the invested capital. The contributors provide funds and know the conditions in which they will recover their investment and obtain benefits (interest rates, terms, guarantees). Due to crowdlending's similarities with traditional loans, it has been noted that the contributors' motivations may be very similar to those of conventional lenders and investors (Agrawal et al., 2011).

1.4   Actors' Incentives

There are three main actors in crowdfunding: (1) *creators*, (2) *funders/investors and* (3) *platforms.* To understand the basics of the crowdfunding model operation, it is imperative to have a clear understanding of their incentives and objectives (Agrawal et al., 2014).

1.4.1   Creators' Incentives

Generally, the main objective of creators is to reach a minimum amount of capital needed for a specific project. Other incentives, though, can drive creators to use crowdfunding to raise capital (Mollick, 2014). Agrawal et al. (2014) offer a twofold classification: (1) *lower costs of capital and* (2) *access to valuable information.*

Lower Cost of Capital
The reasons crowdfunding can be expected to incur lower costs include the following. First, it allows developers to look for sources of financing beyond their location. When the search is directed to a wider geographical area, the funds are more likely to come from contributors with the strongest intention of participating in the project (Agrawal et al., 2011). Second, contributors are willing to accept lower returns, as they can value other qualities of the project, such as early access to products and being part of an innovative initiative. Third, crowdfunding allows promoters to provide much more project information than with other funding alternatives, thus sending confidence signals that reduce the investors' perception of risk and, consequently, the cost of capital (Koch & Siering, 2019). Finally, the existence of several projects in which to invest increases competition between investors and leads to a reduction in the cost of capital (Agrawal et al., 2014).

Access to Valuable Information

Crowdfunding campaigns provide valuable information to promoters. For example, in the rewards-based model, they are used as a type of market research in that they can reveal levels of demand for a product before additional resources and time are invested in it (Mollick, 2014). Unlike conventional market research, crowdfunding campaigns that allow the advance purchase of products reduce uncertainty over demand. This, in turn, can lead to an increase in the number of products sold and enhance the prospects of a successful launch to market.

Moreover, crowdfunding communication channels provide valuable feedback from investors to creators. For example, in the case of product presale, funders can collaborate in the creation of the products they are going to buy. Also, in highly complex projects, funders can boost the project by contributing their experience, knowledge and creativity. This collaboration facilitates the establishment of an 'ecosystem' around the project. This improves the performance of the campaign and opens up the creation of new possibilities and ideas that in other circumstances the creators might not have considered (Agrawal et al., 2014).

Creators' Disincentives

Promoters are prompted to use crowdfunding to obtain financing for a variety of good reasons, but problems and obstacles can and do arise.

Although the information provided by promoters about the project helps to reduce information asymmetries and facilitates investors' decision-making, it can, in certain situations, harm their interests. One example is that important details of their activities and products might be made available to competitors, which is especially unfortunate in projects where imitation might be fatal to the project. The need to maintain the confidentiality of any information given out can seriously discourage promoters from using crowdfunding (Agrawal et al., 2014).

A significant difference between crowdfunding and conventional sources of financing is that the number of investors is usually considerably higher in crowdfunding. While this allows promoters to receive feedback from many more people, it can be difficult and sometimes costly for developers to manage and maintain proper communication with all investors. This problem occurs especially when projects suffer difficulties of some kind, and all investors demand more attention simultaneously (Agrawal et al., 2014).

Finally, opportunity costs exist for the creators choosing crowdfunding over other financing alternatives. In crowdfunding, the investors are not usually professionals, so creators cannot expect to receive the professional feedback, status and contacts that can be obtained through other funding sources, where investors are generally professionals or have at least some knowledge of the project sector.

1.4.2   Funders' Incentives

In crowdfunding, funders' motivations and their relationships with creators will vary according to the project's context, nature and type of model. They will range from the merely economic to the merely social. In the donation-based model, investors act as philanthropists looking to support an idea with social impact. In the loan-based model (crowdlending), they act as lenders who expect to profit in exchange for providing capital. In the rewards-based model, they are early customers who can participate in developing the products they are buying. And in the equity-based model, we can regard the investors as very similar to investors in conventional equity holdings (Belleflamme et al., 2014).

The social factor is the main incentive for many funders. The provision of funds can, in itself, be a social activity, collaborating with the community and obtaining recognition from the creators of the project (Agrawal et al., 2014). One of the main motivations of the crowd is to participate in those projects whose communities have interests and ideals in common (Gerber et al., 2012). Likewise, the desire to be part of an innovative idea or an impact initiative motivates investors to be part of a project (Schwienbacher & Larralde, 2010). Even in projects with mainly economic purposes, investors' intentions can include philanthropy, as it is not unheard of for contributors to agree not to receive rewards in exchange for their contributions (Agrawal et al., 2014). For this reason, it has often been pointed out that crowdfunding and its social qualities fit very well with projects intended to have social and/or ecological impact (Bento et al., 2019; Lehner, 2013).

Although in certain models, altruism and social motivations carry greater weight in investors' decision-making, funders usually choose those projects that reflect a greater probability of success (Agrawal et al., 2011). Therefore, although altruism might be the main incentive, funders will always act as if they were investors by choosing higher-quality projects.

Crowdfunding also serves to formalise, contractually, the loans established between family and friends. When promoters launch campaigns promoting their ideas or projects, the first contributors are often family, friends or acquaintances (Agrawal et al., 2011). Crowdfunding allows businesses to be formalised and platforms to serve as intermediaries of loans that would otherwise be informal. In this way, both parties can benefit from the advantages of social ties without being fully exposed to the high risks associated with investments made between family and friends.

In the investment (equity) and loan (crowdlending) models, crowdfunding provides investment opportunities available to all sections of the population. Conventional people, therefore, can invest in all kinds of projects, large or small, without the need for the large amounts of capital that are usually necessary for conventional investments. Investors also have these opportunities without the locality-linked restrictions of traditional means of financing.

In the rewards-based model, investors have early access to new products and can participate in their development by providing feedback to developers. Their interests can thus be aligned with those of creators, creating an ideal scenario where both parties benefit (Agrawal et al., 2014).

Funders' Disincentives

It is also important to highlight the factors that could discourage contributors from investing through crowdfunding. First, the possible incompetence of the creators: it is common for promoters to have no experience in the logistics management aspects of the project. This is especially common in the rewards-based model and when the demand is greater than expected, since the projects often suffer delays when delivering the products.

Another aspect that investors often consider is the risk of fraud. It is easy to provide false information, and the platforms often do not review or validate a project before publishing it. Therefore, crowdfunding could be a relatively easy target for professional criminals. Furthermore, projects seeking crowdfunding are usually in their initial stages, so they have usually subjected themselves to considerable risks of their own (Agrawal et al., 2014).

When campaigns operate under the All or Nothing model, early investors also face the risk that the project they are supporting will not raise the target amount. This results in the return of contributions and their suffering the opportunity cost of not having those funds available for other purposes for a period of time (Cumming et al., 2020). This risk has become so prominent that platforms have become more selective with the projects they publish, discarding those that reflect a greater risk (Belleflamme et al., 2015).

1.4.3   Platforms' Incentives

Crowdfunding platforms are usually for-profit businesses. They usually charge a percentage of the financed project as a fee. For this reason, the primary motivation of the platforms is to attract as many investors as possible. In order to do this, platforms need to establish the right conditions to create an efficient market, with good communication and insurance against fraud (Agrawal et al., 2014).

Platforms also need to attract successful projects. Because platforms benefit from campaign funding, published campaigns must be successful: a higher success rate makes a platform more attractive to potential investors (Koch & Siering, 2019).

2   Success and Performance Factors

Before going into detail about the critical factors of a project's success, it is necessary to define what is meant by 'success' in the context of crowdfunding. A crowdfunding campaign is considered 'successful' when it achieves the total amount requested and 'overfunded' when it obtains more than the requested amount (Mollick, 2014). As shown in Fig. 1, a set of variables observable at the end of the campaign are usually used to evaluate the performance of the campaigns. These include the total amount collected, the total number of contributors or investors and the collection ratio, the amount collected divided by the amount requested (Cumming et al., 2017; Mollick, 2014). The time taken to achieve success and the average pledge per investor are also usually taken into account when comparisons are made of performance and research (Ahlers et al., 2015; Mollick, 2014).

In response to the growing popularity of crowdfunding, there has been a special interest in gathering knowledge on how to improve the performance and results of campaigns. The aim is to increase the likelihood of obtaining funding, with funders more attracted to make contributions. To this end, many studies have been conducted

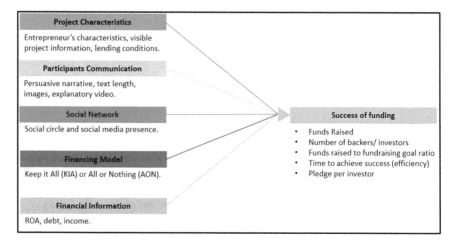

Fig. 1 Success and performance factors in crowdfunding campaigns

to identify specific key factors that have a direct impact on campaign results. The success of a project is strongly linked to the signals it sends about its quality. Those projects perceived to be of higher quality are usually more likely to obtain funding (Mollick, 2014). Most of the most recurrent factors mentioned in the literature deal with this perception of quality (see Fig. 1). We will explore some of them in the next section:

2.1 Project Characteristics

The importance of the creator characteristics in the success of obtaining financing has often been highlighted. Among these factors, quality and prestige have been mentioned (Bento et al., 2019). More specifically, investors' decisions can be influenced by variables such as team size, experience, career path, education, skills, professional ties, geographical proximity to potential contributors and the age of the business (Agrawal et al., 2011; Ahlers et al., 2015; Bento et al., 2019; Mollick, 2014).

Real-time information on the current status of the project has a considerable impact on the performance of a campaign. A 'U' shaped pattern of behaviour is usually observed in project collections: this means that most of the collections are captured at the beginning and end of the campaign. This pattern has been observed in all kinds of projects: successful or not, for large and small amounts and in various categories (Kuppuswamy & Bayus, 2013). The acceleration in contributions received at the end of the campaign is explained by the final impulse to reach the target amount. However, particular emphasis has been placed on the importance of early contributions. The size of the proportion of contributions obtained at the beginning of the project is closely linked to the success of a project (Colombo et al., 2015). Empirical evidence suggests that the success of a project can be predicted on the basis of the amounts raised during the first part of a campaign. It is therefore imperative that creators promote their projects to the maximum from the initial stages.

Early contributions have a significant impact on the results of a campaign because the behaviour of funders is strongly affected by the observable state of project collection. This includes information on the amount raised up to that time, the number of investors participating and the period over which this collection has been achieved (Kuppuswamy & Bayus, 2013). Therefore, the decisions of some people influence the decisions of others, a phenomenon that is known as 'herd behaviour' (Herzenstein et al., 2011). It is a rational action in which individuals evaluate the quality and risk of a proposed idea based on the decisions of others (Kuppuswamy & Bayus, 2013). Such behaviour has been observable even in the loan-based model, where participants seek economic returns. Therefore, when a project has attracted considerable contributions and a large number of funders in a short time, potential new funders perceive it as a positive sign of the quality of the project and are more willing to make contributions or investments.

As mentioned in Sect. 1.4, the motivations of contributors may vary according to the crowdfunding model of the campaign. In models based on loans or investments (crowdlending and equity), contributors adopt the position of investors and consider the economic benefit. Therefore, it is important to emphasise that the information about the investment conditions offered in the projects has a direct impact on the decision-making of investors and, consequently, on the performance of the campaigns. Below, the relationship of some of these aspects with the performance of the campaigns is detailed in greater depth.

Crowdlending
In the case of crowdlending, the key factors in the performance of the campaigns are the characteristics of the loan, because they are direct determinants of the potential benefits of the investment and its conditions. The most noteworthy characteristics are the interest rate, the amount and the term of the loan (Slimane & Rousseau, 2020).

A higher interest rate can have a positive impact on campaign results by providing a higher return to investors (Ahlers et al., 2015). However, paradoxically, in a market with information asymmetries, loans with higher rates can be associated with a higher risk, causing them to be less attractive (Yum et al., 2012). Also, smaller loans are considered more attractive because loans of larger amounts are associated with greater risk (Feng et al., 2015). Although projects with higher target amounts tend to attract a larger number of investors and obtain higher levels of funding in absolute terms, they tend to have a lower probability of success (Hörisch & Tenner, 2020). Longer-term loans are less attractive due to the inherent risk of the lower liquidity they entail.

Equity Crowdfunding
With high levels of uncertainty, developers need to send signals about the quality of the project in order to reduce perceived risk and attract funding. It is a sign of quality

in the equity-based model when developers invest indirectly in their own projects by acquiring considerable stakes (Ahlers et al., 2015). By taking on a significant portion of the risk, they signal confidence in the project. Another factor that makes equity projects attractive is the benefit of participation. Greater benefits make projects more attractive. However, this model is recommended to finance projects that need larger amounts. In projects of reduced amounts, the benefit for participation is very low and the project may lack attractiveness (Belleflamme et al., 2014).

2.2 Participants' Communication

One of the most critical conditions for a campaign's good performance is effective communication between all its participants (Ribeiro-Navarrete et al., 2021). One of the most common reasons why developers fail to obtain funding is that they do not connect and communicate appropriately with investors (Mitra & Gilbert, 2014). The functionalities and structures of most crowdfunding platforms are similar. Generally, the project description is the first, and the main, channel through which creators provide information to potential investors. In this, creators often use text, images and videos to inform the crowd about the project (Koch & Siering, 2019). By using these elements effectively, creators can reduce uncertainty, send confidence signals and improve investors' decision-making capacity. These factors attract more funders and increase their willingness to invest (Ahlers et al., 2015; Koch & Siering, 2015).

Media richness theory states that certain media send certain types of information more effectively (Koch & Siering, 2015). Thus, it is of the utmost importance to choose the correct elements to convey the different aspects of the projects. The elements of the description can then complement each other when all the information behind a project is being communicated.

Text is usually the element that occupies the most space in the description and is one of the most considered factors when evaluating the determinants of the performance of campaigns (Koch & Siering, 2019). Creators should take the writing of texts very seriously because there are indications that a persuasive description increases the probability of success (Mitra & Gilbert, 2014). The impact of characteristics such as the number of times the creator is mentioned or the type of language used in the performance of the campaigns has also been pointed out. However, an especially recurrent aspect is the size of the text, which is linked to the amount of information provided and the usefulness perceived by users. Therefore, a lengthy text may increase the probability of success. However, excessive length can lose the readers' attention (Barbi & Bigelli, 2017).

Text information can be reinforced by graphic elements such as images and videos. The use of these elements in online platforms increases the attention captured by users and enriches communication. Incorporating images requires some level of effort and resources, especially in the initial stages of the project. Its presence in the description demonstrates preparation, commitment and a certain level of development, aspects that justify its impact on the performance of the campaigns (Mollick,

2014). The correct number of images is also an important factor in capturing users' attention and improving the likelihood of success (Borello et al., 2019). While images are static, videos show movement and audio and are more dynamic media for transmitting information. The use of explanatory videos is especially effective in certain types of projects, ones that need processes or ideas to be explained in ways that images or texts cannot manage (Koch & Siering, 2019). Therefore, their presence can enrich the description more than the text and images, increasing the degree of perceived quality and generating more confidence. Consequently, the inclusion of an explanatory video in the description can positively impact the results of the campaigns (Koch & Siering, 2015; Mollick, 2014).

2.3   Social Networks

The importance of the social ties of creators when attracting investors and raising capital has been emphasised on numerous occasions. Scholars often refer to this set of links as 'social capital' and define it as the set of potential resources derived from the social contacts of an individual or organisation (Battaglia et al., 2020; Colombo et al., 2015).

An entity's social contacts can be measured through its social media presence (Colombo et al., 2015). The number of contacts of their official accounts on social networks is usually used to determine the size of the creators' set of social links. There is evidence of a positive relationship between the size of creators' social networks and campaign results (Belleflamme et al., 2014; Colombo et al., 2015; Mollick, 2014). This relationship has been highlighted both in models without economic return, based on rewards and donations (Mollick, 2014; Ordanini et al., 2011), and in investment-based models (Slimane & Rousseau, 2020; Vismara, 2015). However, the network selected depends on the perspective adopted by the studies: Facebook and Twitter have been used to measure the impact of more personal links (Koch & Siering, 2019; Mollick, 2014), and LinkedIn has been used to measure the influence of purely professional links (Colombo et al., 2015; Slimane & Rousseau, 2020).

Social ties are important because, often, most contributors belong to the creators' social circle: friends, family or friends of friends (Kuppuswamy & Bayus, 2013). Such behaviour is especially pronounced in the initial stage of the funding process (Ordanini et al., 2011). Support at this stage is critical to attracting attention to the project, sending messages of trust to the crowd and attracting more contributors through herd behaviour (Herzenstein et al., 2011). Social ties are important also because links between creators and potential investors reduce information asymmetries: this helps investors make decisions on which projects to support and how much to contribute. People close to the creator, therefore, play a pivotal role in attracting further input by providing their support from the earliest stages of the project (Battaglia et al., 2020).

2.4   Financing Model

The choice of funding mechanism is a crucial one when launching a campaign because it has a direct impact on the potential benefits of funding and the campaign's chances of success. The selected mechanism, Keep it All (KIA) or All or Nothing (AON), not only affects how capital is raised but also directly influences how the risk is distributed if the target amount is not raised.

In the KIA mechanism, the promoter receives the funds raised even if the campaign does not reach the target amount. In this way, the promoter does not assume the risk of not obtaining financing. In the AON mechanism, on the other hand, the promoter receives the funds only if the campaign reaches the target amount. This model represents a greater risk for the promoter since there is the possibility of receiving nothing, but, some evidence suggests, it is more likely to succeed. By using this model, developers send the crowd the signal that they consider their project viable. The crowd also gets the guarantee that the project will be carried out only if the campaign reaches the amount necessary for it to proceed correctly and that the promoters will not go ahead with inadequate funds. For example, when selecting this model in reward-based campaigns, if the amount raised does not cover the costs, the promoter has the option of not carrying out the project, including distributing rewards (Cumming et al., 2020).

2.5   Financial Information

In general, in crowdfunding models, funders act as investors supporting those projects that demonstrate higher quality and greater chances of success. The economic profile of the promoter is an element that contributors consider when making decisions, especially in crowdlending, as this is the model that most closely resembles traditional banking (Leboeuf & Schwienbacher, 2018). In this model, investors act like any traditional lender, such as a bank, evaluating the financial situation of borrowers and paying attention to aspects such as their leverage (level of existing debt) or their profitability (Slimane & Rousseau, 2020).

The financial aspects of companies have been shown to have a considerable impact on the success and performance of campaigns (Duarte et al., 2012). Some authors argue that good financial performance is the most important variable for investors since it constitutes a direct demonstration of ability to pay and, therefore, low risk (Greiner & Wang, 2010). This behaviour has been especially noted in models with economic benefits, where the quality of projects can be an even more important determinant of success than social motivations (Hörisch, 2015). Also, in projects with a focus on sustainability, investors usually prefer solid and larger companies. Therefore, although they may have social and ecological motivations, their main goal is still to profit from their investments (Slimane & Rousseau, 2020).

The possibility of directly observing the quality of a project explains why investors consider these indicators for their evaluation. If quality cannot be observed directly, analysts or investors usually evaluate them by looking at other attributes that are considered related to and indicative of quality. For example, investors can make a better judgement on whether or not a project will work based on the characteristics of the promoter. Companies that appear to be more reliable tend to have the best credit assessments and the best financial results in their activities (Duarte et al., 2012).

Among the indicators most used by investors to evaluate financial situations are return on assets (ROA) and leverage. ROA is the ratio of gross earnings to total average assets. It is used to measure a company's actual or potential profitability (Flórez-Parra et al., 2020). A larger ROA is more attractive to investors because it reflects a greater capacity to generate profits.

The borrower's leverage is an indicator of their ability to repay and is a determining factor in obtaining financing (Greiner & Wang, 2010). Empirical evidence shows it has a negative relationship with fundraising capacity (Herzenstein et al., 2011). The putative borrowers' credit ratings and leverage can have a direct, negative impact on the results of campaigns, so the perception of debt in crowdfunding is very similar to that of traditional banking.

Investors rely on their own judgment when they have sufficient information (Yum et al., 2012). Thus, platforms can considerably improve the decision-making capacity of investors and make projects more attractive by providing financial information in a complete, clear and reliable way.

3 Crowdfunding and Sustainability

Entrepreneurship today is no longer focused purely on economic success. Sustainable entrepreneurs orient all their activities around the search for the 'triple bottom line'. This concept directs business management to search for benefits in three dimensions: social, economic and environmental. The potential of crowdfunding for this type of entrepreneurship has been highlighted because it embraces both the economic and the non-economic motivations of the participants (Martínez-Climent et al., 2020). In this sense, sustainable initiatives benefit from the ethical relationship between platforms and stakeholders by allowing the crowd to finance projects with which they share interests and ideals (Gerber et al., 2012). Investors may place more importance on the ideas and values behind the projects than on guarantees or business plans. For these reasons, crowdfunding and sustainable initiatives fit together very well (Lehner, 2013).

The positive relationship between the sustainability of companies and their performance has been stressed on numerous occasions. In the context of crowdfunding, a sustainable orientation considerably increases a project's attractiveness and its chances of obtaining financing, regardless of the type of investment or reward (Bento et al., 2019). Therefore, it is recommended to highlight this orientation in all possible ways (Hörisch & Tenner, 2020).

It has been argued that crowdfunding, in general, is a very interesting alternative way of financing sustainable projects. This can be explained largely by the 'warm-glow theory', which states that people do good deeds to feel good about themselves and, therefore, support projects that they consider to be impactful (Schwienbacher & Larralde, 2010). Warm-glow motivation encompasses those actions performed to feel the pleasure of 'doing good'. Such behaviour can extend both to the social and to the environmental dimensions (Hörisch & Tenner, 2020).

Although the literature linking sustainability with the results of crowdfunding campaigns is relatively scarce (Slimane & Rousseau, 2020), its positive impact has become evident. There are already crowdfunding platforms that provide corporate social responsibility reports that allow investors to consider the environmental and social impact of the projects they might support (Martínez-Climent et al., 2020). Therefore, both promoters and platforms must focus on improving how this information is presented and choose the appropriate means to transmit it (Hörisch & Tenner, 2020).

4   Future Prospects

The global crowdfunding market grew substantially between 2015 and 2020 and is expected to maintain this pace over the next 5 years. Its compound annual growth rate is estimated to be around 17%, catalysed by technological development, the launch of new functionalities through new platforms and the increase of social networks' influence globally. An extra reason for growth recently is that during the COVID-19 pandemic many non-profit organisations have chosen this alternative to provide financial aid (IMARC Group, 2020).

Part of the success and growth of crowdfunding is due to its peculiar characteristics. Its business model allows the creation of a direct market between contributors and recipients of funds, eliminating the need for conventional intermediaries and creating potential benefits for all its participants. Although these benefits have been much explored, it is important to learn more about how its different models operate and the motivations of its participants. Then regulators can establish an environment of minimal uncertainty where all participants benefit.

At the same time, we must also continue to explore the factors that determine success in securing funding, improving creators' and platforms' understanding of what measures will maximise the chance of obtaining the required funds. A deeper knowledge of crowdfunding will establish it more solidly as a financing alternative. At the micro level, this means having an alternative that increases the range of financing options for individuals and companies. At the macro level, it means having a new financing mechanism aligned with the common interests of society.

Among the main interests of society, global warming stands out. Faced with the world's current environmental problems and the need for significant investments in sustainability between now and 2050 (IRENA, 2021), crowdfunding stands as a strong potential alternative source of finance for projects aiming to contribute positively to the goals of the Paris Agreement (Slimane & Rousseau, 2020). By allowing the entire population (the crowd) to participate in projects, environmental and social initiatives can benefit from the motivations of individuals with shared interests and ideals. This idea forms a consistent basis for future efforts in finding alternative sources of financing for building a more sustainable world.

References

Agrawal, A., Catalini, C., & Goldfarb, A. (2011). *The geography of crowdfunding*. Working paper no 16820; working paper series. National Bureau of Economic Research. https://doi.org/10. 3386/w16820

Agrawal, A., Catalini, C., & Goldfarb, A. (2014). Some simple economics of crowdfunding. *Innovation Policy and the Economy, 14*(1), 63–97. https://doi.org/10.1086/674021

Ahlers, G. K. C., Cumming, D., Günther, C., & Schweizer, D. (2015). Signaling in equity crowdfunding. *Entrepreneurship Theory and Practice, 39*(4), 955–980. https://doi.org/10. 1111/etap.12157

Barbi, M., & Bigelli, M. (2017). Crowdfunding practices in and outside the US. *Research in International Business and Finance, 42*, 208–223. https://doi.org/10.1016/j.ribaf.2017.05.013

Battaglia, F., Busato, F., & Manganiello, M. (2020). Signaling success factors in alternative entrepreneurial finance. In C. Cruciani, G. Gardenal, & E. Cavezzali (Eds.), *Banking and beyond: The evolution of financing along traditional and alternative avenues* (pp. 169–190). Springer International. https://doi.org/10.1007/978-3-030-45752-5_8

Belleflamme, P., Lambert, T., & Schwienbacher, A. (2014). Crowdfunding: Tapping the right crowd. *Journal of Business Venturing, 29*(5), 585–609. https://doi.org/10.1016/j.jbusvent.2013. 07.003

Belleflamme, P., Omrani, N., & Peitz, M. (2015). The economics of crowdfunding platforms. *Information Economics and Policy, 33*, 11–28. https://doi.org/10.1016/j.infoecopol.2015. 08.003

Bento, N., Gianfrate, G., & Thoni, M. H. (2019). Crowdfunding for sustainability ventures. *Journal of Cleaner Production, 237*, 1–11. https://doi.org/10.1016/j.jclepro.2019.117751

Borello, G., De Crescenzo, V., & Pichler, F. (2019). Factors for success in European crowdinvesting. *Journal of Economics and Business, 106*, 1–19. https://doi.org/10.1016/j. jeconbus.2019.05.002

Colombo, M. G., Franzoni, C., & Rossi-Lamastra, C. (2015). Internal social capital and the attraction of early contributions in crowdfunding. *Entrepreneurship Theory and Practice, 39*(1), 75–100. https://doi.org/10.1111/etap.12118

Cumming, D., Leboeuf, G., & Schwienbacher, A. (2017). Crowdfunding cleantech. *Energy Economics, 65*, 292–303. https://doi.org/10.1016/j.eneco.2017.04.030

Cumming, D., Leboeuf, G., & Schwienbacher, A. (2020). Crowdfunding models: Keep-it-all vs. all-or-nothing. *Financial Management, 49*(2), 331–360. https://doi.org/10.1111/fima. 12262

Duarte, J., Siegel, S., & Young, L. (2012). Trust and credit: The role of appearance in peer-to-peer lending. *The Review of Financial Studies, 25*(8), 2455–2484. https://doi.org/10.2307/23263634

Feng, Y., Fan, X., & Yoon, Y. (2015). Lenders and borrowers' strategies in online peer-to-peer lending market: An empirical analysis of ppdai.com. *Journal of Electronic Commerce Research, 16*(3), 242–260. Scopus.

Fernandez-Blanco, A., Villanueva-Balsera, J., Rodriguez-Montequin, V., & Moran-Palacios, H. (2020). Key factors for project crowdfunding success: An empirical study. *Sustainability, 12*(2), 599. https://doi.org/10.3390/su12020599

Flórez-Parra, J. M., Rubio Martín, G., & Rapallo Serrano, C. (2020). Corporate social responsibility and crowdfunding: The experience of the colectual platform in empowering economic and sustainable projects. *Sustainability, 12*(13), 1–20. https://doi.org/10.3390/su12135251

Gerber, E. M., Hui, J. S., & Kuo, P. Y. (2012). *Crowdfunding: Why people are motivated to post and fund projects on crowdfunding platforms*. In Computer supported cooperative work 2012

(Vol. 2). Workshop on design influence and social technologies: Techniques, impacts and ethics, Seattle, WA.

Greiner, M. E., & Wang, H. (2010). Building consumer-to-consumer trust in E-finance marketplaces: An empirical analysis. *International Journal of Electronic Commerce, 15*(2), 105–136. https://doi.org/10.2753/JEC1086-4415150204

Herzenstein, M., Dholakia, U. M., & Andrews, R. L. (2011). Strategic herding behaviour in peer-to-peer loan auctions. *Journal of Interactive Marketing, 25*(1), 27–36. https://doi.org/10.1016/j.intmar.2010.07.001

Hörisch, J. (2015). Crowdfunding for environmental ventures: An empirical analysis of the influence of environmental orientation on the success of crowdfunding initiatives. *Journal of Cleaner Production, 107*, 636–645. https://doi.org/10.1016/j.jclepro.2015.05.046

Hörisch, J., & Tenner, I. (2020). How environmental and social orientations influence the funding success of investment-based crowdfunding: The mediating role of the number of funders and the average funding amount. *Technological Forecasting and Social Change, 161*, 120311. https://doi.org/10.1016/j.techfore.2020.120311

IMARC Group. (2020). *Crowdfunding market: Global industry trends, share, size, growth, opportunity and forecast 2021-2026* (p. 107). IMARC Group. https://www.asdreports.com/market-research-report-562392/crowdfunding-market-global-industry-trends-share-size-growth-opportunity-forecast

IRENA. (2021). *World energy transitions outlook: 1.5°C pathway (preview)*. https://irena.org/publications/2021/March/World-Energy-Transitions-Outlook

Koch, J.-A., & Siering, M. (2015). *Crowdfunding success factors: The characteristics of successfully funded projects on crowdfunding platforms*. SSRN scholarly paper ID 2808424. Social Science Research Network. https://papers.ssrn.com/abstract=2808424

Koch, J.-A., & Siering, M. (2019). The recipe of successful crowdfunding campaigns. *Electronic Markets, 29*(4), 661–679. https://doi.org/10.1007/s12525-019-00357-8

Kuppuswamy, V., & Bayus, B. (2013). Crowdfunding creative ideas: The dynamics of project backers in Kickstarter. *SSRN Electronic Journal, 2013*. https://doi.org/10.2139/ssrn.2234765

Leboeuf, G., & Schwienbacher, A. (2018). Crowdfunding as a new financing tool. In D. Cumming & L. Hornuf (Eds.), *The economics of crowdfunding: Startups, portals and investor behaviour* (pp. 11–28). Springer International Publishing. https://doi.org/10.1007/978-3-319-66119-3_2

Lehner, O. M. (2013). Crowdfunding social ventures: A model and research agenda. *Venture Capital, 15*(4), 289–311. https://doi.org/10.1080/13691066.2013.782624

Martínez-Climent, C., Guijarro-García, M., & Carrilero-Castillo, A. (2020). The motivations of crowdlending investors in Spain. *International Journal of Entrepreneurial Behaviour and Research, 27*(2), 452–469. https://doi.org/10.1108/IJEBR-05-2020-0304

Mitra, T., & Gilbert, E. (2014). The language that gets people to give: Phrases that predict success on kickstarter. In *Proceedings of the 17th ACM Conference on Computer Supported Cooperative Work & Social Computing* (pp. 49–61). https://doi.org/10.1145/2531602.2531656.

Mollick, E. (2014). The dynamics of crowdfunding: An exploratory study. *Journal of Business Venturing, 29*(1), 1–16. https://doi.org/10.1016/j.jbusvent.2013.06.005

Ordanini, A., Miceli, L., Pizzetti, M., & Parasuraman, A. (2011). Crowdfunding: Transforming customers into investors through innovative service platforms. *Journal of Service Management, 22*(4), 443–470. https://doi.org/10.1108/09564231111155079

Ribeiro-Navarrete, S., Palacios-Marqués, D., Lassala, C., & Ulrich, K. (2021). Key factors of information management for crowdfunding investor satisfaction. *International Journal of Information Management, 59*, 1–10. https://doi.org/10.1016/j.ijinfomgt.2021.102354

Sajardo, A. (2016). El Nuevos instrumentos de financiación para el sector no lucrativo. *Cooperativismo & Desarrollo, 24*(108), Article 108. https://doi.org/10.16925/co.v24i108.1259

Schwienbacher, A., & Larralde, B. (2010). *Crowdfunding of small entrepreneurial ventures*. SSRN scholarly paper ID 1699183. Social Science Research Network. https://doi.org/10.2139/ssrn.1699183

Slimane, F. B., & Rousseau, A. (2020). Crowdlending campaigns for renewable energy: Success factors. *Journal of Cleaner Production, 249*, 1–13. https://doi.org/10.1016/j.jclepro.2019.119330

Vismara, S. (2015). Equity retention and social network theory in equity crowdfunding. *SSRN Electronic Journal, 46*(4), 579–590. https://doi.org/10.2139/ssrn.2654325

Yum, H., Lee, B., & Chae, M. (2012). From the wisdom of crowds to my own judgment in microfinance through online peer-to-peer lending platforms. *Electronic Commerce Research and Applications, 11*(5), 469–483. https://doi.org/10.1016/j.elerap.2012.05.003

A Prospective Analysis of the Advantages of Crowdlending to Startups

Eva Porras González, José Manuel Guaita Martínez, and José María Martín Martín

1   Definition and Key Characteristics

Crowdlending systems are intermediation services carried out through online platforms by which a large number of investors make small contributions in the form of loans to finance projects (Mollick & Robb, 2016). Crowdlending is also known as peer-to-peer lending (P2P) or peer-to-business lending (P2B) to refer to the moneylending actions that use online platforms to match lenders with borrowers, whether individuals or businesses (Pierrakis & Collins, 2013). This name highlights the fact that capital is obtained directly from the original source of funds rather than from a third party (Schneuwly, 2014). In this system, the lending is done by private individuals who seek to make their relatively small investments profitable. In exchange for their monies, these lenders hope to obtain interest payments in addition to the return of their initial capital.

Although the history of crowdlending goes back hundreds of years, it is the access to the Internet and to specialised websites, together with a renewed belief in participatory processes, that have resulted in a steep increase of this mode of financing. This has become particularly true after the birth of *Web 2.0* as this technology eliminated the costs of disseminating information in a *one-to-one* fashion (Martín et al., 2019). After the implementation of this technology, it became easy to

E. Porras González
Department of Fundamentals of Economic Analysis, Universidad Rey Juan Carlos, Madrid, Spain
e-mail: eva.porras@urjc.es

J. M. Guaita Martínez (✉)
Department of Economics and Social Sciences, Universitat Politècnica de València, Valencia, Spain
e-mail: jogumar@esp.upv.es

J. M. Martín Martín
Department of International and Spanish Economy, Universidad de Granada, Granada, Spain
e-mail: martinmartin@ugr.es

© The Author(s), under exclusive license to Springer Nature Switzerland AG 2022
C. Lassala, S. Ribeiro-Navarrete (eds.), *Financing Startups*, Future of Business and Finance, https://doi.org/10.1007/978-3-030-94058-4_4

access platforms through which to obtain information, as well as devices for interaction that reduce the costs of finding peer groups with similar interests. In this way, for more than a decade now, the Internet has significantly reduced transaction costs and increased its forum as people with no special skills can now easily access a myriad of services (Guaita et al., 2021). Crowdlending is a part of the FinTech 'revolution' that hopes to disintermediate financial services (Moenninghoff & Wieandt, 2012). This word links *finance* and *technology* hinting at the offering of financial services through new technologies. But the precise definition of the term is elusive as it is often debated whether fintech is a type of company, a type of service, or a series of people. Overall, it just refers to innovation through technology in the financial industry.

With respect to crowdlending, the P2P/P2B online lending platforms have challenged traditional banks and intermediaries by awarding more cost-efficient offerings due to the scaling of the newly adopted technologies. As a result, these services can offer higher returns for lenders and lower interest rate costs for borrowers (Cumming & Hornuf, 2018). Overall, the business model of these platforms varies substantially with respect to traditional financial institutions in several aspects. For instance, the platforms do not take credit risks but rather decentralise these by spreading them to the crowdlenders (Duarte et al., 2012; Lenz, 2016). We now list some of the common characteristics of these platforms and processes.

In crowdlending, there are three basic types of participants:

• The entity or person requesting the funds and which needs to be approved by the platform.
• The people willing to lend money in exchange for some profit and the return of their initial capital.
• The intermediary responsible for bringing together the borrower with the lenders.
• The following is a list of common characteristics of the crowdlending processes:
• There is no need for a prior relationship between lenders and borrowers.
• The intermediation takes place online, through the crowdfunding platform.
• Borrowers typically obtain better and more flexible terms than with the traditional intermediaries.
• Lenders select the project of interest among those publicised at the site and, if qualified, may invest in more than one to diversify risk.
• The loans can be unsecured or secured and are mostly not protected by any government insurance.
• Typically, the crowdlending platforms provide the following services:
  – Find and attract lenders and borrowers.
  – Gather and verify information such as borrower's identity, bank account and other data.
  – Perform credit checks and filters out the unqualified borrowers.
  – Develop credit models for loan approvals and pricing.
  – Help borrowers find adequate lenders and investors identify and purchase loans according to their investment criteria.

- Process and forward payments to lenders according to the agreed upon terms.
- Deal with a myriad of issues such as trying to collect payments from delinquent borrowers, legal compliance, and reporting.

There are also different types of crowdlending depending upon who is the borrower, the lender and the purpose of the loan or the guarantees. The most common are:

- Loans to companies.
- Loans with an asset as collateral.
- Loans with a mortgage guarantee.
- Commercial credit discount.
- Consumer loans without a buyback guarantee.
- Consumer loans with buyback guarantee.

Conceptually, crowdlending derives from crowdfunding in that it refers to a collective form of financing. Here, the collective contributions to finance projects shape into different types of contracts each delivered under different formats. The better know are reward-based, equity-based, donation-based and lending-based crowdfunding. The differences among those lie on the type of return obtained by the lender, whether it is a small-value gadget related to the project, a stake in the company, no reward whatsoever or an interest rate in the case of the latter. Hence, it is necessary to differentiate crowdlending from other types of crowdfunding as, in the former, the lender only invests in specific loan requests. And this contrasts with other forms of crowdfinancing such as the mentioned crowd equity where investors acquire a portion of a company; donation or reward-based crowdfinancing, which includes more altruistic motives and does not involve a legal claim to an asset as already stated.

2   Crowdlending Is Important for Startups

After the 2008 international financial crisis, as banks needed to deleverage their balance sheets, financing startups and small and median-size enterprises (SME) became ever so more difficult. The reason is that the bank's ledgers reflected devalued assets to support a given level of debt acquired before the said devaluation. That is why, even though governments flooded the markets with cheap money, very little of it—if any—ever reached this niche. In this funding environment, loans intermediated by online platforms grew dramatically and the traditional financial industry began to encounter serious competition due to the disaffection generated by the financial system (Cai et al., 2016; Lundahl et al., 2009; Manrai & Manrai, 2007). Thus, alternative financing options started to play a crucial role in raising capital for small companies and startups. In particular, this latter group aggregates a number of circumstances that turns it into *specifically* undesirable during financial challenging times; primarily because a startup is most often an untested entrepreneurial proposition as the business concept of the nascent group needs to be proven, as well as the market insight and capabilities of its management team. Furthermore, as of 2019, the failure rate of startups was around 90%: 21.5% in the first year, 30% in the second, 50% by the fifth and 70% in the 10th (Embroker, 2021). These statistics are typical of the failure rate of businesses at this time of their life cycle.

Thus, during the 2008 crises, as banks became more unable and unwilling to take further debt, venture capitalists and angel investors come to the rescue. One advantage provided by these, is that most often they do not request the return of their capital until the company is making money. On the other hand, they require a portion of the equity of the funded company and they extract enormous returns. Also, typically, they do not fund startups from the onset. Instead, they target firms looking to commercialise an idea. They then buy a stake, nurture its growth and cash out when the time comes. The circumstances surrounding the 2008 crises, became a time of opportunity for lending platforms that invested heavily to position themselves as capital attraction centres (Rogers, 2003). During these times, they upgraded their offer to ensure potential borrowers encountered a user-friendly engine and a flexible scheme capable of providing finance fast at reasonable rates (Maier, 2016). In a symbiosis, the number of borrowers that a platform attracts influences the number of investors who will select that platform, and the funds available will attract the projects (Havrylchyk & Verdier, 2018). In fact, crowdlending platforms have *democratised* the investment opportunity landscape by providing access to small investors wishing to participate in financial markets. But, in addition to becoming the small investor gate-of-entry to the financial markets, a second reason for the platforms' success is that they allow the participation in projects of the investors' liking. And yet a third reason is that they contribute to the success of nascent projects because of the advantageous conditions this sector offers to starting entrepreneurs. Furthermore, these systems help investors finance the various stages of the life cycle of firms further providing options. Hence, investors will choose whether their loans go to startups and new business ideas or more mature projects. With social media and specialised websites easing the entry for both lenders and borrowers, crowdlending platforms have multiplied in developed and emerging economies worldwide filling-in a void in the lending landscape. Unfortunately, it is difficult to obtain reliable data on the total volume traded through these platforms. However, Statista (2021) has estimated their annual volume traded will reach $302 billion by 2025.

3   Background

As already stated, crowdlending is a form of collective financing that brings together multiple investors to contribute towards the funding of companies, projects or individuals. Etymologically, this word refers to the lenders' role in a category of *crowdfunding*, argued to be a particular type of crowdsourcing (Rouzé, 2019). This neologism designates activities performed on specialised web platforms by Internet users. These novel business strategies rely on communities to develop content, solve problems and 'innovate' through the concerted effort of a large participatory crowd. Considering these actions, Howe's (2006) perspective refers to the strategic and economic aspects of outsourcing tasks to a group of people in resolving a problem or creating a project. In his words:

> ...the act of a company or institution taking a function once performed by employees and outsourcing it to an undefined (and generally large) network of people in the form of an open call. This can take the form of peer-production (when the job is performed collaboratively), but is also often undertaken by sole individuals. The crucial prerequisite is the use of the open call format and the wide network of potential labourers.... (Howe, 2006)

There are many reasons why companies could use crowdsourcing as defined by Howe's. One mentioned by Surowiecki (2004) 'is that in the right circumstances, groups are remarkably intelligent, and are often smarter than the smartest people in them'. In this author's opinion, aggregating information can offer results that are superior in terms of cognition, coordination and cooperation to those that could be offered by any single member of the same group. Corney et al. (2009) propose that crowdsourcing can be defined in terms of three dimensions:

• The nature of the tasks (for instance, creation, value creation or organisation).
• The nature of the crowd (what individual, collective and expert skills are needed).
• The nature of the payment (whether the work will be voluntary or paid, for instance).

To this list, Huberman et al. (2009) added productivity and efficiency in the relations between the objectives to be achieved, the people involved and the returns and *open innovation*. And Doan et al. (2011) spoke about the impact that the collaborative nature of labour could have on the objectives to be achieved. Once this latter consideration is included, the number of potential definitions extends to at least 36 across disciplines (Estellés-Arolas & González-Ladrón-de-Guevara, 2012). As a result, crowdsourcing became an *umbrella* term used to describe multiple activities, including non-digital ones often rendering the term inoperative (Geiger et al., 2011; Ridge, 2014; Belleflamme et al., 2010). That is why, often, the definition used is the one by Jenkins (2006), as most others appear to converge in it. According to this author, the participative culture, the new-found *empowerment* and the collective intelligence, enables the transformation of industrial logic. This is how the financial aspect takes a back seat and the collaborative dimensions take the stage.

4   The History of Crowdlending

Collective financing for social and cultural projects exists in all cultures under various formats and names (Fernández-Olit et al., 2020). In Africa, for instance, many communities collect money for funerals, marriages, building houses and starting the businesses of those who need it. This finds its equivalent in the actions of multiple faiths, religious organisations and non-governmental organisations (NGOs) across the world who led by their leaders organise help for the most needy within their communities and abroad. The modern term crowdfunding is defined by the use of the Internet. However, collaborative financing is many centuries old and has taken place worldwide in form of gift-giving, patronage, tontine, fundraising and others. In Europe, one precedent of patronage is that of Cardinal Cisneros, founder of the University of Alcalá de Henares in Spain and promoter of the Complutense Polyglot Bible (1517), written in Greek, Latin and Hebrew. Also in Spain, patrons would finance the publication of written works. A few examples include the Duke of Sessa who helped Lope de Vega, the Duke of Osuna with Quevedo or the Count of Lemos with the Argensola brothers (Dadson, 2011).

One case of cooperative cultural patronage, was the sixteenth-century emergence of publishing associations through which individuals shared the financial risks and potential profits of printing and book distribution. A related instance is the seventeenth-century start of publication by subscription. This business model involved the subscription of potential buyers to future works to be developed by publishers. This model was used to release some of Jane Austen's and Mark Twain's works (Pemberley, 2021). More recently, other instances that involved the collective mobilisation and wide participation of crowds in the funding of art, include Joseph Pulitzer's 1884 call to the American people to fund the pedestal for the Statue of Liberty through micro-donations (Rouzé, 2019). Even closer, is the case of the 1959 independent film Shadows, by John Cassavetes who made calls for financial contributions on late-night radio shows (Carney, 2003). However, even though numerous forms of collaborative financing have existed for centuries and probably in every culture as the above examples show, in its current form, this innovation started in the late 1990s after the Internet was used to finance charity events and musical projects. Thus, the newness in this concept resides in the technology and frame of mind that conform to a framework of participative projects involving the organisation of a community and an Internet *culture*. Since then, the modern use of the neologisms *based on the crowd* has entered the managerial vocabulary to describe practices whose novelty resides on the recourse to the Internet (Castrataro, 2011) as well as in the ideological participative, Do It Yourself (DIY) environment of its precursors.

As per Méric et al. (2016), the expression crowdsourcing was first used in Wired (14 June 2006) by Jeff Howe (Brickfunding, 2021). The authors highlight that the ingeniousness of the term resided in replacing *out* by *crowd* in *outsourcing* to denote a new managerial philosophy: entrusting a 'crowd' the task of providing funds, bringing out ideas or even spontaneously expressing an opinion. On the other hand, the term crowdfunding is credited to Michael Sullivan who in August 2006 used it while working in 'fundavlog', a failed incubator for videoblog projects and events (Marillion, 2021).

The modern history of crowdfunding can be divided into four periods:

- The late 1990s and early 2000s when Internet campaigning and charity fundraising started.
- The Mid 2000 when microlending platforms and P2P/P2B lending were born.
- The late 2000s when consolidation of these practices occurs.
- The second decade of the 2000s when equity-based crowdfunding began.

The Late 1990s and Early 2000s After AOL Instant Messenger and SixDegrees platforms facilitated the creation of online profiles, creative artists with sizable followings began to request the participation of their fan-base to finance their projects. One example is Marillion (Marillion, 2021), an English rock band, which in 1997 raised $60,000 for their US tour (BBC News, 2001). A second example is JustGiving, a fundraising institution started in 2000 with the mission: 'no great cause goes unfunded' (JustGiving, 2021). Other relevant actions that helped the sector form, include jazz composer Maria Schneider's crowdfunding campaign to produce her 2003 work (Freedman & Nutting, 2015). She was the first to use ArtistShare to launch a campaign to finance a new record. Following this call, she raised $130,000 and her album became the first in history to earn a Grammy Award (in 2005) without being available in retail stores.

The Mid 2000s In February 2005, Zopa became the first P2P lending company in the UK that *directly matched individuals looking for a low rate loan with investors looking for a higher rate of return* (Zopa, 2021). Also in 2005, Kiva was started as a crowdlending platform, the first that helped entrepreneurs lend money worldwide (Kiva, 2021; Flannery, 2006). This model was replicated in 2006 by organisations such as Prosper Marketplace, and the LendingClub in the USA, and other P2P lending sites which posted funding requests by individuals who submitted their projects' proposals.

The Late 2000s Years of consolidation and growth. During the first few years of the twenty-first century, crowdfunding was loosely described as 'the act of informally generating and distributing funds, usually online, by groups of people for specific social, personal, entertainment, or other purposes' (Spellman, 2008; web). This method worked most often as a sort of a patronage. For example, Barack Obama's crowdfunding campaign raised close to three-quarters of a billion dollars over the Internet (Bradley, 2008). Kappel (2009) uses this example as one of 'ex ante crowdfunding', of this period because the support was provided to help achieve a future common objective. The ex ante method was also increasingly used in the entertainment industry to bypass the traditional relationship with record labels. Usually, the *patrons* would lend the money in exchange for perks, such as autographed copies of the work in advance of the market release, t-shirts or back-stage access at one of the artists' shows (Oliver & Armit, 2018). If the fundraising campaign was promoted by a politician, the contributor would probably get a signed note of appreciation as a perk.

Ex ante crowdfunding is in contrast with ex post facto crowdfunding, which would be used when the support provided is in exchange for a 'finished' product. For example, the British rock band Radiohead was able to record their album *In Rainbows* and use ex post facto crowdfunding to recover the costs (ComScore, 2007). To make this work, on 01 October 2007 Radiohead posted on their website the release of *In Rainbows* and announced it could be downloaded in MP3 format for free. The fan base was asked to obtain a registration code and contribute any amount from US$0.00 to US$99.99 for downloading the record. In this way, more than 1.2 million downloads were counted during the next few weeks and 38% of the fans contributed an average of US$6 per album adding to US$2.4 million in revenue. During these years, crowdfunding in music began to develop more sophisticated models. So, in addition to differentiating the timing when the funds were received with respect to the complete product, the recording industry started to develop other forms of ex ante crowdfunding. These did not rely exclusively upon patronage perks, but also offered an opportunity to earn a monetary return on each contribution based on sales of future recordings (Tozzi, 2007). A new business model was then born by distinguishing this last *patronage-plus* ex ante crowdfunding, from the earlier *pure patronage* model. This mechanism had the added benefit of involving fans in the success of their favourite artists and exposing them to illegal downloading and other sector problems. In addition, these models were further modified to obtain the appearance of new categories such as the *Betting Model* and the *Investing Model* (Bandstocks, 2021).

The Second Decade of the 2000s When Equity-Based Crowdfunding Began and Crowdlending Expanded As already stated, the three dimensions of crowdsourcing defined by Corney et al. (2009) were enlarged by Huberman et al. (2009) with the notions of productivity and 'efficiency' in the relations between the objectives to be achieved, the people involved and the returns and 'open innovation'. And later in 2011, it was further expanded by the nature of the collaborative labour, and its impact on the objectives to be achieved (Doan et al., 2011). As a result of the combined consideration of these, there is a symbiosis between practice and theory that results in derivations of the original concepts.

5   Corporate Funding and the Legal Aspects of Crowdlending

5.1   Company Funding Is Recorded as a Liability

Company funding is recorded as a liability on the right side of the accounting balance sheet, where the net worth and the callable liabilities are also found. We want to differentiate between:

- Non-callable liabilities: Financing through partners and company profits.
- Callable liability: Loans and credits a company must repay as those negotiated in the crowdlending platforms.

The exact position of the given loan in the right side of the balance sheet speaks as to its repayment period. These can be:

- Short-term financing: To be repaid in less than 1 year. This includes pending payments to suppliers, customer advances, short-term loans and credits with financial institutions, and discounts of commercial bills.
- Long-term financing: To be repaid after 1 year. This refers to longer-term loans with financial institutions, leasing contracts, reimbursable grants from the public administration and issuance of shares and bonds in the financial markets. All these have due times over 1 year.

Sometimes a medium-term financing is also used to denote those funding sources with lives of 1–5 or 6 years. At any rate, these sources of financing are available and will be used according to the firms' needs and capacities. Legally, the only obligations are with respect to the formation of net worth. As there needs to be a:

- Minimum endowment of social capital will depend on the legal form of the company.
- Minimum legal reserve to be endowed once the company has benefits.

5.2   Regulation Is Country Specific

The regulators' predicament is to protect against systemic risks while maintaining a fair and competitive market. This balance will require determining the optimal regulatory level and this, in turn, will depend upon numerous variables. Thus, worldwide, the regulation that governs P2P/P2B lending has evolved in different manners so that anyone trying to work in different jurisdictions will be faced with a diversity of regulatory responses. For instance, in some countries platforms that rate and intermediate in loans but do not hold the risk of these loans will face problems. On the other hand, the investors' perception of risk will be diminished if the returns are guaranteed by the platforms. In some places with inadequate legislation, P2P/P2B platforms work as Ponzi schemes and old investors are paid off with the funds new investors bring in. But at the same time, in territories where stringent regulation is enforced, the market will not be able to benefit from a fully competitive environment. Furthermore, startups and small businesses will face additional constraints to develop. P2P/P2B lending has many advantages but also carries inherent risks. Hence, becoming aware of every aspect of the legal environment is a must for both lenders and borrowers. This might not be easy because there may be different legal organisms ruling over different aspects of the process. Below we provide a list of the most relevant ones.

5.3   Funding Portal Regulation and Taxes

In the USA, in addition to those established by FINRA (Finra, 2021), the *Rule 400* series of Regulation Crowdfunding contains the norms that specifically apply to these portals. Thus, in trying to determine which crowdlending platform to use, the first step should be to ensure it has the legal permits. Funding portals register by filing an application on *Form Funding Portal* through the SEC's Electronic Data Gathering, Analysis and Retrieval (EDGAR) system. The required information for registration, amendments, and withdrawal is set out in *Instructions to Form Funding Portal* and in the text of the rules of the securities and exchange commission (Sec, 2021). An entity registering as a funding portal must also become a member of a registered national securities association at FINRA. For any funding portal that has an effective registration with the Commission *one can* search the EDGAR system. FINRA also maintains a list of all FINRA funding portal members on its website.

But as said, legislation is country specific, so for instance in Mexico these platforms are regulated by the Fintech Decree Law and one would be checking into the AFICO standards. In the case of Spain, these portals are overseeing by the CNMV and have been regulated by Law 5/2015 on the Promotion of Business Financing Act. These laws will cover many topics including the definition of *accredited* and *non-accredited investor* which will rule the maximum capital each investor can offer for one and all crowdlending platforms. When reviewing country-specific normative one should also check into the tax rules as they are not necessarily intuitive. One should learn how the normative works with respect to profits or benefits obtained and how to include these, if any, in the income tax return either at the company or at the personal level.

5.4   Privacy and Data Protection

In addition to the general legal aspects of crowdlending, there are other relevant matters pertaining to the portal to be used that one should be aware of before sharing any information. For instance, one could wonder what type of information would appear on the platform after a request for funds has been completed or after arranging to become a registered qualified lender. Given that transparency is a key aspect of the process that helps create investor confidence, matters of privacy and data protection are sensitive. For potential lenders, sufficient information should be available so that he/she can consider financing a given project. So most likely the borrower will have to disclose: project name, loan amount, term and risk classification, sector, location, legal form of the firm, year of foundation, number of employees and so on. Overall, these data will not be detailed enough to allow the identification of the company. However, given that a certain measure of discretion is also necessary, the platform may offer to publicise the project without giving away the name of the company. Or it may propose that only qualified registered investors can see relevant details such as company name and other key information to the funding of the project.

6 Performance and Commissions

The performance of each loan will depend upon the duration and risk classification of the project. The longer the duration and the higher the risk, the more profit the lender can expect. This is reflected on the risk/returns categories that any crowdlending platform should disclose. We provide an example in Table 1. As we see, the least risky category of projects is A+ and the most risky is E. Within these lie the range of attainable returns. The final yield to the lender will deduct the commission charged monthly by the platform, in this example 1%. The tax agency will also keep a portion of this, further reducing the lender's return.

7 Risk

The crowdlending platform in our example publishes a loan solvency classification and the expected average probability of default for each risk category in order to help investors in their decision-making process. Table 1 shows the risk/return spread of our example where the crowdlending platform classifies projects into one of six risk asset classes according to their probability of full or partial default (see the Yearly Expected Loss Rate column). Of these, the most conservative investments in terms of risk are grouped within the A+ category, and the riskier are those contained in the E one. Within this range, the average risk that arises in the payment of a loan over 12 months increases steadily and significantly. For instance, if we choose A+ loans, the combined probability of full or partial default will stay around 0.6%, whereas if we choose projects in the E category, this probability will jump to 8.6%. These represent the probabilities that the borrower will not repay according to the established term and conditions. To minimise future losses, the lender can diversify in addition to scrutinizing carefully each project. A simple explanation of how diversification works, is to imagine that an investor puts all her savings into an A+ company and the owner of the firm dies with no successor. More likely than not, this will imply the derailment of all earlier plans and the inability of the company to meet its obligations. In this case, the investor will not be able to recover a significant part of her/his investment, even though the initial probability of default was less than 1%.

Table 1 Risk/return spread

Categories	Type of interest rate (%)	Yearly expected loss rate (%)
A+	5.58–9.40	0.6
A	6.15–10.90	1.8
B	7.23–12.56	2.5
C	9.05–14.20	3.7
D	11.05–16.43	5.5
E	14.05–21.97	8.6

Note: Yield = Interest rate − 1% commission

By spreading the investment across unrelated projects, say different regions, sectors etc. the risk of loss is minimised.

Crowdlending platforms need to satisfy a number of conditions before accepting an investor or deciding to support any given project. Being strict in the procedure to assess veracity in the information provided will be the first step. One aspect of this commitment is the need to verify the provenance of the funds. The *know-your-customer* (KYC) preconditions will ask for identity disclosure, proof of legal residency and a national bank account, among other. Most likely, all information and data will be checked with external sources. A second step will be to study the accounting information received to estimate ratios and other indicators as well the client's public information in rating agencies and other. Third, the financial strength and earning capacity of the company is also assed using metrics and microeconomic data. These analyses help the firm estimate the loans' average probability of default. In our example, if less than 1% of the loans in the A+ classification is not met, it is understood that these risk assessment measures are working correctly.

Another way to project investors is to request that the managers and owners of the borrowing projects, provide personal guarantees and back up the loans with their personal assets. This is important for two reasons. First, because the willingness to back up the loans with their own personal assets can be used as a measure of trust in the project and of the commitment on the part of the management team. And second, because, these assets will be used to minimise the investor's losses if or when necessary. Thus, in addition to great scrutiny, transparency and diversification, this platform mitigates risks by asking borrowers put personal guarantees in the form of tangible assets to help cover some of the eventual losses if at all needed. In this scenario, the management or the owners will be personally liable in the event of non-payment. Of course, the crowdlending platform's collections department also tries to minimise the loss margin if the borrower does not make payments according to the said schedule. If this occurs, they will intervene to help speed up the collection process in a multiple step procedure that focuses on trying to avoid default and the related charges. Crowdlending platforms may also hire external agencies in order to protect the investors' rights. Ultimately, the final loss will depend upon the timing of interruption of the payments, the ability of the collections' office and the value of the guarantees at that time. So most often the probable loss is less than the estimated probability of default.

8 Advantages and Disadvantages of Crowdlending for Startups

Startups as well as small and medium size companies have struggled historically to obtain adequate funds to facilitate their growth. Nonetheless, after the 2008 financial crisis, their access to financial resources was reduced even further forcing the nascent companies turn to new intermediaries. The crowdlending platforms that surged at the shade of the crowdsourcing movements provided a series of advantages for these entrepreneurs. Crowdlending is associated to lower costs, more diversification, comparatively better returns, fewer inefficiencies, speed, adaptability and a high number of potential investors including those in less privileged environments (Dorfleitner & Braun, 2019). Furthermore, this system has recently increased its potential based on the security advantages provided by blockchain technology (Porras et al., 2019). In addition, it decentralises credit risks by distributing them among collective lenders (Lenz, 2016). These advantages have allowed the sector grow significantly in a very short time making meaningful contributions in the development of social finance and the startup sectors (Astrauskaitė & Paškevičius, 2018).

For all the reasons proposed, crowdlending is considered a sustainable investment option associated with financial and social performance (Schweizer et al., 2017). Of course, the system also has weak aspects and some of these have been analysed by the literature. For instance, according to Sanchís-Pedregosa et al. (2020), its main disadvantage derives from insolvency situations that prevent a borrower from recovering his/her investment. But, in response, this adaptable system has created new models in which the recovery of investment and interest is guaranteed by the platform itself or the collateral provided (Ahern, 2018). A second important problem relates to the asymmetric information that can condition operations on these platforms (Agrawal et al., 2014).

Among the many, let us highlight the following advantages of crowdlending platforms:

- Provide an efficient channel for a broad class of small investors and borrowers.
- Allow borrowers to access capital on faster and more flexible and inexpensive conditions.
- Let lenders choose projects closer to their hearts and select among different projects according to the risk profile.
- Provide investors with accurate information about credit risks and other relevant data.
- Bolster diversification.
- Help fight overreliance on few and limited sources of funds.
- It proofs socially useful and serves the real economy.

P2P/P2B lending has many advantages but also carries inherent risks. Below we list some of the more relevant:

- P2P/P2B platforms charge a percentage of the loan volume originated. Furthermore, they rate the borrowers' credit themselves, but are not being exposed to the consequences of defaults. Hence, they receive incentives to maximise the loan volume, and this can hurt their credit standards.
- Because platforms are reliant on the investors' confidence, they are also incentivised to obscure information these might consider negative.
- Because 'opinion' is so relevant to obtaining investors, platforms run the risk of suffering mass withdrawal of funds if investors lose confidence.

- Investors are not protected by deposit insurance, as it is often the case with bank deposits.
- Lending can be pro-cyclical, with cheap loans supporting unprofitable projects and good businesses being priced out by high-interest rates when credit turns expensive.
- Possibility that the borrower does not obtain the whole required capital and of default for the investor.
- Risk of selecting a scam platform or that it disappears.

9   Lines of Research and Key Findings in Crowdlending

Even though the published literature of fintech is at its infancy, different strands have started to conform this new area of research. One of them, has looked into the various forms of collective *crowd intelligence* (Berkowitz & Souchaud, 2019; Chanal & Caron-Fasan, 2010) which we follow to focus on the scant P2P business tract (Adhami et al., 2019). Having said that, the work published has started to shed light into this nascent area. Here, we highlight just a few of the relevant findings. The relationship between the arrival of lending platforms and traditional banking has been analysed in the literature. In particular, one question assessed is whether crowdlending platforms have partially replaced bank lending. To investigate this issue, using data from a P2P lending portal named Prosper, the work of Havrylchyk et al. (2018), did confirm that these types of platforms have taken a part of the lending business of traditional financial institutions. A second contention scrutinised, is the impact that the growth of the innovative platforms could have on the (in)solvency and (il)liquidity risks of banking. Related to the aforementioned, the conclusions of Yeo and Jun (2020) summarise that banks are less exposed to risky loans and interim liquidity requirements because the needs of the smaller investors are attended by the platforms. Another engaging result is that the competition between these organisms is bound to diminished the combined risk, a benefit that would disappear if banks were to participate in P2P lending. These findings are interesting because of their economic impact, but also because other works have suggested that the differences between crowdfunding and conventional finance are almost nil (Moss et al., 2015). For instance, Tang (2019) found that P2P platforms are virtually bank substitutes, which serve the same borrower population. Thus, to further examine the coexistence of these lending institutions, Thakor and Merton (2018) looked into the matter of 'trust' to determine that banks are more incentivised to manage this variable, even though the platforms will suffer the more severe effects from its loss. De Roure et al. (2019) concluded that P2P lenders aim at bottom fishing. Hence, P2P loans are riskier, and their adjusted interest rates lower than those of the banks.

Lending platforms' earnings are directly related to the number of borrowers and lenders they attract. This circumstance has been blamed for the lowering of the requirements on borrowers. In this respect, a work by Vallee and Zeng (2019) looked into the informational role of P2P lending and its relationship with investors and banks. This analysis is thought-provoking in that in maximizing loan volume, the platform balances two forces. On the short-run they benefit from lowering standards; but on the long-run their reputation is damaged as the number of unpaid loans increases. Their findings recognise that as the platforms develop, they optimally raise their prescreening intensity, but also decrease the information provision to investors. In addition, the authors' results show that sophisticated investors systematically outperform, but this outperformance shrinks when the platform reduces the information provision to them.

In reference to the relationship with banking, studies such as those by Cusumano (2015), Einav et al. (2016), and Sundararajan (2016) highlight that the benefits of competition enhance efficiencies in the lending platforms' economies. But a more recent strand of the banking literature using games of incomplete information has looked into additional aspects. In Goldstein and Pauzner (2005), a global game-based bank run model extends Bryant–Diamond–Dybvig (BDD) (Bryant, 1980; Diamond & Dybvig, 1983) by incorporating the actual interim liquidity needs of consumer depositors. While in the global game-based bank run model of Rochet and Vives (2004), the authors focus on depositors' speculative runs on unprotected bank deposits. The competitive implications for the case of P2P are difficult to assess, but given the lack of deposit protection and liquidity relief for lenders, a separate regulatory framework could be advisable to promote the sustainability of alternative lending.

Crowlending provides important benefits to financial markets. According to Bofondi (2017), three of the most significant are (1) diminished costs of financial intermediation, (2) higher degree of diversification for small lenders and (3) larger volumes of debt capital available for SMEs. There are also some key reasons that explain the success of P2P lending such as (1) borrowers obtain credit with lower interest rates, (2) they can raise funds rapidly and (3) they do not need to provide strong guarantees (Pignon, 2017). Also, crowdlending platforms provide lenders better returns than those that could be obtained from bank deposits (Lin et al., 2013). In addition, it helps small lenders diversify and combine investments to finance different projects (Bruton et al., 2015).

The lack of data on loans limits the number of empirical studies available (Coakley & Huang, 2020). However, some databases have been utilised repeatedly to assess a number of issues. For instance, using information on potential and realised loans on the United States Lending site Prosper, for years 2007–2008 Lin and Viswanathan (2016) find evidence of *home bias* behaviour and conclude that the special characteristics of crowdlending do not eliminate this bias. This finding contrasts with the expectation that information and communication technologies would produce a *flat world* (Friedman, 2005). A possible explanation is that funders of projects locate in proximity to each other (Gunther et al., 2017), that local funders are more likely to contribute larger amounts, and earlier (Agrawal et al., 2015), and that they are likely to have personal connections in close geographical proximity to each other.

Furthermore, an earlier study by Lin et al. (2013) using the same Prosper site found that online friendship networks of borrowers signal credit quality to lenders.

These networks reduce the probability that a loan is not funded, they lower the interest rates paid, and they are correlated with smaller default rates of the loan thereafter. In line with these findings and using the same data pool site, Iyer et al. (2016) investigate and analyse the role four soft factors play on loan performance in marketplace lending. Their results show that lenders predict an individual's probability of default with 45% greater accuracy than the credit score of the borrower would suggest. However, lenders do not solely consider soft factors when funding a loan. In Herzenstein et al. (2011) who again use the Prosper database, the evidence suggests that verifiable hard factors related to borrowers also play an important part in funding decisions. Furthermore, they conclude that the identities of borrowers which are considered more trustworthy or successful are associated with a higher probability of funding success as well as poorer loan performance. In this respect, Serrano-Cinca et al. (2015) use information from Lending Club to investigate the performance of individual loans. Their findings show that the debt level of the borrower helps predict the accuracy with which the default rate is estimated and also that the loan rating is most predictive of a default.

Other studies have investigated the role of physical appearance, gender, age and race in marketplace lending. Results are sometime conflicting. For example, some works have found that female borrowers have a higher probability of funding success, pay lower interest rates, and have lower default rates (Pone & Sydnor, 2011). However, using data from the German peer-to-peer lending platform, Barasinska and Schäfer (2014) find no evidence that female borrowers have a better chance of obtaining funding. Within the area of *appearance*, some works have looked into the impact that the project description of proposed loans have on their success. For instance, again with Prosper, Lin et al. (2013) find that an extensive loan description with shorter sentences have a positive effect on funding success. While Dorfleitner et al. (2016) find that spelling errors, text length and keywords evoking positive emotions predict funding success on the German database Auxmoney, while on Smava only specific keywords do. Moreover, the text length has an inversely u-shaped impact on funding success, with too short or too long texts decreasing the probability that a loan is funded.

Another strand of literature has centred on the impact of portal design. This is of particular interest because the lending process, be it via traditional financial institutions or P2P lending portals, suffers from significant agency problems due to information asymmetries that can lead to adverse selection and moral hazard (Jensen & Meckling, 1976). New and small entrepreneurial initiatives can be quite susceptible to information asymmetry problems but different works have established the importance of signalling in mitigating the agency costs (Cassar 2004; Blumberg & Letterie, 2007; Rostamkalaei & Freel, 2016) and help overcome some of the agency problems in P2P lending (Bruton et al., 2015). Additional studies have suggested that the image of the provider with regard to the amount of information disclosed about the company, solvency and experience in other campaigns is very important (Yan et al., 2015). Appearance has also been used to assess the impact that the description of the projects had on the obtained loans. For instance, in 2016, Dorfleitner et al. (2016) found that spelling mistakes, text length and words evoking positive emotions predicted success for the portal Auxmoney, while for Smava only specific keywords helped. In this line, Lin et al. (2013) noticed a correlation between longer loan description written with short sentences and a positive impact on funding success. Interestingly, the length of the text had an inversely u-shaped impact, with too long or too short sentences decreasing the probability of obtaining funding.

Some the research has focused on the factors involved in attracting and maintaining investors (Serrano-Cinca et al., 2015) as well as the reasons for leaving the traditional financing systems for the crowdlending models (Coakley & Huang, 2020). For instance, Belleflamme et al. (2010) looked into the motivations that lead entrepreneurs to use these platforms while Sanchís-Pedregosa et al. (2020) focused on the analysis of the characteristics of investors and their relationship with the success of the projects. The success factors of a loan request such as the credit rating, the interest rate, the period of time, the amount to invest, the image of the entrepreneur or the previous experience etc. have also been analysed (Sanchís-Pedregosa et al., 2020; Cumming & Hornuf, 2018; Cummins et al., 2018; Franks et al., 2020).

The information transmission processes between investors have also been studied, as well as the information asymmetries that are generated in intermediation based on these platforms (Greiner & Wang, 2010; Yum et al., 2012). For instance, mispricing is present in some crowdfunding platforms (Jagtiani & Lemieux, 2017; Freedman & Jin, 2017). In this line, the risk-pricing models of P2P lending portals have been analysed to assess if the signaling of risk/pricing information is relevant to the platforms' abilities to fund projects. One question that derives from the mispricing findings is whether credit quality signals can be derived from participation on the portal. In this respect, Herzenstein et al. (2011) propose that strategic herding takes place in crowdlending and show that, in as long as the loan is not yet fully funded, a 1% increase in bids boosts the probability of more bids by 15%. In addition, this herding also has a positive and significant effect on how the loan performances.

10 Conclusions

This chapter has reviewed a series of key matters that construe the crowdlending market history and current reality. We have differentiated among the various crowdsourcing products and services to distinguish the main characteristics that set crowdlending apart. We have also listed the advantages these platforms provide entrepreneurs trying to set their startups, as well as the small investors willing to enter the funding markets. These few pages have not been exhaustive. Nonetheless, they have provided a sufficient overview so that the reader can navigate the subject on his/her own and, depending upon the source of his/her interest, revise the updated situation. We have insisted in the locality of the laws and the geographical proximity of much of the decision-making. Thus, it is of utmost importance to understand the reality of the territories where decisions are made.

We have also summarised some of the academic works published in this area. But this incipient literature has significant voids. For instance, more quantitative works with updated data are needed to uncover disparities in the findings of earlier research. In addition, some results point to the fact that traditional funding sources and crowdlending platforms do serve the same customer base. Thus, it would be insightful to assess whether crowdlending is supplementary or an alternative to traditional lending services. It would also be necessary to discern if the conditions offered for such loans are indeed better than those that can be obtained elsewhere for the same risk class. Finally, future research may also analyse the impact of this type of indebtedness on individuals and organisations. Of particular interest, would be to shed light on the true contribution of crowdlending in wealth creation through its support to startups.

References

Adhami, S., Gianfrate, G., & Johan, S. (2019). *Risks and returns in crowdlending.* Retrieved April 15, 2021, from https://ssrn.com/abstract=3345874

Agrawal, A., Catalini, C., & Goldfarb, A. (2014). Some simple economics of crowdfunding. *Innovation Policy and the Economy, 14*(1), 63–97.

Agrawal, A., Catalini, C., & Goldfarb, A. (2015). Crowdfunding: Geography, social networks, and the timing of investment decisions. *Journal of Economics and Management Strategy, 24*(2), 253–274.

Ahern, D. M. (2018). *Regulatory arbitrage in a FinTech world: Devising an optimal EU regulatory response to crowdlending.* European Banking Institute Working Paper Series, 24. Retrieved March 1, 2021, from https://ssrn.com/abstract=3163728

Astrauskaitė, I., & Paškevičius, A. (2018). An analysis of crowdfunded projects: KPI's to success. *Entrepreneurship and Sustainability Issues, 6*(1), 23–24.

Bandstocks. (2021). *See generally Bandstocks.* Retrieved April 10, 2021, from http://www.sellaband.com/site/faqbeliever.html

Barasinska, N., & Schäfer, D. (2014). Is crowdfunding different? Evidence on the relation between gender and funding success from a German peer-to-peer lending platform. *German Economic Review, 15*(4), 436–452. https://doi.org/10.1111/geer.12052

BBC News. (2001). *Marillion fans to the rescue.* Retrieved April 15, 2021, from http://news.bbc.co.uk/2/hi/entertainment/1325340.stm

Belleflamme, P., Lambert, T., & Schwienbacher, A. (2010). *Crowdfunding: An industrial organization perspective.* Digital Business Models Workshop, París, pp. 25–26.

Berkowitz, H., & Souchaud, A. (2019). Intelligence collective et organisation codépendante: le rôle de l'expert-comptable dans le crowdlending. *Accounting Auditing Control, 3*(25), 41–67.

Blumberg, B. F., & Letterie, W. A. (2007). Business starters and credit rationing. *Small Business Economics, 30*(2), 187–200.

Bofondi, M. (2017). Il lending-based crowdfunding: opportunità e rischi. *Questioni di Economia e Finanza, 375,* 80–94.

Bradley, T. (2008). *Final Fundraising Figure: Obama's. 2008.* Retrieved April 10, 2021, from http://www.abcnews.go.com/Politics/Vote2008/Story?id=6397572&page=1

Brickfunding. (2021). *¿Qué es el Crowdfunding?.* Retrieved April 15, 2021, from https://www.brickfunding.com/es/que-es-crowdfunding/

Bruton, G., Khavul, S., Siegel, D., & Wright, M. (2015). New financial alternatives in seeding entrepreneurship: Microfinance, crowdfunding, and peer-to-peer innovations. *Entrepreneurship Theory and Practice, 39*(1), 9–26.

Bryant, J. (1980). A model of reserves, bank runs, and deposit insurance. *Journal of Bank Finance, 4*, 335–344.

Cai, S., Lin, X., Xu, D., & Fu, X. (2016). Judging online peer-to-peer lending behavior: A comparison of first-time and repeated borrowing requests. *Information Management, 53*(7), 857–867.

Carney, R. (2003). *Chapter on the making of shadows*. Retrieved April 15, 2021, from http://people.bu.edu/rcarney/cassoncass/shadows.shtml

Cassar, G. (2004). The financing of business start-ups. *Journal of Business Venturing, 19*, 261–283.

Castrataro, D. (2011). A social history of crowdfunding. In D. Castrataro (Eds.), *A social history of crowdfunding*. Retrieved April 15, 2021, from https://socialmediaweek.org/blog/2011/12/a-social-history-of-crowdfunding/

Chanal, V., & Caron-Fasan, M. L. (2010). The difficulties involved in developing business models open to innovation communities: The case of a crowdsourcing platform. *M@N@ Gement, 13*(4), 318–340.

Coakley, J., & Huang, W. (2020). P2P lending and outside entrepreneurial finance. *The European Journal of Finance*. https://doi.org/10.1080/1351847X.2020.1842223

Comscore. (2007). *Press release, ComScore, for Radiohead fans, does "Free" + "Download" = "Freeload"?* Retrieved April 15, 2021, from http://www.comscore.com/press/release.asp?press=1883 (discussing a study of online sales of Radiohead's new album).

Corney, J. R., Torres-Sánchez, C., Jagadeesan, A., & Regli, W. C. (2009). Outsourcing labour to the cloud. *International Journal of Innovation and Sustainable Development, 4*(4), 294–313.

Cumming, D. J., & Hornuf, L. (2018). *The economics of crowdfunding: Startups, portals and investor behavior*. Palgrave Macmillan.

Cummins, M., Macan Bhaird, C., Rosati, P., & Lynn, T. G. (2018). The lending performance of non-Bank financial institutions in online credit markets. *SSRN Electronic Journal*. Retrieved April 15, 2021, from https://www.ssrn.com/abstract=3137177

Cusumano, M. A. (2015). How traditional firms must compete in the sharing economy. *Communications of the ACM, 58*, 32–34.

Dadson, T. (2011). *La difusión de la poesía española impresa en el siglo XVII*. Retrieved April 15, 2021, from https://journals.openedition.org/bulletinhispanique/1307

De Roure, C., Pelizzon, L., & Thakor, A. V. (2019). *P2P lenders versus banks: Cream skimming or bottom fishing?* SAFE Working Paper No. 206. Goethe University Frankfurt, SAFE-Sustainable Architecture for Finance in Europe, Frankfurt.

Diamond, D. W., & Dybvig, P. H. (1983). Bank runs, deposit insurance, and liquidity. *Journal of Political Economy, 91*, 401–419.

Doan, A., Ramakrishnan, R., & Halevy, A. Y. (2011). Crowdsourcing systems on the world-wide web. *Communications of the ACM, 54*, 86–96.

Dorfleitner, G., & Braun, D. (2019). Fintech, digitalization and blockchain: Possible applications for green finance. In *The rise of green finance in Europe* (pp. 207–237). Palgrave Macmillan.

Dorfleitner, G., Priberny, C., Schuster, S., Stoiber, J., Weber, M., de Castro, I., & Kammler, J. (2016). Description-text related soft information in peer-to-peer lending. Evidence from two leading European platforms. *Journal of Banking and Finance, 64*, 169–187.

Duarte, J., Siegel, S., & Young, L. (2012). Trust and credit: The role of appearance in peer-to-peer lending. *Review of Financial Studies, 25*(8), 2455–2483.

Einav, L., Farronato, C., & Levin, J. (2016). Peer-to-peer markets. *The Annual Review of Economics, 8*, 615–635.

Embroker. (2021). *106 Must-Know Startup Statistics for 2021*. Retrieved April 15, 2021, from https://www.embroker.com/blog/startup-statistics/

Estellés-Arolas, E., & González-Ladrón-de-Guevara, F. (2012). Towards an integrated crowdsourcing definition. *Journal of Information Science, 38*(2), 189–200.

Fernández-Olit, B., Martín, J. M., & Porras, E. (2020). Systematized literature review on financial inclusion and exclusion in developed countries. *International Journal of Bank Marketing, 38*(3), 600–626.

Finra. (2021). *Filing & reporting.* Retrieved April 15, 2021, from http://www.finra.org/industry/funding-portals

Flannery, M. (2006). Kiva at four. *Innovations, 4*(2), 31–49.

Franks, J. R., Benigno, N. A., & Sussman, O. (2020). *Marketplace lending, information aggregation, and liquidity.* European Corporate Governance Institute—Finance Working Paper, 678, Review of Financial Studies. Retrieved April 15, 2021, from https://ssrn.com/abstract=2869945 or https://doi.org/10.2139/ssrn.2869945

Freedman, S., & Jin, G. Z. (2017). *The information value of online social networks: Lessons from peer-to-peer lending.* Retrieved April 15, 2021, from https://www.nber.org/system/files/working_papers/w19820/w19820.pdf

Freedman, D. M., & Nutting, M. R. (2015). *A brief history of crowdfunding.* Retrieved April 15, 2021 from https://pdf4pro.com/view/a-brief-history-of-crowdfunding-david-m-freedman-219ec7.html

Friedman, T. L. (2005). *The world is flat: The globalised world in the twenty first century.* Farrar, Straus & Giroux.

Geiger, D., Seedorf, S., Schulze, T., Nickerson, R. C., & Schader, M. (2011). Managing the crowd: Towards a taxonomy of crowdsourcing processes. In *AMCIS 2011 proceedings, paper 430.*

Goldstein, I., & Pauzner, A. (2005). Demand–deposit contracts and the probability of bank runs. *Journal of Finance, 60,* 1293–1327.

Greiner, M., & Wang, H. (2010). Building consumer-to-consumer trust in E-finance marketplaces: An empirical analysis. *International Journal of Electronic Commerce, 15,* 105–136.

Guaita, J. M., Martín, J. M., Ostos, M. S., & de Castro, M. (2021). Constructing knowledge economy composite indicators using an MCA-DEA approach. *Economic Research-Ekonomska Istraživanja, 34*(1), 331–351.

Gunther, C., Johan, S., & Schweizer, D. (2017). Is the crowd sensitive to distance? How investment decisions differ by investor type. *Small Business Economics, 50*(2), 1–17.

Havrylchyk, O., & Verdier, M. (2018). The financial intermediation role of the P2P lending platforms. *Comparative Economic Studies, 60,* 115–130.

Havrylchyk, O., Mariotto, C., Rahim, T., & Verdier, M. (2018). *What has driven the expansion of the peer-to-peer Lending?* Retrieved April 15, 2021, from http://ssrn.com/abstract=2841316

Herzenstein, M., Dholakia, U. M., & Andrews, R. L. (2011). Strategic herding behavior in peer-to-peer loan auctions. *Journal of Interactive Marketing, 25*(1), 27–36.

Howe, J. (2006). *The rise of crowdsourcing.* Retrieved April 15, 2021, from https://www.wired.com/2006/06/crowds/

Huberman, B. A., Romero, D. M., & Wu, F. (2009). Crowdsourcing, attention and productivity. *Journal of Information Science, 35*(6), 758–765.

Iyer, R., Khwaja, A. I., Luttmer, E. F., & Shue, K. (2016). Screening peers softly: Inferring the quality of small borrowers. *Management Science, 62,* 1554–1577.

Jagtiani, J. A., & Lemieux, C. (2017). *Fintech lending: Financial inclusion, risk pricing, and alternative information.* FRB of Philadelphia Working Paper No. 17-17. Retrieved April 15, 2021 from https://ssrn.com/abstract=3005260

Jenkins, H. (2006). *Convergence culture: Where old and new media collide.* New York University Press.

Jensen, M., & Meckling, W. H. (1976). Theory of the firm: Managerial behavior, agency costs and ownership structure. *Journal of Financial Economics, 3*(4), 305–360.

Justgiving. (2021). Retrieved April 15, 2021, from https://www.justgiving.com/

Kappel, T. (2009). Ex ante crowdfunding and the recording industry: A model for the U.S., 29 Loyola Law School L.A. *Entertainment Law Review, 29,* 375.

Kiva. (2021). Retrieved April 15, 2021, from https://www.kiva.org/about

Lenz, R. (2016). Peer-to-peer lending: Opportunities and risks. *European Journal of Risk Regulation, 7*(4), 688–700.

Lin, M., & Viswanathan, S. (2016). Home bias in online investments: An empirical study of an online crowdfunding market. *Management Science, 62*(5), 1393–1414.

Lin, M., Prabhala, N., & Viswanathan, S. (2013). Judging borrowers by the company they keep: Friendship networks and information asymmetry in online peer-to-peer lending. *Management Science, 59*(1), 17–35.

Lundahl, N., Vegholm, F., & Silver, L. (2009). Technical and functional determinants of customer satisfaction in the bank-SME relationship. *Journal of Service Theory and Practice, 19*(5), 581–594.

Maier, E. (2016). Supply and demand on crowdlending platforms: Connecting small and medium-sized enterprise borrowers and consumer investors. *Journal of Retailing and Consumer Services, 33*, 143–153.

Manrai, L. A., & Manrai, A. K. (2007). A field study of customers' switching behavior for bank services. *Journal of Retailing and Consumer Services, 14*(3), 208–215.

Marillion. (2021). Retrieved April 15, 2021, from https://www.marillion.com/index.htm

Martín, J. M., Ostos, M. S., & Salinas, J. A. (2019). Why regulation is needed in emerging markets in the tourism sector. *The American Journal of Economics and Sociology, 78*(1), 225–254.

Méric, J., Jardat, R., Mairesse, F., & Brabet, J. (2016). La foule. *Revue Française de Gestion, Lavoisier, 42*(258), 61–74.

Moenninghoff, S. C., & Wieandt, A. (2012). *The future of peer-to-peer finance.* Retrieved April 15, 2021, from http://ssrn.com/abstract=2439088

Mollick, E., & Robb, A. (2016). Democratizing innovation and capital access: The role of crowdfunding. *California Management Review, 58*(2), 62–87.

Moss, T. W., Neubaum, D. O., & Meyskens, M. (2015). The effect of virtuous and entrepreneurial orientations on microfinance lending and repayment: A signaling theory perspective. *Entrepreneurship Theory and Practice, 39*, 27–52.

Oliver, P. G., & Armit, B. (2018). *Crowdfunding and the DIY artist: The influence of Web 2.0 on DIY music communities.* Retrieved April 15, 2021, from https://ssrn.com/abstract=3297206 or https://doi.org/10.2139/ssrn.3297206

Pemberley. (2021). Retrieved April 15, 2021, from https://pemberley.com/

Pierrakis, Y., & Collins, L. (2013). *Crowdfunding: A new innovative model of providing funding to projects and businesses.* Retrieved April 15, 2021, from https://ssrn.com/abstract=2395226 or https://doi.org/10.2139/ssrn.2395226

Pignon, V. (2017). Regulation of crowdlending: The case of Switzerland. *Journal of Applied Business and Economics, 19*(2), 44–49.

Pope, D. G., & Sydnor, J. R. (2011). What's in a picture? Evidence of discrimination from Prosper. com. *Journal of Human Resources, 46*(1), 53–92.

Porras, E., Martín, J. M., & Guaita, J. M. (2019). A critical analysis of the advantages brought by blockchain technology to the global economy. *International Journal of Intellectual Property Management, 9*(2), 166–184. https://doi.org/10.1504/IJIPM.2019.100214

Ridge, M. (2014). *Crowdsourcing our cultural heritage.* Ashgate.

Rochet, J. C., & Vives, X. (2004). Coordination failures and the lender of last resort: Was Bagehot right after all? *Journal of the European Economic Association, 2*, 1116–1147.

Rogers, E. M. (2003). *Diffusion of innovations.* Free Press.

Rostamkalaei, A., & Freel, M. (2016). The cost of growth: Small firms and the pricing of bank loans. *Small Business Economics, 46*(2), 255–272.

Rouzé, V. (2019). *Crowdfunding: Platform capitalism, labour and globalization.* University of Westminster Press.

Sanchís-Pedregosa, C., Berenguer, E., Albort-Morant, G., & Sanz, J. A. (2020). Guaranteed crowdlending loans: A tool for entrepreneurial finance ecosystem sustainability. *Amfiteatru Economic, 22*(55), 775–791.

Schneuwly, A. (2014). *Crowdfunding from a legal perspective.* Universität St. Gallen. Retrieved April 15, 2021, from https://bit.ly/3dOkoPl

Schweizer, A., Schlatt, V., Urbach, N., & Fridgen, G. (2017, December 10–13). Unchaining social businesses—Blockchain as the basic technology of a crowdlending platform. In *Proceedings of*

38th International Conference on Information Systems. ICIS Seoul, South Korea. Association for Information Systems.

Sec. (2021). Retrieved April 15, 2021, from http://www.sec.gov/forms

Serrano-Cinca, C., Gutierrez-Nieto, B., & López-Palacios, L. (2015). Determinants of default in P2P lending. *PLoS One, 10*(10), 0139427.

Spellman, P. (2008). *Crowdfunding-arts patronage for the masses.* Retrieved April 15, 2021, from http://www.knowthemusicbiz.com/index.php/BIZBLOG/CROWDFUNDINGARTS-PATRONAGE-FOR-THE-MASSES

Statista. (2021). *Crowdlending business.* Retrieved April 15, 2021, from https://www.statista.com/outlook/dmo/fintech/alternative-lending/crowdlending-business/worldwide

Sundararajan, A. (2016). *The sharing economy: The end of employment and the rise of crowd-based capitalism.* MIT Press.

Surowiecki, J. (2004). *The wisdom of crowds: Why the many are smarter than the few and how collective wisdom shapes business, economies, societies, and nations.* Doubleday.

Tang, H. (2019). Peer-to-peer lenders versus banks: Substitutes or complements? *The Review of Financial Studies, 32*, 1900–1938.

Thakor, R. T., & Merton, R. C. (2018). *Trust in lending.* NBER working paper no. 24778. National Bureau of Economic Research. Retrieved April 15, 2021, from http://www.nber.org/papers/w24778

Tozzi, S. (2007). Scoring money from an online crowd. *Businessweek.* Retrieved April 15, 2021, from http://www.businessweek.com/smallbiz/content/sep2007/sb20070910_540342.htm

Vallee, B., & Zeng, Y. (2019). Marketplace lending: A new banking paradigm? *The Review of Financial Studies, 32*, 1939–1982.

Yan, F., Fan, X., & Yoon, Y. (2015). Lenders and borrowers' strategies in online peer-to-peer lending market: An empirical analysis of PPDai.com. *Journal of Empirical Research, 16*, 242–260.

Yeo, E., & Jun, J. (2020). Peer-to-peer lending and bank risks: A closer look. *Sustainability, 12*, 6107.

Yum, H., Lee, B., & Chae, M. (2012). From the wisdom of crowds to my own judgment in microfinance through online peer-to-peer lending platforms. *Electronic Commerce Research and Applications, 11*(5), 469–483.

Zopa. (2021). Retrieved April 15, 2021, from https://www.zopa.com/about/our-story

The Financing of Minority Entrepreneurial Efforts in the USA

Derek Abrams

1 Minority Entrepreneurial Efforts in the USA

The Minority Business Development Agency (MBDA) is the primary federal agency committed to the competitiveness and the growth of Minority-Owned Business Enterprises (MBEs). The MBDA defines MBEs as those businesses controlled and operated by Pacific Islanders, African Americans, Asian Americans, Hasidic Jews, Hispanic Americans and Native Americans. Members of these underrepresented ethnic groups must own 51% of the equity to certify the company as a MBE (Minority Business Development Agency, n.d.).

In the USA, the term 'minority' has consisted mainly of underrepresented ethnic groups. But, over the years, the definition of a minority has expanded to some extent to include gender. Although women make up approximately half the US population, they do not share the same power, privileges, rights and opportunities as men. For these reasons, the classification of Women-Owned Business Enterprises (WBEs) emerged. Similar to MBEs, WBEs refer to certified companies where women maintain a controlling interest of at least 51% equity. At both the federal and state level, MBEs and WBEs share many of the same business development and funding opportunities while still retaining their own exclusive support programmes.

2 Traditional Funding Sources

Traditional funding sources refer to those long-established funding sources which have a substantive track record of providing funding for MBEs.

D. Abrams (✉)
University of Texas Rio Grande Valley, Edinburg, TX, USA
e-mail: derek.abrams@utrgv.edu

71

2.1   Bootstrapping

The term 'bootstrapping' is the process of building a business from scratch without attracting investment or with minimal external capital. Bootstrapping is a way to finance small businesses by purchasing and using resources at the owner's expense without sharing equity or borrowing huge sums of money from various funding sources. Bootstrapping could entail the entrepreneur exhausting all personal bank savings and retirement savings, utilising all credit available on credit cards and taking out all possible loans.

2.2   US Government Agencies

Many federal agencies set aside some of their contracts for MBEs, WBEs and Veteran-Owned Small Businesses. In addition, federal agencies provide all grants to MBEs through a federal government grant website. Two major federal agencies that play central roles in funding MBEs are the US Department of Commerce and the US Department of Treasury.

The *US Department of Commerce* is responsible for creating the conditions for economic growth and opportunity across the USA. Two key agencies within the Department of Commerce with major supporting roles are the Small Business Administration (SBA) and the MBDA (U. S. Department of Commerce, n.d.).

- The *Small Business Administration (SBA)* provides loan programmes for small businesses through its 7(a) Loan Program, its 504 Loan Program and its Micro Loan Program. The SBA also has an 8(a) Business Development Program to provide a mentor-protege relationship with established firms to help grow the MBEs (U. S. Small Business Administration, n.d.).
- The *MBDA* does not offer loan programmes directly, but the agency directs MBEs to available loan sources (Minority Business Development Agency, n.d.).

The *US Department of the Treasury* is responsible for maintaining a strong economy and promoting the conditions that enable economic growth and stability at home and overseas. Within the US Department of the Treasury, there is a fund called the Community Development Financial Institutions Fund (CDFI). The CDFI Fund invests federal dollars along with private sector capital of CDFI-certified financial institutions to help promote economic growth and opportunity in distressed communities (Community Development Financial Institutions Fund (CDFI), n.d.; U.S. Department of the Treasury, n.d.):

- The *NMSDC Business Consortium Fund (BCF)* is a fund, certified by the US Treasury Department and managed by the National Minority Supplier Development Council (NMSDC), which provides financing to MBEs. Funds are provided to NMSDC certified businesses in the form of term loans or lines of credit ranging from $100,000 to $750,000+. Loan terms may not exceed 5 years (NMSDC Business Consortium Fund (BCF), n.d.).

2.3   Traditional Banks

Today, there are numerous banks, large and small, which will provide both personal and business loans to all citizens throughout the USA. Historically, traditional bank options were limited for minorities due to a federal redlining policy where banks would collect bank deposits from minorities but not lend money to invest in businesses operating in minority communities. As a result, minority entrepreneurs turned to numerous small, black-owned banks to finance MBE development and growth in minority precincts. The names and descriptions of a few current minority-owned banks are:

- *One United Bank* is the nation's largest black-owned and FDIC-insured bank with offices in Los Angeles, California; Boston, Massachusetts; and Miami, Florida. Over the past 2 years, One United has financed over $100 million in loans mostly in low-income communities such as South Central and Compton, California; Roxbury, Massachusetts; and Liberty City, Florida (One United Bank, n.d.).
- *Citizens Trust Bank* is a bank based in Atlanta, Georgia, which supports not only Atlanta, Georgia but also the Birmingham and Eutaw communities in Alabama. With over a 100-year legacy, Citizen's Trust is committed to promoting community economic growth and stability in its served communities (Citizens Trust Bank, n.d.).
- *Greenwood Bank* is a new digital bank that is majority owned, managed and operated by Blacks and Latino employees and management (Greenwood Bank, n. d.).

2.4   Charitable Foundations

Many charitable foundations provide grants to fund MBEs operating in underserved communities. A few of the major foundations include:

- *JPMorgan Chase Foundation* provides investment to entrepreneurs servicing underserved communities (JPMorgan Chase Foundation, n.d.).
- *Wells Fargo Foundation* provides grants to local nonprofit firms that support low-income communities by addressing racial and social equity issues (Wells Fargo Foundation, n.d.).
- *Techstars Foundation* has invested more than $1 million and helped 30 nonprofits deliver scalable impact for entrepreneurs from underrepresented communities. In 2020, the Techstars Foundation's grant contributions totalled more than $445,000 to mostly MBEs (Techstars Foundation, n.d.).

- *Bank of America Foundation* plans to invest $1.25 billion over 5 years to advance racial equality and economic opportunity in underserved communities (Bank of America Charitable Foundation Philanthropic Strategy, n.d.).
- *WK Kellogg Foundation* provides grants to organisations that support low-income families and communities to help create the conditions that enable vulnerable children to become productive members of society and achieve individual success (WK Kellogg Foundation, n.d.).

2.5   Business Grants

A business grant is a source of funding that does not require repayment. There are countless grants from a wide range of organisations, including government agencies, private businesses and nonprofits. Important grant resources include:

- *Grants.gov* is the main federal website that lists all federal agencies (Grants.gov, n.d.).
- *Native American Business Development Institute (NABDI) Grant* provides $25,000 to $75,000 to business owners of Native American or Alaskan Native descent (Native American Business Development Institute (NABDI) Grant, n.d.).
- *MBDA* provides some grant funding opportunities through the:
  - *American Indian, Alaska Native, and Native Hawaiian (AIANNH) Competition* supports projects that enhance job creation, economic development in US Tribal areas.
  - *Enterprising Women of Color Business Center Competition* aids U.S. minority women entrepreneurs by helping them to obtain business contracts to grow their enterprises.
  - *MBE Inner City Innovation Hub Grant Competition* fund programmes that provide technical and management educational support to innovative entrepreneurs located in minority urban areas.
  - *Entrepreneurship Education Program for Formerly Incarcerated Persons* supports minority entrepreneurs with criminal records (WK Kellogg Foundation, n.d.).
- *Cartier Women's Initiative Award* provides $30,000 to $100,000 to women-run and women-owned businesses from any country who seek to have a strong and sustainable social and/or environmental impact (Cartier Women's Initiative, n.d.).

3   More Recent Funding Sources

Technological innovation, more inclusive societal attitudes and changing business priorities have helped lead to the development of 'modern day' crowdfunding, financial technology firms and minority or diversity-focused investment.

3.1   'Modern Day' Crowdfunding

By leveraging the capability of the internet and social networking platforms, 'modern day' crowdfunding has transformed the traditional fundraising landscape by making it possible for people to offer direct financial support to individuals or businesses in need of funds. Four categories of crowdfunding providing minority funding are:

- *Equity-based crowdfunding* involves investors receiving a piece of equity in exchange for their financial support to individuals or companies looking to invest, typically to help launch a business.
- *Rewards-based crowdfunding* provides donor funds to an individual or business, usually offering a product or service, in exchange for some reward.
- *Donation-based crowdfunding* involves people searching for and financially supporting a single cause or multiple causes by directly donating to them. The cause could be for a personal issue and community-focused issues. The donor does not receive anything for his or her donation.
- *Crowdlending* or *peer-to-peer lending* allows investors to loan funds to individuals or businesses at an interest rate with the promise to pay them back in the future.
- *Real estate crowdfunding* allows investors to put their money in real estate, without the hassle of getting a traditional loan or the obligation of owning all of a single property. Investors will then receive quarterly payouts, depending on how much revenue the property generates.

Several important 'modern-day' crowdfunding platforms are:

- *Indigogo* is a crowdfunding platform that allows investors to support entrepreneurs with new technology products from the earliest stages of development. Investors evaluate the stage of development and any potential production risks—and then fund the projects that you want to help succeed (Indigogo, n.d.).
- *Seedinvest Technology* is a leading equity crowdfunding platform that provides public access to venture capital and angel investing (Seedinvest Technology, n. d.).
- *Mightycause* is online fundraising software for empowering nonprofits, people and the causes they choose to support (Mightycause, n.d.).
- *Startengine* is the largest equity crowdfunding platform in the U.S. and the first mover in the industry. To date, Startengine has raised over $350 million for over 500 company offerings and helped more companies raise capital than any other platform (Startengine, n.d.).
- *Gofundme* is the world's largest social fundraising platform designed to help people fundraise for personal, business and charitable causes (Gofundme, n.d.).
- *Patreon* utilises a subscription-style payment model to allow fans of creators to pay creative artists a monthly fee of their choice in exchange for exclusive access, extra content, or a closer look into their creative journey (Patreon, n.d.).

3.2   Financial Technology (FinTech) Lenders

Financial Technology pertains to the technology and innovation that aims to compete with traditional financial methods in the delivery of financial services. The financial technology industry is quickly emerging and seeks to improve financial processes and activities particularly with the use of computers and smartphones such as mobile banking, investing, borrowing services and cryptocurrency. FinTech firms are made up of startups, established financial institutions and technology companies seeking to replace or improve the usage of financial services provided by existing traditional banks and other financial institutions. Several key fintech companies that provide loans are:

- *Prosper*, founded in 2005, as the first peer-to-peer lending marketplace in the United States. Since its inception, Prosper has facilitated more than $18 billion in loans to more than 1,100,000 people. Prosper offers unsecured, fixed rate loans from $2000 to $40,000. Individuals or established business institutions can invest in the loans and earn attractive returns. Interest rates are based on loan seeker's credit score (Prosper, n.d.).
- *Upgrade* provides personal loans up to $50,000 at fixed interest rates (Upgrade, n. d.).
- *On Deck* makes available business term loans and lines of credit (On Deck, n.d.).
- *Lendio* offers to finance to small business owners. Lendio provides startup capital, business lines of credit, accounts receivable financing, equipment financing, business term loans, merchant cash advance and commercial mortgage financing (Lendio, n.d.).
- *Avant* provides personal loans to borrowers ranging from $2000 to $35,000. Interest rates for loans range from 9.95 to 35.99%. Avant also provides credit cards with limits ranging from $300 to $1000 to help individuals start to build their credit scores (Avant, n.d.).
- *LendingClub* is a peer-to-peer lender which provides fixed term and fixed interest rate loans to individuals and business. LendingClub also provides retirement and insurance products (LendingClub, n.d.).

3.3   Minority-Focused and Diversity-Focused Investment

A Harvard Business Review (2018) article concluded that although diversity in Venture Capital significantly improves financial performance on individual investment profitability and overall fund returns, the VC industry has remained largely homogenous in terms of employment and investment. Today, the VC industry has begun to diversify in terms of ownership and more actively seeks investment in women and minority-owned companies (Gompers & Kovvali, 2018). Several VC firms that have a minority investment focus are:

- *Fearless Fund* invests in women of colour-led businesses seeking pre-seed, seed level or series A financing. Fearless Fund's mission is to provide venture capital funding for minority women founders building scalable, growth aggressive companies (Fearless Fund, n.d.).
- *EchoVC* is a technology-focused early-stage VC firm focused on investing in underrepresented founders and underserved markets (EchoVC, n.d.).
- *Harlem Capital* is a venture capital firm seeking to invest in 1000 diverse founders over the next 20 years (Harlem Capital, n.d.).
- *baMa* provides pre-seed, seed and series A funding to minority-founded technology firms and other technology firms that service the minority community. These firms operate in the industries of education, consumer goods, finance, medicine, or clean technology (baMa, n.d.).
- *New Voices Foundation* provides direct funding and pitch competition funding awards to minority women-owned businesses (New Voices Foundation, n.d.).
- *Backstage Capital* actively invests in the very best company founders who identify as women, People of Colour, or LGBTQ (Backstage Capital, n.d.).
- *Impact America Fund* makes early-stage investments in tech-driven businesses that create new frameworks of ownership and opportunity within marginalised communities (Impact America Fund, n.d.).
- *Serena Ventures* invests in early-stage companies that embrace diverse leadership, individual empowerment, creativity and opportunity (Serena Ventures, n. d.).
- *Lightship Capital* invests in firms owned by people of colour, women, members of the LGBTQ community, people with disabilities and others who have been overlooked and underfunded by traditional venture capital. Firms that received funding serviced the consumer products, e-commerce, sustainability, artificial intelligence and healthcare areas (Lightship Capital, n.d.).

4   COVID-19 Impact on US Minority Businesses

According to a McKinsey & Company report surveying 1000 small businesses in the USA, MBEs, already facing vulnerabilities, braced for a disproportionate impact from the COVID-19 pandemic. Structural challenges inherent to MBEs tend to make them more vulnerable than non-minority businesses. MBEs show signs of limited financial health as evidenced by weak profitability, low credit scores, a limited access to credit and the use of retained earnings as a primary funding source. There are two critical reasons possible for the unequal impact on MBEs. First, the structural challenges that MBEs tend to face make it harder for them to run and scale successfully. Second, the MBEs are more likely to be concentrated in sectors most immediately negatively affected by the pandemic (Dua et al., 2020).

The SBA offered several programmes to help support businesses during the COVID-19 pandemic:

- The *Paycheck Protection Program (PPP)* designed as an emergency disaster loan programme to provide funds to small businesses with under 500 employees. This SBA-backed loan helped businesses keep their workforce employed during the COVID-19 crisis. PPP ended on May 31, 2021 (Paycheck Protection Program (PPP), n.d.).
- The *COVID-19 Economic Injury Disaster* provides financial support to small firms and nonprofit organisations that are experiencing a temporary loss of revenue. The loans, approved to start the week of April 6, 2021, delivered 24-months of economic injury funding with a maximum loan amount of $500,000 (COVID-19 Economic Injury Disaster, n.d.).
- The *Restaurant Revitalization Fund Loan* provides free emergency financial assistance for eligible restaurants, bars and other qualifying businesses impacted by the COVID-19 pandemic. Businesses do not have to repay the money as long as the funds are properly spent by March 11, 2023 (Restaurant Revitalization Fund Loan, n.d.).
- The *Shuttered Venue Operators Grant* provides emergency assistance for eligible venues affected by COVID-19. The Shuttered Venue Operators Grant (SVOG) programme was established by the Economic Aid to Hard-Hit Small Businesses, Nonprofits, and Venues Act, and amended by the American Rescue Plan Act. The programme, administered by the SBA's Office of Disaster Assistance, includes over $16 billion in grants to shuttered venues (Shuttered Venue Operators Grant, n.d.).
- The *SBA Debt Relief* provides financial support to current SBA loan recipients whose businesses have been impacted by the COVID-19 pandemic (SBA Debt Relief, n.d.).

5 Summary

Today is an exciting time to start and own a Minority-Owned Business Enterprise (MBE). Although traditional funding sources provide MBEs with funding options, the emergence of minority-focused and diversity-focused funders help to further level the playing field by supporting established, innovative and focused MBEs and minority entrepreneurs more responsibly.

6 Further Reading

The numbers and types of funding sources available to MBEs are constantly changing to meet society's demand. To strengthen MBE knowledge and remain up to date on topics related to MBEs, see:

- Funding Alternatives and Resources for Minority Entrepreneurs (Biewener, 2020)

- Profit First for Minority Business Enterprises (Mariga, 2021)
- Biden's SBA Newsletter (Ransom, Diana@DIANARANSOM, 2021)

References

Avant. (n.d.). https://www.avant.com
Backstage Capital. (n.d.). https://backstagecapital.com
baMa. (n.d.). https://businessangelminorityassociation.com
Bank of America Charitable Foundation Philanthropic Strategy. (n.d.). https://about.
   bankofamerica.com/en/making-an-impact/charitable-foundation-funding
Biewener, D. (2020, October 21). Funding alternatives and resources for minority entrepreneurs.
   Fundbox.
Cartier Women's Initiative. (n.d.). https://www.cartierwomensinitiative.com
Citizens Trust Bank. (n.d.). https://ctbconnect.com
Community Development Financial Institutions Fund (CDFI). (n.d.). https://www.cdfifund.gov/
COVID-19 Economic Injury Disaster. (n.d.). https://www.sba.gov/funding-programs/loans/covid-1
   9-relief-options/covid-19-economic-injury-disaster-loan)
Dua, A., Mahajan, D., Millian, I., & Stewart, S. (2020, May). *Covid-19's effect on small minority
   business in the United States.* https://www.mckinsey.com
EchoVC. (n.d.). http://www.echovc.com
Fearless Fund. (n.d.). https://www.fearless.fund
Gofundme. (n.d.). https://www.gofundme.com
Gompers, P., & Kovvali, S. (2018, July). The other diversity dividend. *Harvard Business Review.*
   https://hbr.org/amp/2018/07/the-other-diversity-dividend?mc_cid=2cef0d7015&mc_
   eid=a7804b60f7
Grants.gov. (n.d.). https://www.grants.gov/web/grants/home.html
Greenwood Bank. (n.d.). https://bankgreenwood.com/
Harlem Capital. (n.d.). https://harlem.capital
Impact America Fund. (n.d.). https://www.impactamericafund.com/
Indigogo. (n.d.). https://entrepreneur.indiegogo.com/how-it-works
JPMorgan Chase Foundation. (n.d.). https://www.jpmorgan.com/solutions/private-banking/online_
   grant_application
LendingClub. (n.d.). https://www.lendingclub.com
Lendio. (n.d.). https://www.lendio.com
Lightship Capital. (n.d.). https://www.lightship.capital/
Mariga, S. (2021). *Profit first for minority business enterprises.* Avant-Garde Project, LLC.
Mightycause. (n.d.). https://www.mightycause.com
Minority Business Development Agency. (n.d.). https://www.commerce.gov/bureaus-and-offices/
   mbda
Native American Business Development Institute (NABDI) Grant. (n.d.). https://www.bia.gov/
   service/grants/nabdi
New Voices Foundation. (n.d.). https://newvoicesfoundation.org
NMSDC Business Consortium Fund (BCF). (n.d.). https://bcfcapital.com/
On Deck. (n.d.). https://www.ondeck.com/
One United Bank. (n.d.). https://www.oneunited.com/
Patreon. (n.d.). https://www.patreon.com
Paycheck Protection Program (PPP). (n.d.). https://www.sba.gov/funding-programs/loans/covid-1
   9-relief-options/paycheck-protection-program
Prosper. (n.d.). https://www.prosper.com
Ransom, Diana@DIANARANSOM. (2021, June 10). Biden's small business administration: More
   lenders, easier terms, fewer hurdles. *Inc Newsletter.*

Restaurant Revitalization Fund Loan. (n.d.). https://www.sba.gov/funding-programs/loans/covid-1 9-relief-options/restaurant-revitalization-fundt Revitalization Fund (sba.gov)
SBA Debt Relief. (n.d.). https://www.sba.gov/funding-programs/loans/covid-19-relief-options/sba-debt-relief
Seedinvest Technology. (n.d.). https://www.seedinvest.com
Serena Ventures. (n.d.). https://www.serenaventures.com/
Shuttered Venue Operators Grant. (n.d.). https://www.sba.gov/funding-programs/loans/covid-19-relief-options/shuttered-venue-operators-grant
Startengine. (n.d.). https://www.startengine.com
Techstars Foundation. (n.d.). https://www.techstars.org
U. S. Department of Commerce. (n.d.). https://www.commerce.gov/
U. S. Small Business Administration. (n.d.). https://www.sba.gov/category/business-groups/minority-owned
U.S. Department of the Treasury. (n.d.). https://home.treasury.gov/
Upgrade. (n.d.). https://www.upgrade.com/home
Wells Fargo Foundation. (n.d.). https://www.wellsfargo.com/about/corporate-responsibility/community-giving
WK Kellogg Foundation. (n.d.). https://www.wkkf.org

Bank Credit in Europe Between Two Crises: From the Great Recession to the COVID-19 Pandemic

Francisco del Olmo-García, Fernando Javier Crecente-Romero, María Sarabia-Alegría, and María Teresa del Val-Núñez

1   Introduction

In the mind of an entrepreneur, two questions often coexist: What idea to launch and how to finance this idea?

On the one hand, and in relation to business ideas, the euro area economy is characterised by a strong dynamism of entrepreneurship, with more than 1.5 million companies being created each year; this has an unequivocal influence on the economic development of the region.

Likewise, if there is one thing that characterises the region's business fabric, it is the prominence of the self-employed and SMEs. In fact, it is significant that 61% of active companies in the euro area are companies without employees, reaching 94% if companies with less than ten employees are added.

Moreover, from an entrepreneurial perspective, 81% of the new companies started up are entrepreneurs who do not generate employment, reaching 98% of the total newly created business fabric if newly created companies that generate up to four jobs are added.

On the other hand, access to finance is a fundamental pillar of business development in the euro area. In this respect, if there is one characteristic that describes the nature of the European financial system today, it is the high degree of bankarisation. Indeed, the weight of the banking sector within the financial system is significant in comparison with financing through financial markets, especially after the economic crisis of 2008.

This is why SMEs and the self-employed need bank financing to be able to carry out their day-to-day business and make investments for growth. Although there is no

F. del Olmo-García (✉) · F. J. Crecente-Romero · M. Sarabia-Alegría · M. T. del Val-Núñez
Department of Economics and Business Administration, Institute of Economic and Social Analysis (IAES), Universidad de Alcalá, Alcalá de Henares, Madrid, Spain
e-mail: francisco.olmo@uah.es; fernando.crecente@uah.es; maria.sarabia@uah.es; mteresa.val@uah.es

doubt that there are financing alternatives, they are still in the minority, although the current dynamic of change favours the emergence of new competitors that take advantage of the opportunities that appear in the financial environment.

However, the fact that the first 20 years of the twentieth century have seen the two worst economic crises since the Great Depression has had direct effects on the financing of SMEs in the euro area, a region particularly hard hit by the 2008 crisis and the COVID-19 pandemic.

In this regard, recent literature has investigated the effect of the economic crisis on bank lending in the euro area. On the one hand, Aisen and Franken (2010) show that the fall in bank lending in the 2009 crisis was due to factors such as the boom in financing granted in the pre-crisis period and lower economic growth, albeit alleviated by countercyclical monetary policy measures and liquidity. On the other hand, Neri (2013) analyses the influence of sovereign debt tensions on credit conditions in euro area banks, mainly in relation to the cost of finance. In turn, Casey and O'Toole (2014) study the credit crunch in European SMEs, noting that trade credit is more likely to be used by credit-constrained SMEs, with the effect increasing with age and firm size. They also point out that credit-constrained firms are more likely to use informal finance or loans from other firms. Furthermore, Andrieu et al. (2018) find that firm age and size are positively related to obtaining bank loans. Moreover, Fell et al. (2018) find evidence on the influence of the stock of non-performing loans in banks and its influence on credit extension. Finally, Moscalua et al. (2020) point out that credit constraints limit SME growth, although growth is boosted by increased banking integration in the euro area. The aim of this paper is to analyse bank financing to SMEs in the euro area by comparing the information available for the 2008 crisis and the coronavirus crisis. In order to do so, the first step is to analyse the importance of the banking sector within the European financial system from a comparative perspective between the two crises. Emphasis is also placed on the emergence of new players that are developing competition to traditional banks by taking advantage of the opportunities offered by the current environment.

Below, and based on the information provided by the European Central Bank's *Survey on the access to finance of enterprises* up to the first half of 2020, we analyse on both the demand and supply side how SMEs perceive the evolution of bank credit.

Finally, the main conclusions are described, as drawn from the analysis.

2   The Euro Area: A Bank-Based Financial System for the Twenty-First Century

Traditionally, the nature of the European financial system has been described as a highly bank-oriented system, mainly in comparison with other geographies where financial markets predominate over banks, such as the United States (where stock market capitalisation reached 153% of GDP in 2017, compared with 51.6% of GDP for credit granted by banks). This way of differentiating the financial system between

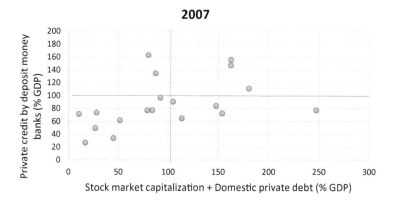

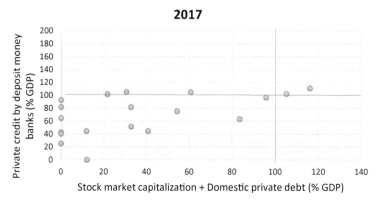

Fig. 1 Euro Area Financial System nature. [Data from World Bank (2020)]

regions is fundamental in the economic literature, which distinguishes between market-oriented financial systems and bank-oriented financial systems, although there are mixed alternatives between the two models [see for example the works of Boot and Thakor (1997), Levine (2000), Torrero (2003), Fecht (2003), Berges and Ontiveros (2014), and Amissah et al. (2016)].

However, describing the European financial system as solely bank-based can lead to a misunderstanding of the nature of the system. In this regard, and in order to base the conclusions of the paper on data, Fig. 1 shows, for the countries belonging to the euro area, the ratio between the weight of the banking sector over GDP and the weight of financial markets (equity and debt) over GDP, differentiating between 2007 and 2017 (the last year available before the appearance of SARS Cov-2). These metrics, based on stock magnitudes, are traditionally used to measure the degree of banking and market orientation of financial systems.

The first conclusion to be drawn from the analysis in Fig. 1 is that, in 2007, the euro area financial system had a high degree of market orientation, not just bankarisation, so that the European financial system cannot be described as simply bankarised, achieving a mixed nature.

However, the most interesting analysis comes from a study of recent developments in the system. Over the last 10 years, the impact of the economic crisis (of financial origin) has led to a reduction in the weight of the banking sector in the economy. Thus, while prior to the onset of the economic crisis in 2008 there were countries with a weight of banking significantly higher than GDP (such as Cyprus, Spain, Ireland, Portugal or the Netherlands with 163%, 155.5%, 147.2%, 134.4% and 111%, respectively), in 2017, the adjustments carried out in the banking sector as a consequence of the crisis itself, but also of the dynamics of a much more complex environment, have led to the banking sector barely exceeding GDP in countries such as the Netherlands, Portugal, Spain, Luxembourg and Greece, reaching shares of 110.9%, 105.1%, 104.9%, 102.4% and 101.7%, respectively.

From the data observed, a number of countries stand out in particular for their radical evolution over 10 years. First, Spain and Ireland stood out in 2007 for their high degree of banking penetration relative to the rest of the euro area; they have seen the weight of their banking systems reduced by 33% and 70%, respectively, mainly due to the profound restructuring of their banking systems since the onset of the 2008 crisis, which had a particular impact on these countries.

On the other hand, while in 2017 only the Netherlands and Luxembourg showed a weight of financial markets above 100%, in 2007 other countries such as Ireland, Spain, Finland, France and Austria did so, although the countries with the greatest weight of market-based financing were also Luxembourg and the Netherlands. Therefore, although in 2007 the importance of the banking system was unquestionable, there had also been a strong development of capital and debt markets in the euro area, with cases such as Ireland, Spain and the Netherlands sharing an important relative importance in both spheres of the financial system.

Only 10 years later, the importance of financial markets was significantly reduced, even in the Netherlands and Luxembourg, where it fell by 36% and 57%, respectively, although the reduction in capitalisation and debt markets was notable in countries with the greatest impact of the 2008 crisis, such as Ireland, Spain, Portugal, Greece and Cyprus, where relative falls of 75%, 63%, 65%, 64% and 85%, respectively, were observed.

Thus, despite initiatives within the European Commission aimed at strengthening the capital market, there has been a strong contraction of this pillar of the European financial system, which is complemented by a reduced weight of the European banking system.

In this regard, over the last decade, the European financial environment has become more complex as a result, among other factors, of the expansive economic policy that has led interest rates to negative levels and the unstoppable development of the digitalisation of financial processes, which implies a cultural and behavioural change among the consumers of financial services.

This dynamic of change has led to the emergence of new players that compete with the banking system in financial activity, albeit on the basis of competitive advantages that banks do not have. Thus, the lack of financial regulation as strict as

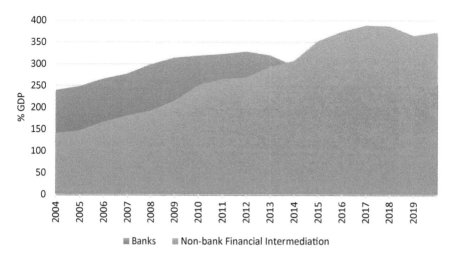

Fig. 2 Banks vs. Non-Banks Financial Intermediation (Assets as %GDP). [Data from Financial Stability Board (2020)]

that which characterises traditional banking activity has led non-financial intermediation institutions (also known as shadow banking) to grow significantly, achieving, as shown in Fig. 2, a size in terms of GDP in the euro area that is larger than that of the banking system as of 2014.

On the other hand, the spread of digitalisation in financial services has led to the emergence of technology companies carrying out financial activities (Fintech), which have steadily gained credit share in the main euro area countries, as shown in Fig. 3, based on the contribution of Cornelli, Frost, Gambacorta, Rau, Wardrop and Ziegler (2020).

There is no doubt, in view of the data shown in Fig. 3, of the strong momentum that Fintechs have experienced between 2013 and 2019 in the main euro area countries, especially in the Netherlands, Germany, France, Italy and Spain.

In short, the European financial system has been undergoing profound change since the onset of the 2008 crisis, so that the COVID-19 pandemic has intensified these changes, mainly those related to the digitalisation of society, accelerating the digital transformation of the financial system and the intensity of competition in the sector, which undoubtedly affects the volume and conditions of credit for smaller companies and start-ups.

3   Bank Lending to SMEs Between Two Crises

The euro area is a region of SMEs. This categorical statement is based on incontrovertible data. Firstly, in 2018 (latest data available from Eurostat), 61% of companies in the euro area had no employees, highlighting the great importance of self-employed entrepreneurs in the business fabric, while 33% had fewer than ten

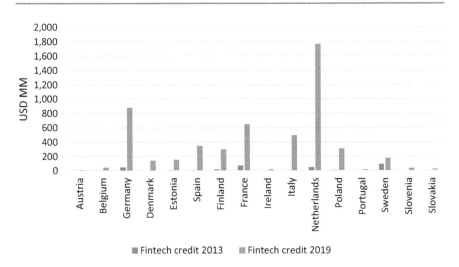

Fig. 3 Fintech credit (USD MM.) 2013–2019. [Data from Cornelli, Frost, Gambacorta, Rau, Wardrop, and Ziegler (2020)]

employees. Secondly, 81% of the enterprises that were created in 2018 were started by self-employed entrepreneurs, without generating employment, while 17% had less than ten employees.

Therefore, the weight of SMEs in the business structure of the euro area is unquestionable, with 94% of companies in the euro area having fewer than ten employees and 98% of new projects undertaken having fewer than ten employees, which makes it necessary to analyse the influence of credit on these companies, as a reflection not only of the business fabric but also of the dynamics of start-up creation.

Figure 4 describes the main problems faced by SMEs in their activity.

As can be seen, both in 2009 and 2020, the main problem for SMEs has been finding customers, although with a downward trend, highlighting that between 2017, 2018 and 2019 the main problem was the need to find talented and experienced workers. Therefore, in times of crisis (2008 but also that resulting from the COVID-19 pandemic), the main difficulty for companies lies in finding demand for their products. The problem of finding demand is mainly rated as a problem among medium-sized companies (30% in 2009 and 23.3% in 2020), while the difficulty of finding talent with the required skills is mainly rated as a problem by small companies (21.4% in 2020 compared to 16.7% of micro-enterprises and 18.6% of medium-sized companies).

It is also worth noting the evolution of access to finance as a problem for SMEs. Figure 4 shows that between 2009 and 2013, the most intense years of the economic crisis, this problem was the second most important for SMEs. However, from 2014 onwards it became the least important problem for SMEs, not only due to improvements in the economic environment but also to the monetary policy measures of the European Central Bank, which have provided an unprecedented volume of liquidity in the financial system while reducing interest rates to levels

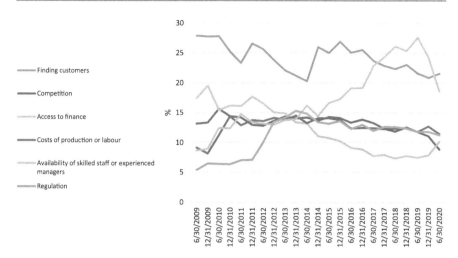

Fig. 4 The most important problems faced by euro area SMEs (% of respondents). [Data from European Central Bank (2020)]

never expected (reaching negative rates in the interbank market). In fact, in 2007, this difficulty was slightly more of a problem for micro-enterprises than for small and medium-sized enterprises, with 17.6%, 17.2% and 17.3%, respectively, which leads to the conclusion that access to financing was not a difficulty when distinguished by size.

However, despite the intensity of the crisis resulting from the COVID-19 pandemic, business financing is the penultimate concern for SMEs. This is not surprising, given the nature of the responses put in place to tackle the crisis, many of which have been based on providing liquidity to companies and facilitating the payment of their obligations. Thus, in 2020, micro-enterprises are the ones that most value access to finance as a problem (11.1%) compared to small and medium-sized enterprises (9.8% and 8.8%, respectively).

Therefore, access to credit has been on a downward trend as a concern for SMEs, mainly due to environmental conditions and economic policies implemented in the last decade.

However, despite its diminishing concern as a problem for SMEs in the euro area, this does not mean that access to finance has ceased to be one of the fundamental pillars of the SME business economy, as shown in Fig. 5.

There is no doubt, in view of the results shown in Fig. 5, that the main source of financing in the last 6 months for SMEs has been credit lines over the last few years, showing the importance of traditional financing in this segment of companies, especially for medium-sized companies, with 36.9% compared to 3.9% and 26.3% for small and micro-companies, respectively.

However, credit lines began to reach their relative importance in 2010, bearing in mind that previously internal resources were the main source of financing for SMEs, also conditioned by the credit crunch that characterised the first phase of the financial

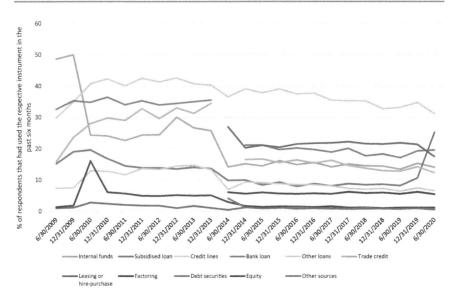

Fig. 5 Use of internal and external funds by euro area SMEs. [Data from European Central Bank (2020)]

crisis in 2009, mainly in the case of medium-sized companies, with 56.8% compared to 48.5% and 44.6% for small and micro-companies. However, the importance of companies' internal resources has followed a decreasing trend over time, ranking at the time of the COVID-19 crisis as the fifth source of company financing. In fact, subsidised loans have become very important in the COVID-19 crisis, increasing by 137% in importance among SMEs, due to the measures put in place to tackle the pandemic, mainly among small (27.2%) and medium-sized enterprises (26.5%).

An issue of great importance for SMEs is the analysis of changes in financing needs (demand), but also in the volume and conditions of supply.

With regard to changes in demand, Fig. 6 shows that the demand that has grown most at the start of the COVID-19 crisis has been for bank loans, mainly for larger companies (with a net percentage of 22.2% for small companies, 20.2% for small companies and 18% in the case of micro-enterprises), credit lines, especially for smaller enterprises (with a net share of 16.8% for small enterprises, 16.3% for micro-enterprises and 13.6% for medium-sized enterprises) and other loans, mainly with 15.2% for micro-enterprises compared to a net share of 12.7% and 12% for small and medium-sized enterprises, respectively.

If we compare the current situation with the previous economic crisis of 2008, we observe the predominance of the demand for credit lines from the moment data is available (2010), showing, together with bank loans, a decreasing trend over time until 2019, when the demand for these banking products grows very significantly (from −0.6% in the first half of 2019 to 8.1% in the second half of the year to 19.9% in the first half of 2020, already in crisis).

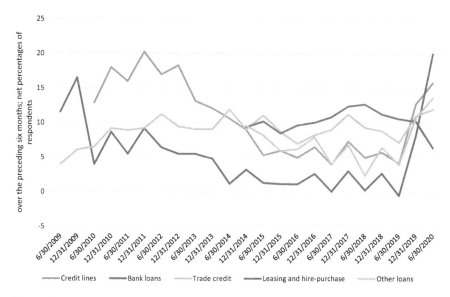

Fig. 6 Change in external financing needs of euro area SMEs. [Data from European Central Bank (2020)]

The data show, once again, the importance of the banking sector in the first moments of the crisis caused by the COVID-19 pandemic, which was characterised by the implementation of measures that paralysed business activity in the euro zone, with bank financing contributing to the availability of liquidity and, in short, allowing a fundamental part of the productive fabric to survive.

On the other hand, in terms of supply, Fig. 7 shows that the percentage of responses indicate an improvement in the availability of bank loans in 2020 compared to the last half of 2019 (6.4% compared to 5.3%), highlighting the improvement observed by micro-enterprises (1% compared to 0.3%) and, especially, small enterprises (9.4% compared to 5.1%). In the case of medium-sized companies, a lower percentage has been observed than at the end of 2019 (11.3% compared to 13.8%). However, for the rest of the financing instruments, a reduction in opinions on improved access is observed. The case of leasing and hire-purchase is particularly noteworthy, with a reduction in the percentage of 8.2 percentage points, although it also stands out that SMEs consider that access to trade credit and other loans has worsened. In the case of credit lines, which is a key product for the activity of SMEs in the euro area, the opinion on the improvement in access to this instrument has fallen by one percentage point since the last half of 2019.

However, in the long-term, there is a substantial improvement in the opinion on access to all financing instruments, taking into account that, in the case of bank loans, in the first half of 2009, the net percentage reached -33.5%.

Therefore, in terms of supply, one can see the difference that SMEs in the euro area is experiencing in access to finance when comparing the two most recent financial crises.

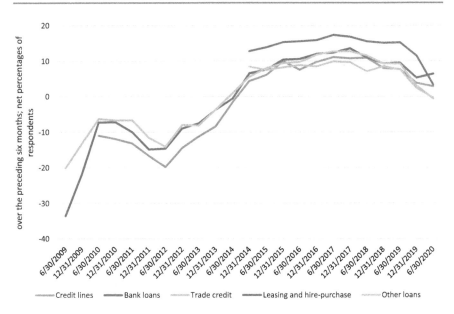

Fig. 7 Change in the availability of external financing for euro area SMEs. [Data from European Central Bank (2020)]

Beyond access to finance, changes in the terms and conditions of such finance should also be considered. As can be seen in Fig. 8, SMEs have observed a decrease in the level of interest rates in 2020, although the percentage of net responses (increase minus decreases) has gone from −9.8% to −4.5%. However, this trend reported by micro and small enterprises is not observed in medium-sized enterprises that report an increase in the level of interest rates, with the net percentage of responses going from −17.8% in the second part of 2019 to 2.3% in the first half of 2020.

This situation is radically opposed to that experienced in the 2008 crisis, where the trend was for interest rate increases, mainly in the case of micro-enterprises, until 2014, after which the trend changed, undoubtedly driven by the expansionary policy of the European Central Bank. However, despite the macro environment, micro-enterprises have reported increases in interest rate levels from 2017 to 2019. In contrast, while small firms have reported increases in interest rate levels in 2018, medium-sized firms have not reported increases in interest rates since 2013, until the onset of the pandemic.

In relation to the rest of the financing conditions, it can be seen how, in the first half of 2020, the trend of increase in other financing costs has continued, but to a lesser extent (from 31.4 to 20%). Despite the general trend showing increases in other financing costs, the percentage of net positive responses has maintained a general downward trend, with the maximum in 2012.

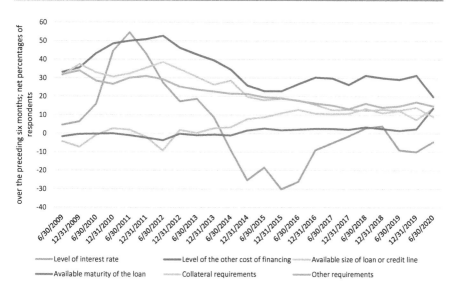

Level of interest rate   Level of the other cost of financing   Available size of loan or credit line
Available maturity of the loan   Collateral requirements   Other requirements

Fig. 8 Change in factors with an impact on the availability of external financing to euro area SMEs. [Data from European Central Bank (2020)]

It is interesting to note that, with the onset of the pandemic, there has been a significant increase in the volume of credit lines granted (especially to small enterprises) and, above all, in the term of operations, mainly for micro and medium-sized enterprises.

This improvement in financing conditions observed by euro area SMEs has been complemented by a reduction in the collateral and other requirements normally needed to obtain financing.

The differences observed when comparing the COVID-19 crisis with the 2008 crisis are therefore appreciable. Thus, while in the early days of the COVID-19 crisis substantial improvements in financing conditions have been observed, in the 2008 crisis SMEs reported a general picture of worsening financing conditions, not only in relation to interest rates (although this is the most notable feature until 2011) and other financing costs (until 2012) but also in terms of collateral and other requirements (especially between 2010 and 2012).

The question underlying this observation is: what are the environmental conditions that lead to these differences? Figure 9 attempts to answer the question.

There is no doubt, in view of the data in Fig. 9, that SMEs in the euro area observed a deterioration in the general economic environment since the second half of 2018, although if we drill down into the differences by size, we observe a generally pessimistic sentiment in micro-enterprises relative to small and medium-sized enterprises (Fig. 10), marking lows in 2009.

Thus, the situation of the general environment seems to be the factor affecting business financing that SMEs perceive most pessimistically.

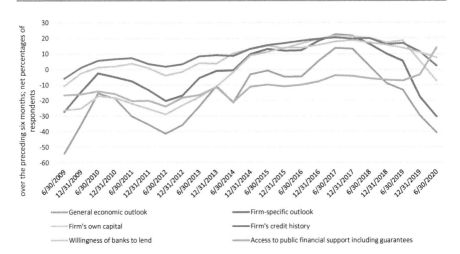

Fig. 9 Change in factors with an impact on the availability of external financing to euro area SMEs. [Data from European Central Bank (2020)]

Fig. 10 Change in general economic outlook. Differences by size. [Data from European Central Bank (2020)]

From an environment-specific perspective, the long-term outlook is less negative, although the sharp decrease caused by the pandemic can be observed, especially among medium-sized and, above all, small companies (with a net percentage of −14.6% and − 15.7%, respectively, in the first half of 2020 compared to the second half of 2019).

On the other hand, there is also a sharp decrease in the net percentage in relation to equity of SMEs in the euro area, from 5.4 to −7.4%, with the reduction in small and medium-sized enterprises (net percentage differences of 15.5% and 13.8%, respectively, in relation to the second half of 2019) standing out. It is worth noting that the second half percentage of micro-enterprises was already at negative levels, which translates into a greater concern in smaller enterprises beyond the incidence of the pandemic.

Finally, the willingness of the banking system to support the business fabric in the face of the virulence of the crisis has led to an increase in the willingness of banks to lend financing, although with a lower net percentage than in previous periods (particularly noteworthy is the reduction in the positive percentage in the case of medium-sized companies). This, together with a strong increase in the outlook for access to public support (including guarantees), has allowed euro area SMEs to survive in an environment of paralysed activity in many sectors. This public support, together with the willingness of the banking system to finance business activity, is undoubtedly the most notable feature that differentiates the COVID-19 crisis from the 2008 financial crisis, where SMEs' perception of bank and public support was negative.

4   Conclusions

Bank financing is one of the fundamental pillars underpinning business activity in the euro area. This is even more important when it comes to SMEs, which account for 94% of active firms in the euro area and 98% of start-ups.

However, the first 20 years of the twentieth century have been accompanied by the two worst crises in living memory since the Great Depression of the 1930s. On the one hand, the 2008 crisis, which had financial origins but quickly mutated into an extremely serious economic crisis that pushed many small European companies to the limit. On the other hand, the crisis resulting from the measures put in place by European governments to curb the spread of the SARS-Cov-2 virus, which has led to the paralysis of business activity in sectors of great importance in the economic structure of the member countries of the Eurozone, entailing an unprecedented economic crisis.

Against this backdrop, bank financing has evolved unevenly in the years between the two crises. On the one hand, the very structure of the euro area's financial system has undergone important changes derived from the loss of weight of the financial markets in corporate financing, but also from a process of adjustment of the banking sector that has led to its loss of relative importance in the European economy, also a consequence of the excess capacity that had accumulated in the years prior to the 2008 crisis, especially in countries such as Spain and Ireland.

On the other hand, changes in the environment have facilitated the emergence of players competing with traditional banks in corporate finance, taking advantage of competitive advantages arising from the strict regulatory banking environment (shadow banking) or from the dynamics of digitalisation that have characterised recent years (Fintech).

Thus, both the competitive environment and the crises that have occurred have influenced the financing of European SMEs over the years, although the differences observed in both crisis periods are significant.

Firstly, access to finance was the second biggest problem for SMEs between 2009 and 2013, years that marked the peak of a crisis that had its causes in the international financial system itself. However, the crisis derived from the COVID-19 pandemic, with very different causes and impact to that of 2008, has not involved a process of credit restriction, but rather the opposite, as the European banking system has risen as a line of defence against the possibility of the disappearance of thousands of companies that were faced with serious liquidity problems derived from the policies put in place by governments to reduce the contagion of SARS-Cov-2.

In fact, and as a direct consequence of the previous aspect, bank credit lines have become the main source of financing for SMEs in the euro area, reaching great importance in the first months of the pandemic, while in the initial stage of the 2008 crisis it was the companies' internal resources that were the main source of their financing, due to the credit restriction that occurred in that initial stage of the crisis.

Second, while the demand for bank loans and credit lines has followed a general downward trend over the last 10 years, in 2020 the dynamics changed, with demand for bank loans and credit lines increasing very significantly as a result of companies' financing needs in the face of the restrictions put in place.

Supply has accompanied demand in the first phase of the COVID-19 crisis in relation to bank loans, although the trend is not similar when looking at other financing instruments.

Likewise, in terms of conditions, financing costs (especially interest rates), showed an upward trend in the first years of the 2008 crisis and subsequently experienced a generalised downward trend, caused by the unconventional monetary policy measures of the European Central Bank. However, despite the exceptional measures implemented by the European Central Bank, SMEs in the euro area, mainly smaller companies, have seen their financing costs increase.

In short, despite the fact that in the 2008 crisis access to business finance was not favourable for a large number of SMEs in the euro area, the COVID-19 crisis has led to a radical change in the business experience, with the banking system proving to be a fundamental pillar for the survival of companies.

However, the challenges faced by the banking system in the euro area are significant, which may condition access to credit for the most vulnerable SMEs, although it is also true that the environment favours the emergence of new players that broaden the alternatives for business financing and which will gain prominence in the coming years.

References

Aisen, A., & Franken, M. (2010). *Bank credit during the 2008 financial crisis: A cross-country comparison.* International Monetary Fund working paper. Retrieved May 12, 2021, from https://www.imf.org/external/pubs/ft/wp/2010/wp1047.pdf

Amissah, E., Bougheas, S., Defever, F., & Falvey, R. (2016). *Financial system architecture and the patterns of international trade.* Centre for Economic Performance Discussion Papers CEPDP. 1448. https://cep.lse.ac.uk/pubs/download/dp1448.pdf

Andrieu, G., Staglianò, R., & van der Zwan, P. (2018). Bank debt and trade credit for SMEs in Europe: Firm-, industry-, and country-level determinants. *Small Business Economics, 51,* 245–264. https://doi.org/10.1007/s11187-017-9926-y

Berges, A., & Ontiveros, E. (2014). Financiación de la economía: bancarización frente a mercados. *Mediterráneo económico, 25,* 195–211.

Boot, A. W. A., & Thakor, A. V. (1997). Financial system architecture. *The Review of Financial Studies., 10,* 693–733. https://www.jstor.org/stable/2962201

Casey, E., & O'Toole, C. (2014). Bank lending constraints, trade credit and alternative financing during the financial crisis: Evidence from European SMEs. *Journal of Corporate Finance., 27,* 173–193. https://doi.org/10.1016/j.jcorpfin.2014.05.001

Cornelli, G., Frost, J., Gambacorta, L., Rau, R., Wardrop, R., & Ziegler, R. (2020). *Fintech and big tech credit: A new database.* BIS Working Papers. 887.

European Central Bank. (2020). *Survey on the access to finance of enterprises.* Retrieved May 12, 2021, from https://www.ecb.europa.eu/stats/ecb_surveys/safe/html/ecb.safe202011~e3 858add29.en.html

Fecht, F. (2003). *On the stability of different financial systems.* Discussion Paper Series 1: Economic Studies. Deutsche Bundesbank 2003, 10. https://www.econstor.eu/bitstream/1041 9/19598/1/200310dkp.pdf

Fell, J., Grodzicki, M., Metzler, J., & O'Brien, E. (2018). Non-performing loans and euro area bank lending behaviour after the crisis. *Financial Stability Review, 35,* 7–28. https://repositorio.bde. es/handle/123456789/11262

Financial Stability Board. (2020). *2020 global monitoring report on non-bank financial intermediation.* Retrieved May 12, 2021, from https://www.fsb.org/2020/12/global-monitoring-report-on-non-bank-financial-intermediation-2020/

Levine, R. (2000). Bank-based or market-based financial systems: Which is better? *Journal of Financial Intermediation, 11,* 398–428. https://doi.org/10.1006/jfin.2002.0341

Moscalua, M., Girardone, C., & Calabrese, R. (2020). SMEs' growth under financing constraints and banking markets integration in the euro area. *Journal of Small Business Management, 58,* 707–746. https://doi.org/10.1080/00472778.2019.1668722

Neri, S. (2013, February 15). *The impact of the sovereign debt crisis on bank lending rates in the euro area.* In Paper presented at the Workshop "The Sovereign Debt Crisis and the Euro Area" organized by the Bank of Italy.

Torrero, A. (2003). Intermediarios bancarios frente a mercados financieros. *Ekonomiaz: Revista vasca de economía., 54,* 158–169.

World Bank. (2020). *Global financial development.* Retrieved May 12, 2021, from https://datacatalog.worldbank.org/dataset/global-financial-development

Part II

Startup Innovation

Emerging Technologies in Financing Startups

Antonio de Lucas Ancillo, Sorin Gavrila Gavrila, and Julio Cañero Serrano

1 Digitisation and Digitalisation as Financing Accelerators

The concepts of digitisation and digitalisation, despite their similarity, are often misunderstood; while they seem to refer to the same subject matter, they actually resemble more of a relationship (Fig. 1): where digitisation implementation leads to digitalisation deployment, and digitalisation demands more and more digital infrastructure for its operations.

1.1 The Digitisation Concept

Digitisation can be seen as the process of transforming information from analogue to digital format, such as paper letters to email communications, or paper receipts to digital receipts. The content remains the same; however, the format is different. Alternatively, it can also be seen as a digital procurement process, where organisations replace existing analogue or obsolete hardware and software infrastructure with newer technological equipment, usually with greater processing capacities, sensors and faster connectivity.

Startups, on the other hand, are not required to go through this process, since by their nature they can be considered as digitally born. However, their technological procurement process involves a higher risk, as it usually forces them to seek larger amounts of financing in order to afford the acquisition of all the hardware and software elements. Therefore, during their digitisation process, startups need to struggle with multiple difficulties:

A. de Lucas Ancillo (✉) · S. G. Gavrila · J. Cañero Serrano
University of Alcala, Alcalá de Henares, Spain
e-mail: antonio.lucas@uah.es; sorin.gavrila@uah.es; julio.canero@uah.es

© The Author(s), under exclusive license to Springer Nature Switzerland AG 2022   99
C. Lassala, S. Ribeiro-Navarrete (eds.), *Financing Startups*, Future of Business and
Finance, https://doi.org/10.1007/978-3-030-94058-4_7

Fig. 1 The digitisation and
digitalisation lifecycle

Fig. 1 The digitisation and digitalisation lifecycle

- Business model implementation, which is still experimental and normally not fully validated on the market
- Lack of financing that stops them from fully developing their ideal solution
- External investors and financial agents must be persuaded about the high potential but limited resources, in order to get access to more financing.

1.2   Digitalisation or the Digital Transformation Concept

Undoubtedly, by converting analogue information into digital format, organisations can keep better control of business activity and the capability of starting some basic automation. However, this does not necessarily mean it has any impact on the business model, where its internal processes, customer and supplier relationships remain unchanged. Traditional organisations, despite investing in digitisation, do not seem to reach the projected expectation as they do not take full advantage of all the technology as they keep doing business in the same analogue fashion.

Startups highlight the fact that technology requires a solid business model or a disruptive transformation in order to absorb all the potential automation efficiency and growth capacities. Therefore, this leads to the concept of digitalisation, where organisations need to align and digitally transform their business model (hence the alternative name of digital transformation) to shift towards a customer-centric approach, where technology stays at the core of the daily business operations, deeply integrating the business activity with customers and suppliers. This digital-friendly approach, coupled with agile management, grants startups their growth potential and versatility in attracting potential investors and securing financing.

1.3   IT Outsourcing as a Financing Accelerator

One of the key success factors regarding startups' business model and scalability derives from the digitisation and digital transformation capacity. Thanks to the existing internet and technological infrastructure to externalise computing functionalities, startups can accelerate the development of their business model by means of IT outsourcing, which basically comprises shifting the existing on-premises hardware and software towards an external service provider, under an agreed monthly or yearly fixed fee, based on a contractual agreement. Based on the amount of outsourced elements, startups can distinguish between multiple levels: On-Premises (no outsourcing), IaaS (Infrastructure as a Service), PaaS (Platform as a Service) and SaaS (Software as a Service).

Therefore, outsourcing improves financing risk scoring as it drastically reduces hardware and software procurement, maintenance and infrastructure costs and time, bringing an earlier market-ready solution (Table 1).

As reflected in Fig. 2, if the startup is following an on-premises approach it will ultimately lead to higher costs of operation and ownerhip, as compared to the available outsourcing options. By outsourcing the IT infrastructure, the startup can focus on its business model, exponential growth capacity and dynamic customer scalibility; however, this comes at the expense of relaxing the control over its data and platform as a single point of failure risk.

2   Technological Enablers

The digitisation and digital transformation processes have pushed academia and industry to innovate and develop new hardware and software solutions, where some startups are adopting the use of Industry 4.0's potential Digital Enablers and more recent digital trends, such as Data Cybersecurity and Robotic Process Automation, establishing the concept of Technological Enablers (Fig. 3). This set of technologies is of great interest for startups, since, on one hand, they can generate disruptive business models leading to the raising of financing, and on the other hand, can optimise their business operations towards growth scalability and financing cost efficiency.

2.1   Cloud and Cloud Computing

Incipient online storage services made the term 'cloud' popular, whose origin is derived from the initial use of 'uploading data to the cloud', referring to a location considered irrelevant. However, the term is not limited to storage, and it actually provides a more generic meaning that encompasses multiple solutions, where the data is normally generated locally within the organisation and sent for processing towards external Cloud service providers. Therefore, Cloud Computing can be conceptualised as the multiple services that the Cloud providers can supply to

Table 1 Outsourcing—key aspects and implications

Key aspects	Implications
On-Premises	The startup is responsible for all hardware installation and network cabling; hardware and software maintenance and upgrades; OS (Operating System) and application security updates and patches; Licensing of all software; Helpdesk support; etc. The equipment is physically located within the startup's premises and fully administrated by the organisation Requires qualified technical personnel running on a 24 h support model
IaaS (Infrastructure as a Service)	The startup outsources the hardware layer to the external service provider but keeps control over the OS and applications layers. Serves as a contingency or business continuity plan in case of fire or natural disasters Can easily scale according to business needs (example: from 5 to 100 virtual workstations or servers in a matter of seconds) Requires qualified technical personnel running on a 24 h support model, as only the hardware has been outsourced. Helpdesk, OS and user application remain the responsibility of the startup
PaaS (Platform as a Service)	Hardware and OS layers are outsourced to the external service provider The startup only focuses on the applications required for the business activity. Everything else is the responsibility of the external service provider Some qualified technical personnel are still required to ensure the applications operate properly, but not on a 24 h basis
SaaS (Software as a Service)	Hardware, OS and application layers are outsourced to the external service provider, which is in charge of all hardware, software, maintenance, cybersecurity and helpdesk aspects Some qualified technical personnel with knowledge between the external service provider and the startup's business model is required, but not on a 24 h basis Is the most efficient and scalable option since the startup can dedicate itself entirely to its business model and dynamically adapt to its number of customers Is the least flexible option as many times the startup has to adapt its business model to the external service provider, as some changes or configurations are not available as a standard solution, forcing the adoption of PaaS or IaaS for more hardware or software control

organisations and can be considered as the natural evolution of their on-premises Information Systems.

Today, there are thousands of Cloud Computing services, and many others yet to be created, such as: Cloud Computing, Artificial Intelligence, artificial vision services, voice recognition services, translation services, data analytics services, remote work platforms, contingency solutions or cybersecurity reinforcement. As a consequence, this novel technological delivery manner is almost mandatory for virtually all startups due to its cost-effectiveness, growth and scalability acceleration, together with an ease of day-to-day operations (Table 2).

	On-Premises	IaaS	PaaS	SaaS
Application Layer	Startup	Startup	Startup	External Provider
Operating System Layer	Startup	Startup	External Provider	External Provider
Hardware Layer	Startup	External Provider	External Provider	External Provider
Costs & Ownership	Full			
Outsourcing Level	None			

Fig. 2 Outsourcing relationships

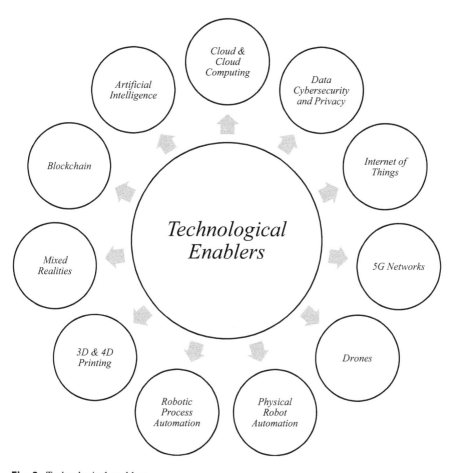

Fig. 3 Technological enablers

Table 2 Cloud and cloud computing—key aspects and implications

Key aspects	Implications
Almost unlimited storage and scalable processing power	Leaner business models as configurations are dynamically adapted to the needs of each particular startup requirement, by means of few clicks and a matter of seconds to make it effective Startups simply focus on their financing aspects, product or services and can easily scale their business models from a few thousands of clients to millions
Reduced costs and maintenance	All the hardware, software, cybersecurity, maintenance and helpdesk infrastructure are outsourced to the Cloud provider under a monthly or yearly agreed rate (OPEX) Long-term investment (CAPEX) is not required, thus reducing the startup's risks and financial stress
Secure and always updated to the latest version	Startups are protected as the Cloud provider takes care of keeping everything secure and running at the latest version, which could ultimately improve the financial risk scoring as unless a startup is specifically dedicated to cybersecurity, it is highly unlikely to contract a specialist solely for this purpose
High-speed connection required	Unless the connection to the Cloud provider meets the minimum requirements, it is very difficult or almost impossible for startups to continue operations, as either the organisation itself or their customers will suffer network connectivity drops, leading to potential economic losses, worsening the financial risk scoring
Single point of failure	The startup's business activity is linked to a permanent connection to the Cloud provider, where a failure of the line or downtime of the provider itself results in catastrophic consequences

2.2 Data Cybersecurity and Privacy

Data and information are considered the most valuable assets, especially for startups. Despite their continuous effort in maintenance and investment in their cybersecurity solutions, malicious software and threats are constantly evolving, adding a latent economic risk which in the unlikely event of a failure or security breach will ultimately affect the operations and consequently their customers.

Startups that undergo an on-premises approach are required to consider contracting dedicated cybersecurity experts and solutions, while if they follow an outsourcing approach, they should be aware that not all Cloud services are equal, and that confidential documents or patents cannot be published just anywhere. Therefore, from the point of view of data cybersecurity and privacy aspects, startups can distinguish between three main categories of Clouds (Fig. 4): Public Cloud, Private Cloud and Hybrid Cloud.

Although Cloud providers are considered secure and undergo exhaustive audit processes, startups need to evaluate and select the option that fits them best from finance raising and risk scoring: (1) *the economic perspective*, where Public Cloud

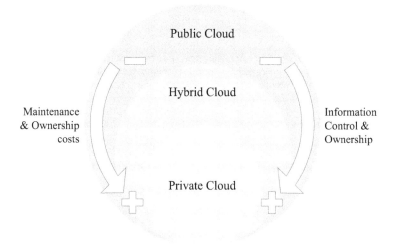

Public Cloud

Hybrid Cloud

Maintenance
& Ownership
costs

Information
Control &
Ownership

Private Cloud

Fig. 4 Data cybersecurity

solutions cost significantly less as compared to Private Cloud solutions due to their shared hardware, software licenses, maintenance and cybersecurity expenses; and (2) *the ownership perspective*, where Public Cloud solutions provide less control over the information and ownership as compared to Private Cloud solutions where virtually full control and ownership is provided (Table 3).

2.3   Internet of Things

Internet of Things (IoT) refers to the concept of having all kinds of objects and devices connected to public or private networks. The main objective is to continuously monitor and collect data from these sensors to understand better the reality based on solid data, improve decision-making and even automate repetitive actions, such as automatically ordering supplies if a sensor detects a threshold is below a defined minimum.

There are virtually no limits regarding IoT applications, and startups normally include them either as a support to their business activity or as part of disruptive business models, such as:

- Personal objects, such as a jacket that regulates heat based on the current temperature, an umbrella to quantify air quality, or a pair of sneakers to quantify the effort made
- Smart Home objects, such as monitoring plant watering or wellbeing of pets, internet-connected refrigerators, or security and automation ecosystems

Table 3 Data cybersecurity and privacy—key aspects and implications

Key aspects	Implications
Public Cloud	The Cloud provider offers the startup a shared architecture and datacentre for multiple customers under a logical separation, based on user accounts and strict access permissions that avoid unintended access and security; however, all the data is stored on the same shared machines As an example: When a file is uploaded to a Cloud drive, the server will store the file under a specific directory linked to the account and apply certain permissions to restrict the crossing of files between users
Private Cloud	On the other hand, the opposite of the Public Cloud is the Private Cloud approach, where the Cloud can be considered as exclusive to the startup, where no other organisation shares access or resources Depending on the required Cloud services, the solution can be supplied by the Cloud provider at an extra cost or on-premises dedicated hardware and software with Cloud functionalities, however requiring additional resources such as technical maintenance, permanent internet access connectivity or cybersecurity expertise
Hybrid Cloud	This is considered as a middle point between the Public Cloud and the Private Cloud where there is a logical and physical separation (non-shared hardware and software) for certain services; however, some others (normally considered non-critical) are still operating under a shared architecture As an example: The mail service is operating on a shared server; however, the Cloud storage is isolated on dedicated hardware

- Smart City objects, such as street furniture where a litter garbage can is able to alert municipal services if it is full, or dynamic traffic lights counting the volume of traffic
- Healthcare objects, such as health monitoring of elderly people
- In industry and agriculture, such as sensors that report on the number of finished products, quality monitoring, logistics purposes, among many other sectors (Table 4).

2.4   5G Networks

5G networks are the natural evolution of current mobile communication technologies as a response to the existing limitations in terms of capacity, latency and reliability, by means of more efficient design, additional antennas, more frequency spectrums and easier deployment using low-powered indoor devices, among other improvements.

Despite consumers benefitting from 5G networks, these changes are motivated by ever-growing business and industry needs to absorb the millions of forecast computing devices, IoT sensors and connected robots. As a novel addition to existing communication networks, 5G is also designed for private purposes, where startups can deploy their own private 5G network for their own IoT devices and users, in a similar fashion to a Wi-Fi network.

Table 4 Internet of things—key aspects and implications

Key aspects	Implications
Quantify and monitor	The primary objective of IoT is to connect, quantify and monitor physical objects, where startups can check their status and evolution on a timeline
Automate decisions	Based on the obtained data, startups can automate decisions and anticipate businesses' and customers' needs. These automations can be done regarding internal processes or related to actual business models
Better decision-making	Startups gain competitive advantage as decisions are based on real data obtained from direct sources, enabling the possibility of more reliable forecasts and estimates
Irrelevant information risk	The fixation of attaching a sensor to absolutely all physical objects provides the risk of quantifying things that are not required or very obvious duplication of data, leading to poor value information, increases of unnecessary costs and even generating inefficient business models
Cybersecurity and privacy	Startups underestimate the fact that the majority of IoT devices are basically a small form factor computer and are left behind with outdated operating systems or lacking basic cybersecurity protection. This makes IoT appealing as a vector for cyber-attacks leading to data theft, falsifying data, or directing cyber-attacks elsewhere

Table 5 5G networks—key aspects and implications

Key aspects	Implications
Lower latency for IoT	This is considered as the biggest advantage for startups, as it will allow remote devices and IoT to be controlled in almost real time, generating new business models and business opportunities
Faster download and upload speeds	5G technical papers promise organisations and consumers 20 times the maximum speed of 4G, up to a theoretical 20 Gbps, allowing startups to create innovative services and products, such as connected virtual reality experiences (high potential business models)
More stable connections	5G deployment promises startups better coverage due to the new types of antenna arrangement and emitters, both for outdoors and indoor purposes
New cybersecurity threats	Due to the increase of ultra-connected devices and high-speed connectivity, startups are more exposed to cyber-attacks regarding the IoT or internal infrastructure
Infrastructure costs	In general, 5G deployment, due to new frequencies and overlapping bands (television 800 MHz and Wi-Fi 2.4 GHz/5 GHZ), requires new antennae installation and compatible devices, leading to an increase in cost to both organisations and consumers

Due to its high cost, patent issues and commercial litigations between governments and 5G network device manufacturers, its deployment is relatively slow, forcing operators to implement intermediate solutions, such as 4.5G/LTE, and plan a future upgrade to 5G when the technology is available (Table 5).

2.5   Drones

A drone is a simple electronic device capable of flying in any direction and maintaining stability in both vertical and horizontal axes. The drone can be directly controlled by an operator by means of a radio frequency joystick or smartphone application, or indirectly by means of a remote control centre. Due to its high versatility in different industry fields and even for leisure purposes, it has become a very sophisticated technological product of great interest to startups and investment market demand, including:

- Short-range RF remote control within hundreds of metres range
- Long-range RF remote control or 4G/5G mobile network within kilometres range
- GPS satellite positioning modules or combination with ground stations
- Autonomous flights based on GPS coordinates virtual routes
- Connectivity modules for un-manned or manned flights from dedicated remote control centre
- Auxiliary modules, such as long-range batteries, video cameras, infrared cameras, laser sensors (LIDAR), speedometres (speed radar) or devices for military purposes
- Advanced functions, such as 'follow-me' function, 'autonomous mode' in case of signal loss or negative weather conditions, and 'return home' in case of low battery (Table 6)

Table 6   Drones—key aspects and implications

Key aspects	Implications
New business models	Due to its commoditisation, from both the economic and technological point of view, provides startups with new and innovative business models, especially regarding service-related ones: Logistics, medical, surveillance, etc.
Longer range	The low cost of drones and automation makes it possible to cover more distance, such as power lines; terrain, such as agricultural fields; or height, such as for building maintenance purposes
Simplification of tasks	As drones reach remote and geographically difficult sites, they simplify the execution of tasks, providing startups with a highly competitive advantage over traditional methods, making them attractive for investment purposes
Increased safety for operators	The use of drones directly reduces the Health & Safety related risks for operators and brings direct economic benefits to organisations, especially those related to heights or working with very high voltages
Costs optimisation	Startups can increase their efficiency as the same number of staff can absorb and better employ the obtained financing, as well an increase of capacity as they can reach more customers
Confusing legal framework	Despite drones' potential, from the legal point of view there are many limitations regarding organisation liabilities and lack of a common legal framework that governments need to agree: Licenses, operators, risks, mandatory insurance, civil and criminal aspects

2.6 Physical Robotic Automation (PRA)

Physical robots are technologically sophisticated devices that can help startups in their automation process. These robots are normally designed for specific tasks only and require a major initial investment; however, depending on the industry and targeted purposes, it can range from partial up to complete automation, where a higher ratio requires more financing but, on the other hand, ensures a higher return of investment, by way of:

- Enormous productivity and precision increasing the overall quality aspects
- Data regarding the production rate and quality parameters
- Dynamic adaptation to the required production rate

In order to work cooperatively with humans, they come equipped with all kinds of sensors, such as 'touch' pressure to manipulate objects, or artificial vision to identify objects and people to ensure an accident-free environment.

Despite the use of robots being associated with the manufacturing industry, their use is no longer limited to industrial applications in that they have crossed over to other startup segments in the form of electronic pets or personal assistants (Table 7).

2.7 Robotic Process Automation (RPA)

When organisations require the automation of physical object handling, they are highly likely to make use of a physical robot. However, when discussing computer software, instead of developing a physical robot to type and interact with the mouse and keyboard, a virtual robot is designed, leading to the creation of the RPA (Robotic Process Automation) concept. A virtual robot is piece of software, such

Table 7 Physical robotic automation—key aspects and implications

Key aspects	Implications
New business models	Due to its commoditisation, from both an economic and technological point of view, provides startups with new and innovative business models with high disruptive potential and financing appeal
Increased productivity	Startups, on one hand, can take advantage of the fact that machines can operate on a continuous basis without the need to stop or rest; on the other hand, they have more production capacity than a human being
Quality improvement	Due to the new generations of sensors and high precision, startups can make use of robots to ensure that all products are produced with the same characteristics and properties
Performs dangerous jobs	Robots have tremendous potential within certain industries, such as chemical, electricity, or nuclear, where they can avoid exposing humans to certain hazards, such as gases, high voltages or radiation
Potential to destroy jobs	The intensive use of physical robots has a highly destructive potential as the production process automation usually involves a reduction of the required number of workers

Table 8 Robotic process automation—key aspects and implications

Key aspects	Implications
Business model scalability	RPA supports the startup's business model scalability by easily automating repetitive tasks and accommodating virtually any number of customers
Increased productivity	In addition, RPA relieves the startup's workload by providing additional time and resources to focus on the tasks that matter for the business, such as spending more time with the customer or better product and service personalisation
Resources optimisation	Startups benefit from RPA as the repetitive tasks do not require overstaffing for one particular task and are always execute the task properly, eliminating human error
Cloud integration	This keeps the organisation's systems updated and synchronised, with great importance for startups from the point of view of Cloud service integration

as an application, process or script, designed and programmed for a specific function, where time-consuming and repetitive tasks, such as repetitive manual inputs, manual file synchronisation, manual database synchronisation (copy/paste from a spreadsheet to the main customer database) only require supervision.

RPA has the potential to drastically reduce the amount of required resources, such as workforce and time, leading to cost optimisation and lower financing requirements, critical for virtually any startup (Table 8).

2.8   3D and 4D Printing

The additive manufacturing process, more commonly known as 3D Printing, comprises a technological device capable of creating physical objects out of a computer-designed 3D object using rigid materials, such as ABS filament, other composite materials, metals or cements. Typical plastic filament 3D printers consist of an extruder that is heated up to 200 °C to melt the filament, and by means of moving the motors in XYZ coordinates (left, right, height) it places the liquid filament according to the designed object properties. Finally, a fan attached to the extruder cools and solidifies the filament.

An evolution of additive manufacturing is 4D Printing, where academia and industry are researching the possibility of mixing some materials to create objects with special physical properties, such as those which self-assemble or change shape based on designed temperature, humidity, sound or light conditions.

Ultimately, the health industry has extended the concept of additive manufacturing to the medical field by experimenting with organic materials, exploring the possibility of future printing of human tissues and organs (Table 9).

Table 9 3D and 4D printing—key aspects and implications

Key aspects	Implications
Cost reduction	A 3D printer provides startups with the capability of printing any object, without requiring an industrial assembly line or an expensive mold or cast
Fast prototyping	Startups can innovate, test new products and make design improvements at very fast pace, skipping traditional industrial processes
True customisation	Brings new competitive advantages to startups' business model by offering the possibility of adapting the product to the customer's needs, such as colour, shape or size, without having to depend on a third party or change the production process
Copyright and royalties	Startups must be aware that the moment their product becomes a 3D computer object, there is a cybersecurity risk and piracy issues, where anyone having a copy of the file could print a copy at home without paying for the object or copyright
Malicious uses	Startups need to be aware that employees may use printers for illicit purposes, such as printing firearms, sharp objects, even making modifications to the internal structure of the object to make it fail or cause damage

2.9 Virtual, Mixed and Augmented Reality

The Augmented Reality concept and technology has been present in the industry since the 1960s where a projection system, usually known as HUD (Heads Up Display), simply overlays additional information over real elements and has been widely used in the aviation and automotive sectors. Thanks to CPU (Computer Processing Unit) computing capacities, GPU (Graphic Processing Unit) rendering capacities, and the development of new sensors to determine position within the environment, HUDs have evolved into so-called 'mixed reality' glasses and 'virtual reality' glasses.

From the user perspective, Mixed Reality blends real elements with virtual elements, allowing interaction with both of them, while on the other hand, Virtual Reality provides a total immersion and interaction within completely different virtual environments, without mixing any real elements.

This technology provides tremendous potential for startups, not only for their business models but for disruptive tools that innovate and optimise their internal processes, allowing them to become more competitive and profitable (Table 10).

2.10 Blockchain

From a technological point of view, Blockchain is a decentralised node-based system consisting of a set of blocks linked together under unique identifiers. From a startup's utility point of view, this is essentially a secure system that certifies the authenticity of the data, as once the block has been forged the contained data cannot be modified or deleted, and if someone tampers with it, it becomes unusable. Thanks to this system, there is no longer any need for a trusted third party or a certifying

Table 10 Virtual, mixed and augmented reality—key aspects and implications

Key aspects	Implications
Disruptive business models	Startups can build disruptive business models regarding new ways of consuming online content, interacting in social networks, virtual gaming, virtual environments immersion within architecture/ construction, etc.
Innovation in prototyping	Startups have the ability to detect potential design errors far ahead before going to actual production processes, as the final product can be analysed in 3D. In addition, startups have the flexibility of modifying creating multiple iterations leading to more mature solutions
Continuous innovation	Startups can continuously innovate their internal processes or as a product by means of virtual trainers, virtual classes, virtual maintenance manuals, virtual stores, virtual fitting rooms, etc.
Disruptive experiences	The use of mixed realities not only provides an innovation source for disruptive content, but a major differential advantage as startups can create disruptive experiences that involve and engage their customers
Emerging technology	Due to the novelty of the technology, current solutions on the market still have to overcome major barriers such as price, size, performance, etc., although recent smartphones support VR/MR/AR frameworks
Cost and dependence on third parties	Despite the commoditisation of the mixed reality development frameworks, additional hardware, graphic designers and programmers are required to carry out the whole development process

entity to provide data authenticity, where organisations and consumers benefit from more secure transactions and lower costs as intermediaries are removed.

Cryptocurrencies, such as Bitcoin, are based on Blockchain because it allows certifying the unique number of each coin as it is equivalent to the serial number of a banknote. The data can be duplicated, just like photocopying a banknote, but cannot create value as it is considered worthless. These novel cryptocurrency applications provide startups with the possibility of creating not only new disruptive financial business models but also achieving disruptive financing options by means of ICO (Initial Public Offering) or STO (Security Token Offering) (Table 11).

2.11   Artificial Intelligence

Thanks to the continuous increase of computational performance, software optimisation and Cloud Computing services, many repetitive analysis tasks are being automated and even support automatic decision-making. Artificial Intelligence is a set of technologies and algorithms that can help startups to transform data inputs into manageable information outputs. There are several different types of AI, such as:

Table 11 Blockchain key aspects and implications

Key aspects	Implications
New business models	Due to its commoditisation, from both an economic and technological point of view, provides startups with new and innovative business models regarding certification and cryptocurrencies
Independence from third parties	Startups can reduce costs as third party trusted authorities are no longer needed to certify the veracity of transactions, reducing the financing requirements
Security and transparency	The whole Blockchain concept is based on open mathematical principles, therefore it can be audited and checked for integrity and can be considered secure as it significantly hinders malicious manipulation
Slower than a database	Unlike traditional databases, where changes are almost instantaneous, the majority of Blockchain implementations are periodic, where a block is generated every specific period of time
Misinterpreted as Bitcoin	The industry confuses Blockchain with Bitcoin, a cryptocurrency based on Blockchain implementation, greatly underestimating its financing potential based on ICO and STO options

- *Machine Learning*: refers to the automatic learning process making use of different approaches, such as Deep Learning, using specific algorithms, such as Neural Networks or Decision Trees, to classify data. In general, this field is associated with trained models that already implement some features and weights.
- *Deep Learning*: is generally considered as a subset of Machine Learning, that is making use of specific algorithms, such as Neural Networks, and is capable of modelling features and weights from untrained or unknown input data.
- *Artificial Intelligence*: can be understood as a superset of Machine Learning networks ultimately capable of generating knowledge on its own. This requires a lot of computing power that currently is limited to some supercomputers or future quantum computing.

AI can be applied to virtually all industries and organisations as it increases productivity and reduces costs by automating repetitive tasks, thus becoming a very interesting tool for organisations due to its analysis, optimisation, decision-making and forecasting potential.

However, startups may have some issues regarding developing their required algorithms despite having the available technology to support them: fintech or trading startups may use existing known algorithms, while other segments need to model them from scratch, implying economic risks but also leading to high investment potential.

Finally, there are a lot of open discussions about what the term intelligence really implies, and whether in the future computers will develop their own sort of intelligence, and if that would imply any threat to humans, among many other philosophical questions that go beyond the objective of this book (Table 12).

Table 12 Artificial intelligence—key aspects and implications

Key aspects	Implications
New business models	Due to its commoditisation, from both the economic and technological point of view, this provides startups new and innovative business models, especially regarding service-related ones
Eliminate repetitive tasks	Startups can automate the processing of tables, databases, images or videos with little human intervention, optimising resources and reducing financing requirements
Eliminate human error	Humans make mistakes and biased decisions, such as towards gender, beliefs, opinions or experiences, where an independent AI's decision will be based on the analysed input data, reducing startups' operations risks
Advances in medicine	AI is forecasted to have a great impact on all fields, with high investment ratios on medical-related startups: From detecting possible tumours from an X-ray to finding vaccines and cures for diseases
Job destruction	Intensive AI automation has a highly destructive potential as its implementation involves a reduction of the required number of workers

3   Summary

Table 13 describes the impact of each Technological Enabler regarding its potential impact on financing from the point of view of the business model (in terms of how the technology can create a disruptive idea to obtain financing) and internal operations impact (in terms of how the technology optimises the use of resources to absorb or achieve more financing).

4   Further Reading

An overview of further recommended reading is provided for the following topics:

- Technological Enablers specific: (Sahut et al., 2021; Sathi, 2014; Gavrila & de Lucas Ancillo, 2021)
- Artificial Intelligence specific: (Brynjolfsson & McAfee, 2020; Burgess, 2018; Choi & Huang, 2021; Obschonka & Audretsch, 2020)
- Robotic Process Automation specific: (van der Aalst et al., 2018; Smeets et al., 2021)
- Blockchain specific: (Choi & Huang, 2021; Marco & Karim, 2017)

Table 13 Technological enablers impact on financing aspects

Technological enabler	Potential access to financing opportunities based on disruptive business models	Potential access to financing opportunities based on internal technological efficiency
Cloud and Cloud Computing	High	High potential for financing due to disruptive implications
Data Cybersecurity and Privacy	High	Medium/low potential for financing depending on the business model
Internet of Things	High	Medium/low potential for financing depending on the business model
5G Networks	High	Medium/low potential for financing depending on the business model
Drones	High	Low potential for financing depending on the business model
Physical Robotic Automation	High	Medium/high potential for financing due to increased automation
Robotic Process Automation	High	High potential for financing due to increased IT automation
3D and 4D Printing	High	Low potential for financing depending on the business model
Mixed Realities	High	Medium/high potential for financing due to disruptive experiences
Blockchain	High	High potential for financing due to third-parties reduction
Artificial Intelligence	High	High potential for financing due to disruptive implications

References

Brynjolfsson, E., & McAfee, A. (2020). Artificial intelligence: The insights you need from Harvard Business Review. In *Harvard Business Review Press (Issue February 2019)*. Harvard Business Review Press. http://link.springer.com/10.1007/978-3-030-33447-5

Burgess, A. (2018). The executive guide to artificial intelligence. In *The executive guide to artificial intelligence*. Springer International. https://doi.org/10.1007/978-3-319-63820-1

Choi, P. M. S., & Huang, S. H. (2021). *Fintech with artificial intelligence, big data, and Blockchain*. Springer Singapore. https://doi.org/10.1007/978-981-33-6137-9

Gavrila, S., & de Lucas Ancillo, A. (2021). Spanish SMEs' digitalization enablers: E-receipt applications to the offline retail market. *Technological Forecasting and Social Change, 162*, 120381. https://doi.org/10.1016/j.techfore.2020.120381

Marco, I., & Karim, L. R. (2017). The truth about blockchain. *Harvard Business Review..* https://enterprisersproject.com/sites/default/files/the_truth_about_blockchain.pdf%0A. https://hbr.org/2017/01/the-truth-about-blockchain

Obschonka, M., & Audretsch, D. B. (2020). Artificial intelligence and big data in entrepreneurship: A new era has begun. *Small Business Economics, 55*(3), 529–539. https://doi.org/10.1007/s11187-019-00202-4

Sahut, J. M., Iandoli, L., & Teulon, F. (2021). The age of digital entrepreneurship. *Small Business Economics, 56*(3), 1159–1169. https://doi.org/10.1007/s11187-019-00260-8

Sathi, A. (2014). Technological enablers. In *Engaging customers using big data* (pp. 131–157). Palgrave Macmillan. https://doi.org/10.1057/9781137386199_6

Smeets, M., Erhard, R., & Kaußler, T. (2021). *Robotic process automation (RPA) in the financial sector: Technology—Implementation—Success for decision makers and users.* Springer Fachmedien Wiesbaden.

van der Aalst, W. M. P., Bichler, M., & Heinzl, A. (2018). Robotic process automation. *Business and Information Systems Engineering, 60*(4), 269–272. https://doi.org/10.1007/s12599-018-0542-4

ICOs, IEOs and STOs: Token Sales as Innovative Formulas for Financing Start-Ups

Noelia Romero-Castro, Ada M. Pérez-Pico, and Klaus Ulrich

1 Introduction

Technological advances and the decentralization of finance have fostered the development of innovative financing formulas based on which companies, entrepreneurs or project developers raise funds in open calls through the internet to obtain cryptocurrencies in exchange for digital assets (tokens), which entitle buyers to an exclusive right, reward or financial claim (Adhami & Giudici, 2019). The public sale of these tokens is enabled by the use of distributed ledger technologies (DLTs), such as blockchain, and can be structured as initial coin offerings (ICOs), initial exchange offerings (IEOs) and security token offerings (STOs). ICOs and IEOs are mainly related to the issuance of tokens that do not exhibit security-like features, falling beyond the scope of most financial regulations (Chew & Spiegl, 2021). Tokens that represent ownership of an asset, such as corporate debt and equity, are named security tokens, and their purchase through an STO is considered an investment subject to securities laws (Lambert et al., 2021).

Although a recent phenomenon, more than US$31[1] billion has been raised through more than 2100 ICOs/IEOs/STOs (PwC/Strategy&, 2020) since the first ICO in 2013 (Mastercoin). The lack of regulation and the rapid and low-cost process behind ICOs caused exponential growth over 2017 and the first half of 2018 (PwC/Strategy&, 2020). The ambiguous or inexistent regulation (lack of investor

---

[1]Calculations are based on the currency exchange rates at the end date of the public sale, and only completed offerings with an indicated funding volume are considered.

N. Romero-Castro (✉) · A. M. Pérez-Pico
Santiago de Compostela University, Santiago de Compostela, Spain
e-mail: noe.romero@usc.es; adamaria.perez@usc.es

K. Ulrich
ESIC Business & Marketing School, Valencia, Spain
e-mail: klausjurgen.ulrich@esic.edu

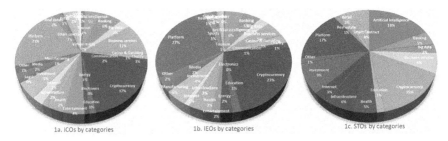

1a. ICOs by categories   1b. IEOs by categories   1c. STOs by categories

Fig. 1 Distribution of ICOs, IEOs and STOs across sector categories. (tokens-economy.com, 2021)

protection, absence of disclosure requirements) and the dubious legitimacy of some operations (OECD, 2019; García-Rodríguez, 2021) motivated a sharp drop in ICOs in the second half of 2018. This drop enabled the development of new issuance schemes such as IEOs and STOs, intended to provide a safer and more regulatory-compliant model for both issuers and investors (Lynn & Rosati, 2021). Nevertheless, whether an offering is considered regulatory compliant will depend on its particular features on a case-by-case basis, based on the regulatory frameworks in the jurisdiction of issuance and in the jurisdictions where the offering is marketed to investors (OECD, 2020).

Since 2019, IEOs and STOs have seen their relevance as alternative forms of issuing tokens increase, although the number of offerings and the volume of funding raised are far behind those reached in 2017 and 2018. According to the sixth ICO/STO Report (PwC/Strategy&, 2020), STOs showed solid but volatile development throughout 2018 and the first half of 2019 (BoltonCoin's STO stands out, raising US$68 million in February 2019) and an overall low funding volume in the second half. A more recent report states that in 2020, STOs raised approximately US$5 billion (Cointelegraph Research & CryptoResearch.Report, 2021). Although the first IEOs (Bread, Gifko) took place in 2017, they did not play a significant role until early 2019, particularly with the Bitfinex IEO (US$1 billion in May 2019). Figure 1 shows the distribution of ICOs, IEOs and STOs across sector categories, with platforms and cryptocurrencies being the top categories. For STO artificial intelligence, smart contracts or investments display a higher percentage than ICOs and IEOs. Figure 2 shows the evolution of ICOs, STOs and IEOs over the 2014–2019 period, confirming the predominance of ICOs until 2018 and the rise of STOs in 2019.

These innovative financing alternatives have come to complete the spectrum of available financing instruments that in recent decades have contributed to the democratization of finance (Chen, 2018; Ackermann et al., 2020). Little more than a decade ago, crowdfunding was also seen as an innovation. Venture capital (VC), private equity, business angels or initial public offerings (IPOs) have consolidated a highly important role in the financing of the start-up and small and medium-sized enterprise (SME) lifecycles. Given that their recent development, it is soon to judge whether ICO/IEO/STO funding models are going to replace these other financing

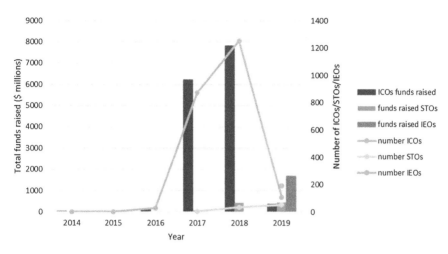

Fig. 2 Evolution of ICOs, STOs and IEOs (total funds raised and number). Source: icodata.io, blockstate.com. The number of IEOs in 2019 is estimated from Coinmarketcap (Slyusarev, 2020)

alternatives, but a complementary role seems more likely (Ackermann et al., 2020; Chew & Spiegl, 2021). ICOs have been mainly related to the initial steps of a start-up (at the seed or early stage), as a vehicle for funding the development of the product or service or even the underlying blockchain technology. Whether these new funding models are suitable for start-ups in any sector or industry is also a relevant issue. As shown in Fig. 1, ICOs have been mainly related to the development of blockchain projects, and there is a consensus with regard to the convenience of securing an alignment between the purpose of an ICO/IEO and the business model and value proposition of a start-up (Massey et al., 2017). In fact, the main value of ICOs has been related to the possibility of creating network effects and a knowledge and user base that fosters the development, adoption, and diffusion of the project (Chen, 2018). Rather differently, STOs have been advocated as a more reasonable option for all types of companies, with a special focus on SMEs (Mazzorana-Kremer, 2019). Chew and Spiegl (2021) confirm that compared to the companies involved in IPOs, STOs are mainly issued by small companies. Nevertheless, both types of token offerings are subject to the interest of speculators relying on an increase in value of the tokens issued (García-Rodríguez, 2021).

ICOs were originally developed as an attractive financing alternative given their unregulated framework and decentralized nature, which significantly lowered the costs of fundraising. Lack of regulation opened the door to scams and frauds that, along with concerns about the impact of these schemes on the whole financial system, led to a variety of regulatory approaches around the world. See Bellavitis et al. (2021) for a complete overview of the international regulatory landscape of token offerings. Some key points are addressed in Sect. 2.2.2. These regulatory approaches have complicated the process of ICOs, IEOs and STOs by forcing issuers to pay special attention to the applicable legal framework in both the jurisdiction of the issuer and that of potential investors (Lynn & Rosati, 2021). Doing so is difficult since the very nature of these offerings hinders the identification of the geographical scope of both (García-Rodríguez, 2021).

2   The Building Blocks

ICOs, IEOs and STOs rely on three main elements or building blocks: the development of digital processes to make and validate transactions in a decentralized network (distributed ledgers), the creation of digital assets or tokens that entitle their buyers to different rights, and the search for innovative and cost-effective new funding sources under the decentralized finance (DeFi) umbrella.

2.1   Distributed Ledger Technology, Blockchain and Smart Contracts

A ledger makes it possible to record and track information about any fact around the world (Holden & Malani, 2019). A distributed ledger is a cryptographically protected, decentralized, single database managed in a peer-to-peer network by multiple participants (nodes) that hold a copy of the ledger and synchronously update it through mining and consensus mechanisms rather than relying on a central authority (Romero-Ugarte, 2018). Thus, DLTs enable the peer-to-peer transfer of information, creating a digital record that is almost impossible to alter (immutability), increasing security and transparency and allowing efficiency gains (i.e. the potential to achieve T + 0 settlement, lower transaction fees) driven by decentralization and disintermediation (OECD, 2019; Chew & Spiegl, 2021). Moreover, a distributed ledger with many nodes is less prone to cyberattacks and fraud than a centralized database (Lambert et al., 2021).

Wadsworth (2018) explains that different DLTs exist depending on their design: (1) permissionless or permissioned; (2) public or private; (3) non-hierarchical or hierarchical; and (4) open source or closed source. Blockchain is a type of DLT originally conceived as a permissionless, public, non-hierarchical, and open-source DLT. Tangle and Hashgraph are other DLTs (Ackermann et al., 2020). Blockchain combines DLT with a variety of block-based encryption technologies (Deloitte et al., 2020a). Individual transactions are processed and stored in blocks that are connected in chronological order to create a chain using cryptographic hash functions (Romero-Ugarte, 2018; Schückes & Gutmann, 2021). Hashing is a cryptographic system for transforming any text of any arbitrary length into a theoretically irreversible string of numbers and letters of fixed length (the 'hash') to provide the security, precision and immutability of records (Adhami et al., 2018). Transactions are recorded in the subsequent blocks and broadcast to nodes for verification of validity. Thus, when consensus is reached, the transactions remain permanently recorded in a transparent and verifiable manner, with no possible modification or deletion (Schückes & Gutmann, 2021).

As explained by Holden and Malani (2019), the validation of transactions (mining) drives the major cost to users from public blockchain ledgers: miner compensation. So-called miners are the entities that are trusted to honestly maintain the ledger in exchange for a reward or compensation so that the return on maintaining the network is greater than the return on manipulating it. This situation can be guaranteed through two main alternative consensus protocols: 'Proof-of-Work' (PoW) and 'Proof of Stake' (PoS). PoW, the algorithm at the heart of Bitcoin[2] requires 'solving a puzzle' for the right to record new transactions to the blockchain, while in PoS, miners bet or stake digital tokens issued by the network. The Ethereum[3] blockchain is moving from PoW to PoS in its 2021 Ethereum 2.0 update. These protocols involve different types of operational (e.g. labour, computers, energy) costs (Miglo, 2021).

The evolution of blockchain has enabled it to be used in the context of public, private, permissionless, permissioned DLTs and even in centralized systems (Amer et al., 2020). Although some of the more well-known blockchains are public (such as Bitcoin, Ethereum, Mastercoin and Litecoin) and anyone can join them, use their protocols and become one of the 'nodes' that write new blocks and perform mining, there are also private or consortium blockchains (such as Ripple, EOS and Stellar) where reading or writing new blocks can be performed only by authorized nodes, offering not only cheaper and faster transactions but also a lower level of security and decentralization (Mazzorana-Kremer, 2019).

Ante and Fiedler (2021) explain that most popular blockchains, such as Bitcoin and Ethereum, are considered pseudo-anonymous and semi-transparent due to their public and private key structure.[4] Private keys are passwords needed to make send transactions from an account. Public keys represent addresses that can receive transactions without permission. In general, they cannot be associated with the owner or holder, but once he or she becomes known, all historic transactions can be accessed.

The non-refutable and unbreakable record of data allowed by DLTs and blockchain improves information flows and allows ownership transparency, which are fundamental features in many markets (Huang et al., 2020). Early blockchains (such as Bitcoin) were designed as simple payment systems, but new and more sophisticated blockchains, such as Ethereum and EOS, have enabled a much wider range of applications (Howell et al., 2020) in the field of financial transactions,

---

[2]In 2008, an individual under the pseudonym 'Satoshi Nakamoto' proposed Bitcoin as the world's first blockchain application for digital payment processing (Adhami & Giudici, 2019; Ackermann et al., 2020). The term bitcoin (with a lowercase letter 'b') refers to the unit of the cryptocurrency, while with a capital 'B', it refers to the peer-to-peer network, the open-source software, the decentralized general ledger (blockchain), and the software development and transaction platform (Ackermann et al., 2020).

[3]In 2015, Vitalik Buterin presented the Ethereum (ether) cryptocurrency and the Ethereum platform based on the concept of decentralized smart contracts (Myalo, 2019).

[4]Private keys are equivalent to pin numbers, and public keys are equivalent to bank account numbers. See OECD (2019) for a complete explanation of how digital crypto-wallets work.

notary, voting, health care, supply chains and logistics, cloud computing and the Internet of Things, energy supply, advertising and media, booking and rental and retail and e-commerce (Mazzorana-Kremer, 2019; Ackermann et al., 2020).

One particularly important use of blockchain is the creation of crypto-assets or tokens, which is enabled by so-called smart contracts. Smart contracts are computer protocols or algorithms that are automatically executed in a decentralized way based on specific events (OECD, 2019; Arner et al., 2020; Ante & Fiedler, 2021), allowing token issuers to fully comply with the clauses of the contracts without any party verifying or fulfilling them (Myalo, 2019), potentially creating perfect disintermediation and close-to-zero transaction costs (Momtaz, 2020). Dividends and coupon payments are practical examples of operations that can be automatically executed through smart contracts (Deloitte et al., 2020a). Smart contracts can also facilitate the enforcement of trading restrictions or lock-up periods, the attribution of different voting rights or the design of sophisticated convertible features of securities (Chew & Spiegl, 2021). Relevant information on transactions (valuation reports, authentication proofs) can also be embedded in a smart contract (Deloitte et al., 2020a, 2020b).

Tokens can be created using an existing protocol instead of creating a new blockchain for each new token (OECD, 2019). Standard templates on a blockchain offer a predefined set of smart contracts that make it possible to easily and quickly issue tokens (Mazzorana-Kremer, 2019; Adhami & Giudici, 2019). The best templates are the ERC-20[5] standard for ICOs and the ERC-14 standard for STOs, which are both linked to Ethereum's blockchain (Ante & Fiedler, 2021). The use of these standards facilitates exchange with other tokens (Massey et al., 2017), their listing on trading platforms (Mazzorana-Kremer, 2019) and interoperability with digital wallets (OECD, 2019).

2.2   Crypto-Assets or Tokens

Crypto-assets or tokens are private digital assets recorded on a cryptographically secured DLT, neither issued nor guaranteed by a central bank or public authority, and they can be used as a means of exchange and/or for investment purposes and/or to access a good or service (Houben & Snyers, 2020; Chamorro Domínguez, 2021). There is no binding or conclusive (regulatory) classification of tokens (OECD, 2019; Ackermann et al., 2020). In general, three types are mentioned in the literature (OECD, 2019; Momtaz, 2020; Miglo, 2021; Ante & Fiedler, 2021): payment tokens (or cryptocurrencies, coins or currency tokens), utility tokens, and security (or investment or asset) tokens. Ackermann et al. (2020) acknowledge four main types, dividing payment tokens to include those backed with real assets (stablecoins). For crypto-assets, Houben and Snyers (2020) make a summa divisio between cryptocurrencies (distinguishing between traditional non-backed coins and

---

[5]ERC stands for Ethereum Request for Comment.

stablecoins) and tokens (differentiating between investment and utility tokens), and they add the consideration of central bank digital currencies (CBDCs) as sovereign (not private) crypto-assets. It is also generally acknowledged that hybrid tokens are very frequent (Houben & Snyers, 2020; Ackermann et al., 2020).

Another relevant classification of tokens distinguishes between native and non-native tokens (OECD, 2020). Native tokens are built directly and live exclusively within the blockchain and are not backed by an off-chain asset. Cryptocurrencies and most tokens issued in ICOs/IEOs/STOs are native tokens. Non-native tokens are related to the concept of asset tokenization, involving the creation of digital tokens that represent real assets (e.g. stocks and bonds, commodities, real estate, fine wines, fine art, intellectual property rights) issued on a blockchain. Tokenization can turn almost any asset, either real or virtual, into a digital token (Stefanoski et al., 2020) so that its ownership can be fractionalized and widely distributed and traded (Deloitte et al., 2020b), increasing liquidity in traditionally less liquid markets and integrating non-bankable assets into the financial system (Ackermann et al., 2020). Tokenization provides investors with new opportunities for portfolio diversification and even hedging (Deloitte et al., 2020a). These non-native tokens can be considered security tokens only if the asset is first securitized and then tokenized (Lambert et al., 2021).

Most utility and security tokens, as well as payment tokens conceived as internal currency for a concrete project, are created based on smart contracts on existing blockchains such as Ethereum in a quick, cheap and standardized process (Adhami & Giudici, 2019). Rather differently, cryptocurrencies are normally built on their own blockchains around their own ecosystem of developers, nodes, users and miners (Ackermann et al., 2020). Tokens can also be transferred, bought, sold and even destroyed ('burned') through the smart contracts coded in their blockchain (Deloitte et al., 2020b). In ICOs/IEOs/STOs, tokens are sold in exchange for fiat currency or cryptocurrencies. Unsubscribed tokens can be burned after the end of the offering to cause an artificial shortage that leads to rising prices (Ackermann et al., 2020). While payment and utility tokens are normally marketed through ICOs to the public at large, regulations on security tokens are forcing STOs to be offered only to accredited investors (Lambert et al., 2021; Chew & Spiegl, 2021). Tokens issued in ICOs/IEOs can be traded 24/7 on specific exchanges that allow the purchase of tokens against many mainstream cryptocurrencies (OECD, 2019; Ante & Fiedler, 2021).

Under the taxonomy of Houben and Snyers (2020), Table 1 provides an overview of the main features of each type of crypto-asset, while the following subsections aim to provide more detailed definitions.

2.2.1 Cryptocurrencies and CBDCs

Traditional non-backed cryptocurrencies or payment tokens (e.g. Bitcoin, Ether, Litecoin) constitute peer-to-peer electronic cash stored and transferred in a DLT or blockchain (Fantacci & Gobbi, 2021). Since they do not represent any underlying asset, claim or liability, they are subject to high price volatility (Houben & Snyers, 2020), which limits their suitability as a (legal) means of payment (Ackermann et al.,

Table 1 Characterization and comparison of crypto-assets

Type of crypto-asset	Private				Sovereign
	Security token	Utility token	Payment token or non-backed cryptocurrency	Stablecoin	CBDC
What it is	A digital representation of an investment product	Gives consumptive rights to access a product or service	A cash equivalent on a blockchain, combining electronic money and cash as an alternative to fiat currency		It is electronic or digitalized official fiat currency for making payments
Why it is bought	Investors expect a profit	To spend it in a community-based ecosystem with features similar to a voucher	As a means of payment in a community-based ecosystem	As a medium of value exchange and storage of wealth on a blockchain with lower volatility than payment tokens	
Who issues the tokens	Start-ups or traditional companies at both early and mature stages, willing to raise funds and to create value for investors by selling products and services to customers	Any type of organization, usually at the early stage, willing to create a community of members who value a specific product or service	Any type of organization that wants to create a community of members who value using a means of payment or value transfer in a blockchain	Private entities that issue stablecoins through a more or less centralized minting process in response to demand sending and receiving the assets used as collateral; they can also be offered through ICOs	Central banks providing electronic money for retail use
How the issuance is launched	Usually through an STO	Usually through an ICO or IEO			
Who oversees supervision and control	Subject to securities laws implemented by the respective financial regulator	In most jurisdictions, not considered securities and subject only to consumer protection and tax laws	In most jurisdictions, covered only by banking and payment services laws	Specific regulatory frameworks are being developed in many jurisdictions	Regulated by the monetary authority of a Country

Lambert et al. (2021)

2020). These payment tokens or cryptocurrencies are means of payment or value transfer in a blockchain-based ecosystem (Lynn & Rosati, 2021; Lambert et al., 2021) and show no other functions or links to specific projects (Ante & Fiedler, 2021).

Houben and Snyers (2020) acknowledge that stablecoins (e.g. Tether, USD Coin, Dai and Paxos) share many features with tokens but must be distinguished from them since they are not issued with a very specific functionality or for a specific purpose, only as a general-purpose medium of exchange or storage of wealth. Fantacci and Gobbi (2021) define stablecoins as 'second-generation' cryptocurrencies that aim to overcome the instability in the value of cryptocurrencies by maintaining a stable value in relation to an official or fiat currency or a basket of currencies or other assets. They are issued by private entities and can be classified into four categories based on the method that they use to stabilize their value (Houben & Snyers, 2020; Fantacci & Gobbi, 2021): (1) fiat tokens (e.g. Monerium, Gemini), which are backed by official currency so that they are in fact a tokenization of official currency; (2) off-chain collateralized stablecoins (e.g. Saga, Tether), which are backed by a portfolio of non-cash regular financial instruments traded on regulated markets, commodities or real estate; (3) on-chain collateralized stablecoins (e.g. BitUSD, Miexcoin), which are backed by other crypto-assets recorded on the same underlying DLT; and (4) algorithmic stablecoins (e.g. Steem, NUBITS), which pursue stability through the use of blockchain algorithms that automatically adjust the supply of tokens in response to their demand. Finally, mention should be made of the June 2019 proposal by Facebook (in a consortium with other major actors) of the first so-called 'global stablecoin' (initially named Libra and recently renamed Diem), with serious potential to emerge as a monetary alternative with global scale and to pose significant risks to financial stability (Houben & Snyers, 2020; Arner et al., 2020). Some stablecoin issuers (GMO, PAX, GEMINI) have adhered to national financial services regulatory frameworks and can be considered e-money issuers (Cermak et al., 2021).

CBDCs can be considered a type of stablecoin issued by a central bank instead of a private entity (Fantacci & Gobbi, 2021) for payment and settlement in retail (general public) or wholesale (selected participants) transactions (Houben and Snyers, 2020). CBDCs can be considered fiat tokens that are directly issued and managed by the same monetary authority that issues traditional fiat money. Thus, they are actually official currency (Fantacci & Gobbi, 2021). According to Stefanoski et al. (2020), 70% of central banks are (or soon will be) engaged in some type of CBDC exploration. The projects of the central banks of Sweden (e-Krona) and Uruguay (e-Peso) are at an advanced stage (Todd & Rogers, 2020; Fantacci & Gobbi, 2021).

2.2.2   Utility Tokens, Security Tokens and Hybrid Tokens

Utility tokens provide digital access to a product, digital application or service created by the token issuer (Lynn & Rosati, 2021) in the form of a software licence or a voucher (Ante & Fiedler, 2021) without any ownership rights attached (Momtaz, 2020). Issued through an ICO, they support and develop a community-based ecosystem by giving consumptive rights to users at a very early stage before any product or service has been developed (Lambert et al., 2021). They are subject to a low degree of regulation (Momtaz, 2020) and should, in theory, be subject only to ordinary consumer protection and tax laws (Lambert et al., 2021). Nevertheless, in the USA, utility tokens might be recognized as securities under US Securities and Exchange Commission (SEC) regulations (Lambert et al., 2021).

Security tokens are analogous to traditional financial instruments such as equities and bonds (Lynn & Rosati, 2021; Ante & Fiedler, 2021). They can confer voting rights and/or rights to income streams such as dividends and interest payments, which can take the form of digital assets instead of fiat currencies (Chew & Spiegl, 2021). Lambert et al. (2021, p. 5) provide a comprehensive definition, i.e. 'a digital representation of an investment product, recorded on a distributed ledger, subject to regulation under securities laws', and they group security tokens into five categories: (1) equity tokens, (2) debt tokens, (3) fund tokens, (4) income-share tokens, and (5) other security tokens. They can be issued through STOs regardless of the development stage of the firm (Lambert et al., 2021).

The most important feature of security tokens is that they should be subject to securities laws, but the hybrid nature of many tokens makes it complicated to truly identify security tokens. Thus, it is generally assumed that security tokens must be designated as such on a case-by-case basis (OECD, 2020). In the USA, the SEC determines through the Howey test whether an investment qualifies as a security, essentially verifying whether money is invested in a common enterprise in exchange for a profit derived from the efforts of a promoter or third party (Momtaz, 2020; Ante & Fiedler, 2021). Requirements can be softened by restricting sales to accredited investors (Deloitte et al., 2020b). The European Union (EU) is developing a legal framework adopting four proposals: the Market in Crypto-Assets Regulation (MiCA), the Pilot DLT Market Infrastructure Regulation (PDMIR), the Digital Operational Resilience Regulation (DORA), and a directive to amend existing financial services legislation (European Parliament, 2020; European Commission, 2020). The proposed regulation will foreseeably be enacted in 2022. According to these regulations, STOs will be subject to the EU's second Markets in Financial Instruments Directive (MiFID II) and other financial market legislation (Chew & Spiegl, 2021). Some European countries, such as France, Luxembourg, the Netherlands, Germany, Italy and the UK, are applying the same legislation for STOs as for securities if certain conditions are met. However, other European countries still have not reached a consensus, and STOs remain unregulated.

Hybrid tokens are single tokens exhibiting features of more than one class of digital assets (Lambert et al., 2021).

2.3 Decentralized Finance (DeFi) and the Search for Innovative Funding Mechanisms

The aforementioned advances related to the use of DLTs and blockchain and the issuance of crypto-assets are at the base of the current trend towards the decentralized and disintermediated provision of financial services. Blockchain technology, together with other technologies such as artificial intelligence and machine learning, big data and cloud computing (Zetzsche et al., 2020), is the core of DeFi. Traditional finance had already been challenged by financial technologies (FinTechs), replacing financial intermediaries with technological companies (Chen & Bellavitis, 2020). DeFi has made it possible to reduce transaction costs, broaden financial inclusion, facilitate open access, encourage permissionless innovation and interoperability, increase transparency, allow borderless finance and create new opportunities for entrepreneurs and innovators (FSB (Financial Stability Board), 2019; Chen & Bellavitis, 2020). Thus, DeFi has been related to the democratization of finance, although Zetzsche et al. (2020) warn that in its purest form, its aim is in fact to develop a financial system without borders, jurisdiction, and centralized (governmental) control, raising important challenges and threats to financial stability. Chen and Bellavitis (2020) distinguish four main business models in DeFi: (1) decentralized cryptocurrencies, (2) decentralized payment services, (3) decentralized contracting based on smart contracts, and (4) decentralized fundraising through ICOs/IEOs/STOs.

Decentralized fundraising promises to improve access to financial markets for companies traditionally left unserved by the financial system, including not only early-stage start-ups and SMEs (Mazzorana-Kremer, 2019; Ante, 2021) but also growth-stage business and new economy/asset-light businesses (Deloitte et al., 2020a). Compared to traditional financial products, the issuance of blockchain-based tokens through ICOs/IEOs/STOs offers improved public tradability, transparency, low entry barriers, efficiency, automation and high cost efficiency (Kondova & Simonella, 2019; Ante, 2021).

These new fundraising instruments come as both alternatives and complements to other innovative sources of financing, such as crowdfunding, business angels and VC, jointly contributing to the democratization of entrepreneurial finance (Ackermann et al., 2020; Chen & Bellavitis, 2020). ICOs/IEOs/STOs present both advantages and disadvantages to issuers and investors. Table 2 gathers the main benefits and risks highlighted in the previous literature. While their advantages have made token offerings extremely attractive to innovators (Howell et al., 2020; Momtaz, 2020), their disadvantages are causing constant development in the crypto-asset community that has driven the evolution from ICOs to IEOs and STOs in the search for greater security and trustworthiness of these token-based fundraising models (Chamorro Domínguez, 2021). Other formulas are initial decentralized exchange offerings (IDOs), which are an alternative to centralized exchanges in IEOs (Chamorro Domínguez, 2021), and decentralized autonomous initial coin offerings (DAICOs), which combine the advantages of decentralized autonomous organizations (DAOs) and classic ICOs to increase transparency and safety (Myalo, 2019).

Table 2 Advantages and disadvantages of fundraising through ICOs/IEOs/STOs

Advantages	Disadvantages
Inclusive SME financing (OECD, 2019) and supporting the initial development of decentralized networks (Howell et al., 2020; Momtaz, 2020); ICO/IEO/STOs can force existing financing sources to compete and provide better terms for SME financing (OECD, 2019)	Risk of 'blockchainizing' every project (Ackermann et al., 2020) and recurring to these fundraising formulas without an alignment with the business value proposition (OECD, 2019)
Cost efficiencies driven by disintermediation (concerning both financial and payment services) and smart contract automation (OECD, 2019; Momtaz, 2020; Deloitte et al., 2020b); ICO/IEOs have lower transactions costs than STOs, and STOs have lower transaction costs than IPOs (Mazzorana-Kremer, 2019)	High blockchain operating costs (Holden & Malani, 2019) and of listing in exchanges with healthy liquidity (OECD, 2019); no ICO platforms (Block et al., 2021) and light supervision of crypto-asset exchanges, with more regulated exchanges needed to support further development of STOs (Chew & Spiegl, 2021)
Value creation through the monetization of network effects (OECD, 2019) and the fair distribution of value across stakeholders (Howell et al., 2020); token offerings make it possible to calibrate demand and secure commitment from future customers (Howell et al., 2020), obtain knowledge to improve platform features (Momtaz, 2020) and inform latecomers (Ribeiro-Soriano et al., 2020), and hasten network effects since token holders are motivated to help the platform succeed (Howell et al., 2020)	Difficult governance caused by conflicts of interest (OECD, 2019) and information asymmetries or the unknown intentions of promoters, which can increase the cost of capital (Ribeiro-Soriano et al., 2020); speculators seem to outweigh believers (Ackermann et al., 2020); low guaranties of profit sharing in ICOs (Mazzorana-Kremer, 2019)
Direct access to a globally diversified and heterogeneous investor pool (OECD, 2019); asset tokenization also facilitates broadening the range of potential investors in traditionally illiquid and difficult to fractionalize assets (Stefanoski et al., 2020; Deloitte et al., 2020a); tokens also offer investors new opportunities for portfolio diversification, investment, trading and even hedging (Deloitte et al., 2020b)	Low investor protection and market integrity (OECD, 2019), and there is a need to account for different regulations in different jurisdictions; institutional investors are not attracted by low trading volumes (Ackermann et al., 2020); still a niche market reserved for technology-interested investors (Block et al., 2021); warnings from financial authorities to retail investors without the necessary financial skills (Chamorro Domínguez, 2021)
Low regulatory burden, disclosure requirements and legal costs, especially in ICOs/IEOs; STOs demand considering the legal implications of the STO for both the issuing company and investors	Legal and regulatory uncertainty derived from unclear and heterogeneous regulatory frameworks for ICOs/IEOs/STOs and unclear rights and obligations of token issuers and holders (OECD, 2019); open door to frauds and scams
Flexibility to invest in a fraction of a token with a high speed of execution and near-immediate liquidity (OECD, 2019); tokens can be traded 24/7 on crypto-asset exchanges, trading platforms (between private individuals) and online brokers (Ackermann et al., 2020), providing rapid liquidity (Howell et al., 2020)	Complexity in defining the most suitable type of tokens (payment, utility, security, hybrid), their monetary policy (*tokenomics*) and their valuation and pricing (OECD, 2019); the underpricing of an ICO and its relation to market liquidity should be considered, as well as the higher volatility of crypto-assets and

(continued)

Table 2 (continued)

Advantages	Disadvantages
and a rapid exit option (Momtaz, 2020); the risk of token depreciation is not substantially different from that of other regulated investments (Ribeiro-Soriano et al., 2020)	their sensitivity to regulations, which can lead to depreciation and even bankruptcy (Ribeiro-Soriano et al., 2020)
No ownership rights necessarily conferred, avoiding dilution for entrepreneurs (OECD, 2019) and aligning the interests of developers, users and miners without giving any party more control over the platform (Momtaz, 2020)	Connections between customer networks and networks of promoters must be carefully analysed; systematic risks may arise from network effects and decentralized organizations (Ribeiro-Soriano et al., 2020)
Blockchain technology enables secure transactions (Ribeiro-Soriano et al., 2020), immutable governance terms since once launched, the platform can exist independently of the issuer (Howell et al., 2020), accurate record-keeping, and ownership transparency, improving information flows and the tracking of asset ownership (Huang et al., 2020)	Operational risks (scaling, network stability, coding errors etc.) and cyber-risks (OECD, 2019); project risks might be transferred to investors (Ribeiro-Soriano et al., 2020)

3 An In-Depth View of ICOs/IEOs/STOs as New Fundraising Models for Start-Ups and SMEs

With the building blocks now having been described, this section delves into the most relevant aspects to understand the contribution of token offerings to the field of entrepreneurial finance. A better delimitation of token offerings is developed by comparing ICOs, IEOs and STOs both between them and in relation to other innovative financing sources.

3.1 Differences Between ICOs, IEOs and STOs

Although ICOs, IEOs and STOs share many features, notably, IEOs and STOs are evolutions of ICOs that attempt to improve upon them or fill in their gaps. This fact makes it important to gain a deep understanding of their differences. In fact, many authors insist on the idea that STOs are not a subset of ICOs (Ante & Fiedler, 2021; Lambert et al., 2021). Although their differences seem subtle when looking at the graphical representation of ICOs, IEOs and STOs in Fig. 3, a thorough review of the main characteristics of each type of token offering can make them more evident.

An ICO is a funding campaign to sell digital tokens specific to a blockchain-based project to raise money in the form of cryptocurrencies or fiat currencies (Momtaz, 2020; Chamorro Domínguez, 2021), normally before any saleable product or service exists but that will afterwards be accessible to users or consumers in exchange for the previously issued tokens (Holden & Malani, 2019; Lambert et al., 2021). The project

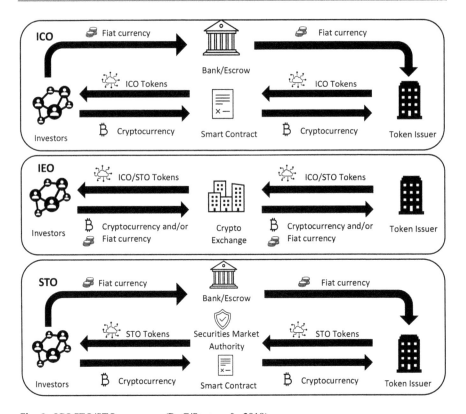

Fig. 3 ICO/IEO/STO processes (PwC/Strategy&, 2019)

development team discloses the technical details on their website and in a so-called white paper that is not overviewed by any third party or regulatory authority. The know your customer (KYC) and anti-money laundering (AML) checks are not mandatory, and only regulated crypto exchanges perform them (OECD, 2019). After the ICO, investors can hold the tokens in their wallets, exchange them for products or services, or trade them if they are listed on cryptocurrency exchanges (Yen et al., 2021). Most ICOs offer utility tokens with no underlying asset tying down their value, making them very volatile and insecure for investors (Mazzorana-Kremer, 2019). This aspect, coupled with poor regulation, has made them risky investments (Fisch, 2019) and has led to greater regulatory scrutiny (Myalo, 2019). Despite the considerable number of scams and frauds attributed to ICOs (Myalo, 2019; Chamorro Domínguez, 2021), Benedetti and Kostovetsky (2021) assert that they were not truly relevant in terms of stolen capital because investors spotted them and did not fund them. Bellavitis et al. (2021) and Huang et al. (2020) offer a complete analysis of the geography of ICOs and how it is conditioned by regulation. Momtaz (2020) provides interesting data on the distribution of ICOs across industries, types of tokens or technical aspects of the ICO process (pre-sale, accepted cryptocurrencies, smart contract standards etc.).

In addition to their fundraising role, one of the most relevant features of ICOs is their ability to build a network, community or ecosystem of stakeholders who support the project (Massey et al., 2017; Chen, 2018; Ribeiro-Soriano et al., 2020). For Lambert et al. (2021), this is a fundamental difference from STOs, which are currently mainly directed to accredited or experienced investors. According to Howell et al. (2020), in ICOs, the decentralized nature of platform management facilitates the accrual of value to token holders, including customers, workers, miners, platform developers and other contributors, making them actively support the success of the project. Fisch (2019) points out that ICO investors are more interested in the technological features of the project than in the financial features.

IEOs are a response to the perceived main drawbacks of ICOs related to the lack of supervision. A cryptocurrency exchange (such as Binance, CoinBene and LBANK) is directly involved in the selection of projects and the launching of the offering, distributing the tokens among verified investors on their trading platform (Myalo, 2019). The crypto exchange offers help with marketing and promotion and backs the offering with its reputation, increasing fundraising success in exchange for listing fees and a percentage of the tokens sold (Anson, 2021; Chamorro Domínguez, 2021). The crypto exchange is expected to give access to a larger set of investors, reject fraudulent or low-quality projects through due diligence, and offer immediate listing after the offering is completed (Myalo, 2019; Chamorro Domínguez, 2021). Nevertheless, IEOs do not reduce concerns about the stability and credibility of token value, especially when it is not backed by underlying assets (Deloitte et al., 2020b). Their development is also limited by the additional burden they place on exchanges (Myalo, 2019) and the regulatory uncertainties related to the consideration of utility or payment tokens as securities and the role of exchanges as brokers/dealers that should act under a licence (OECD, 2020; Chamorro Domínguez, 2021). Only a few crypto exchanges are licenced with local regulators.

Since STOs are directly related to the issuance of tokens qualified as securities (i.e. passing the Howey test in the USA), they face the same regulatory requirements as equity (KYC/AML, disclosure obligations etc.) while retaining the advantages of crypto-assets in terms of liquidity (Lynn & Rosati, 2021). Lambert et al. (2021) highlight that STOs allow start-ups to raise capital through 'traditional' investment products generally reserved for a small group of accredited or experienced investors, but some regulations actually restrict STOs to only these investors. Regardless, security tokens can also involve payment or use functions, thus allowing issuers to access potential customers and investors (Ante & Fiedler, 2021). While ICOs are often developed at very early stages (Chew & Spiegl, 2021), before product or service development, STOs can be undertaken regardless of the development stage of the firm (Lambert et al., 2021). Moreover, ICOs have been labelled 'not the right solution for every project', especially if products or services are not built on DLTs (OECD, 2019); however, STOs are not limited to the existence of DLT-based business models (Ackermann et al., 2020). Ante and Fiedler (2021) verify that information technology, financial services, gaming and gambling, Health care and medicine and real estate are the five most common industry sectors across their sample of STOs.

STOs offer a more secure regulatory framework for both issuers and investors and entitle the latter to more profit rights than ICOs. However, the process is longer, and listing in secondary markets is often delayed due to the need to comply with securities rules (Mazzorana-Kremer, 2019). Myalo (2019) points out that in ICOs, investors are not compensated when the offering fails, whereas in STOs, they bear more rights and are entitled to file a complaint with the appropriate authority. Compared to ICOs, this compliance with securities laws implies a greater regulatory burden on and costs for STO issuers and the need to consider regulations in different jurisdictions. Thus, this fundraising method might be more suitable for larger and established off-chain companies (Myalo, 2019). IEOs are a middle ground between ICOs and STOs, providing a less costly process than STOs for issuers and a more reliable option than ICOs for investors. Despite compliance with securities laws, it is still not common for traditional exchanges to launch an STO (Deloitte et al., 2020b; Chew & Spiegl, 2021).

Now that ICOs, IEOs and STOs have been clearly defined, Table 3 provides a comparative overview of their main features to gain a better understanding of their similitudes and differences. Appendixes 1, 2 and 3 offer an overview of some relevant ICOs, IEOs and STOs.

3.2   Comparison with Other Financing Alternatives (IPOs, Crowdfunding, VC)

Start-ups are subject to risks and information asymmetries that limit their fundraising options, especially in the early stages (Ante & Fiedler, 2021). Traditional financial instruments such as debt (loans or the issuance of private bonds) and equity (private placements or IPOs) are often neither accessible nor affordable to them. Alternative sources of external finance (crowdfunding, business angels, VC) have evolved in the last decade and have seen their relevance increase, but they are hindered by high transaction costs and barriers to access, making token offerings a promising new source of entrepreneurial finance (Ante & Fiedler, 2021).

It is interesting to compare these fundraising alternatives and to think about their potential substitutive or complementary role. Obvious differences related to the implications of using blockchain and DLTs (lower costs, higher transaction speed, transparency, security etc.) and crypto-assets (fractionalization, liquidity etc.) are left aside, as they have been thoroughly explained in Sect. 2. Similar to previous academic studies (Howell et al., 2020; Ackermann et al., 2020; Block et al., 2021), the focus is on comparing token offerings to crowdfunding, VC and IPOs.

Token offerings share features with crowdfunding as a means of raising money from a heterogeneous set of investors (a small 'crowd' and institutional investors) through online platforms (Huang et al., 2020) at a lower cost of entry into the market (Deloitte et al., 2020a). More concretely, the parallels between STOs and equity-based crowdfunding and between ICOs and reward-based crowdfunding (OECD,

Table 3 Comparative overview of ICOs, IEOs and STOs

	ICO	IEO	STO
Risk	High	Medium	Low
Credibility	Low	Medium	High
Costs	Low (technical costs, advisory fees, marketing costs and listing fees)	Medium (ICO costs + crypto exchange fees)	High (ICO costs + legal compliance costs, but these are lower than those under traditional fundraising models)
Crypto-asset	Utility or payment token	Utility or payment token	Security token
Issuer	Start-ups, public companies, SMEs		Start-ups, public companies, SMEs, large companies
Platform	Digital (e.g. website of the issuing company)	Cryptocurrency exchange	STO digital platform
Investor participation	Direct, KYC/AML performed by the issuer	Users of the cryptocurrency exchange with KYC/AML	Direct, KYC/AML by the STO platform, sometimes limited to accredited investors
Listing in secondary markets	Upon request	Immediate in the issuing cryptocurrency exchange	Probably immediate if the STO platform is an exchange
Accepted funds	Fiat and/or crypto-assets		
Initiated	In general, a direct launch to the public without a centralized third party	Cryptocurrency exchange	In general, a direct launch to the public without a centralized third party
Documentation requirements	Whitepaper, website		White paper, prospectus, filings, registration with the regulator, website
Investor rights	Generally limited to digital access to service/application		In general, voting rights, dividends (if structured similar to, e.g. shares)
Controlling authority	None (banned in some jurisdictions)	The regulator if the cryptocurrency exchange is licenced	Regulator (securities laws)
Project assessment	None	Due diligence by cryptocurrency exchange	Due diligence by the regulator on the features of the security token
Marketing costs	Dependent upon the issuer's strategy	Moderate (included in cryptocurrency exchange fees)	Dependent upon the issuer's strategy
Speed	Several months	Several weeks	Up to a year
Underlying	None		Project assets or cash flows
Dividends	None		Depending on the token structure

Myalo (2019), Stefanoski et al. (2020), and Deloitte et al. (2020a, 2020b)

2019; Block et al., 2021; Lambert et al., 2021) are quite straightforward. In STOs, investment is often restricted to accredited investors, while ICOs/IEOs and crowdfunding are directed to the general public (Lambert et al., 2021). Nevertheless, some crowdfunding regulatory frameworks limit contributions from retail investors. This aspect, in addition to the lack of experience and high information costs, prevents investors from conducting in-depth research of crowdfunding projects (Ante & Fiedler, 2021). Both crowdfunding and ICOs/IEOs based on utility tokens can simultaneously attract capital and users and build a community around the project. However, the network effects are probably larger in token offerings (OECD, 2019), which are also completely or almost completely disintermediated (ICOs are not launched on a platform as in crowdfunding since they rely only on the blockchain, while IEOs rely on the crypto exchange) and typically larger in terms of participants and value (Lynn & Rosati, 2021). VC also shows lower network effects (OECD, 2019).

The motivations of investors across the considered fundraising formulas are also different. VC and IPOs involve sophisticated investors mainly driven by financial motives, while ICO and crowdfunding investors are also driven by non-financial motives (Momtaz, 2020). Two particular features of token offerings make them more attractive to investors than crowdfunding or VC: after-market liquidity if tokens are listed and easier and earlier exit options since, in crowdfunding and VC, exits or cash-outs (i.e. through an IPO or acquisition) are not possible in the short run or before reaching a maturity stage, while in ICOs, exiting is possible even before a product or service has been developed (Momtaz, 2020; Miglo, 2021). Nevertheless, Ackermann et al. (2020) point out that some crowdfunding platforms (Crowdcube, Prosser) launched in 2017 are secondary markets.

Some consider ICOs to be a hybrid of IPOs and crowdfunding (Ribeiro-Soriano et al., 2020; García-Rodríguez, 2021). STOs and ICOs are often related to IPOs due to their similar abbreviations, but they share few features (Adhami & Giudici, 2019). Rapid liquidity is a common feature of ICOs and IPOs, although, in ICOs, it has been verified that many tokens remain unlisted (Howell et al., 2020). Insofar as ICOs do not usually grant ownership rights, a comparison with VC, equity crowdfunding or IPOs might not be very relevant. Nevertheless, it is worth acknowledging that ICOs contribute to mitigating the dilution problem of these financial instruments, making it possible to raise capital without sharing ownership (OECD, 2019). STOs make it possible to reach a different (younger) set of investors (Chew & Spiegl, 2021), but the fact that they are often restricted to accredited investors is a major difference between IPOs and STOs (Lambert et al., 2021). Moreover, the largest STOs have been debt offerings instead of equity offerings (Deloitte et al., 2020a). Finally, Massey et al. (2017) state that what truly differentiates a token sale from an IPO is that tokens are a core part of the business of start-ups.

It is also interesting to look at the start-up lifecycle. Different from traditional financial instruments and similar to crowdfunding, token offerings mainly address early-stage projects (Stefanoski et al., 2020), although in crowdfunding, products or services are often in an advanced stage of development (OECD, 2019). For Momtaz (2020), ICOs, similar to VC, could theoretically cover all stages until a firm goes public (Momtaz, 2020). IPOs have been traditionally seen as the last step in the start-up financing lifecycle (Chew & Spiegl, 2021). STOs have also come to fill this stage (OECD, 2019). However, since many tokens remain locked in the wallets of accredited investors, the potential of STOs to represent a growing and liquid alternative to IPOs or crowdfunding to finance SMEs is not clear and greatly depends on the quality of issuers and the existence of specialized trading platforms (Mazzorana-Kremer, 2019).

A higher liquidity of token offerings could be expected to displace equity crowdfunding, but insofar as ICO tokens do not confer ownership, a complementary role between the two has been defended (Huang et al., 2020). Ackermann et al. (2020) believe that crowdfunding and token offerings combined could create added value and overcome inefficiencies. In fact, many ICO projects are meant to support the initial formation of a venture, while equity crowdfunding is better suited to supporting the steady growth of early-stage businesses (Huang et al., 2020). Chew and Spiegl (2021) acknowledge that STOs can be a precursor of an IPO or other fundraising alternatives. VC could be displaced by token offerings and challenged to improve its model (Adhami & Giudici, 2019; Howell et al., 2020). Nevertheless, VC also appears to be complementary to ICO offerings and has been present in some pre-ICO stages, providing additional value in the form of expertise, industry knowledge, connections, or managerial and strategic assistance (OECD, 2019). The increasing interest of VC in after-ICO token purchases raises concerns that utility tokens are held mostly by speculators rather than future customers (Howell et al., 2020).

4   ICO/IEO/STO Ecosystem and Launching Process

This section approaches the ecosystem of the multiple stakeholders involved in token offerings and describes the underlying launching process, establishing a guide or manual for project developers interested in exploring these new financing formulas.

4.1   ICO/IEO/STO Ecosystem

Token offerings involve the creation of a blockchain ecosystem that includes different stakeholders, such as developers, workers, users and miners (Ackermann et al., 2020). The decentralized management of projects distributes value across all of them (Howell et al., 2020). However, beyond these stakeholders, the ICO/IEO/STO ecosystem is a complex environment where many other agents participate, including (OECD, 2019) cryptocurrency exchanges and trading platform operators; digital wallet providers; specialized internet websites; social media; financial, technical and legal advisors; and custodians and regulators.

It is first important to consider that, except for IEOs, token offering campaigns are not developed on specialized platforms as in crowdfunding. Rather, they are developed on dedicated websites created by the development team. Thus, there is no entity making a centralized preselection and creation of a portfolio of token projects, and investors should become informed through each project's website and white paper (Ackermann et al., 2020). Additionally, there is no comprehensive universal database on ICOs (Piñeiro-Chousa et al., 2021). Nevertheless, there are several data aggregators that monitor the crypto-asset market: ICORating.com, ICObench.com, Coinschedule.com, TrackICO.io, ICOmarks.com, ICOholder.com, Rattingtoken. net, CoinLauncher.io, Coin-MarketCap.com, CoinList.co, Token.Security, Tokenmarket.net, STOscope.com, icodata.io, icodrops.com, and ico-check.com have been used as sources of data for empirical studies (Mazzorana-Kremer, 2019; Piñeiro-Chousa et al., 2021; Benedetti & Kostovetsky, 2021). Some of these websites (e.g. ICObench) provide rating services for both upcoming offerings and concluded and actively traded offerings (Adhami & Giudici, 2019). However, they are not comparable to crowdfunding platforms in terms of project preselection and quality assurance, which will surely change in the near future (Ackermann et al., 2020).

The STO ecosystem (which is assumed to contain the ecosystems of ICOs and IEOs) is taken as a reference to further explain the main features of the principal agents supporting token offerings. According to Myalo (2019), this ecosystem consists of four important components: agencies, issuance platforms, custodians and exchanges. Agencies are common to all types of token offerings and include blockchain agencies that provide legal advisory, technical development services, consulting and marketing campaigns (Applicature, New Alchemy, AmaZix, Protos, Fluidity). Legal advisors are increasingly important for ensuring that STOs are regulatory compliant within each jurisdiction. The role of social media and specialized internet websites in the promotion of token projects is also worth mentioning (OECD, 2019).

Issuance platforms aim to attract investors and issue tokens under appropriate open-source protocols for token issuance and, in the case of STOs, under the right framework for legal aspects and KYC/AML verification processes. An important issue is that most platforms are not prepared to comply with the share registration processes and regulations affecting security tokens (Mazzorana-Kremer, 2019). For this reason, many platforms have been specifically created to provide an all-in-one solution for the issuance and trading of STOs (Harbor, Polymath, Swarm, Securitize, Securrency). Custodians (SIX Digital Exchange, Swiss Crypto Vault, PrimeTrust, Coinbase) play the role of third parties (often as special purpose vehicles) to safeguard users' tokens (Deloitte et al., 2020b).

Crypto exchanges (Binance, tZero, Poloniex, Huobi, OKEx, Abacus, Templum, OFB, Kraken) are the central element for making tokens issued in ICOs/IEOs/STOs public through active trading (Chew & Spiegl, 2021). They can either be centralized and managed by a private organization or be decentralized and managed through automated match-making (Adhami & Giudici, 2019). Some cryptocurrency exchanges have obtained legal licences to list security tokens (iSTOX, now ADDX, in Singapore and the Fusang Exchange in Malaysia) or are partnering with traditional stock exchanges (Ante & Fiedler, 2021), such as the SIX Swiss

Exchange and the London, Boston, Malta and Gibraltar Stock Exchanges, which have begun to introduce blockchain technology[6] for the trading of security tokens (Mazzorana-Kremer, 2019; Chew & Spiegl, 2021).

4.2   The ICO/IEO/STO Launching Process

Token offerings demand a structured campaign with, as we have seen in the previous subsection, the involvement of many actors. In broad terms, the development team defines the core aspects of their (blockchain-based) project, prepares a white paper and announces the offering; the sale event makes it possible to raise funds through the exchange of tokens for fiat or cryptocurrency, and after the sale closing, listing on a crypto exchange provides liquidity to token holders (Yen et al., 2021). The different agencies that form the ICO/IEO/STO ecosystem help the development team in defining the legal and technical aspects of the tokens to be issued, marketing the campaign, and managing the exchange of tokens for fiat or cryptocurrencies.

The typical launching process of a token offering involves three main stages: (1) preparation (token design, white paper and marketing campaign), (2) token sale (capital raising through the appropriate technology solutions to perform the crowd sale event), and (3) token listing. In the case of ICOs, a pre-sale or pre-ICO is quite frequent (Momtaz, 2020; Ackermann et al., 2020). In the case of STOs, the main differences from ICOs are related to the need to consider compliance with securities laws and to prepare a prospectus that must be approved by the financial regulator (Lynn & Rosati, 2021). In IEOs, the entire process is greatly supported by the crypto exchange in charge of the issuance (Myalo, 2019). Figure 4 builds on how Ackermann et al. (2020) and Lambert et al. (2021) define illustrative ICO and STO processes, respectively, revealing that the STO process requires a greater involvement of financial and legal advisors and paying attention to regulatory compliance, while ICO processes are more focused on extensive marketing and prospection of the market (pre-announcement, marketing campaign, pre-ICO) to guarantee the success of the ICO.

Adhami and Giudici (2019) also mention a 'zero' step to assess whether an ICO/IEO/STO fits with the strategy and needs of the project, considering whether the project team is willing to disclose sensitive information and whether the project requires a tokenized platform. At this preliminary stage, it could also be important to balance the convenience of an ICO, IEO or STO. Some previous studies have dealt with this decision. For example Gryglewicz et al. (2021) present the ICO as the optimal model when platform value derives from facilitating transactions rather than from generating cash flows and financing needs or when agency frictions or the platform development phase are large. Nevertheless, Miglo (2021) concludes that utility tokens with profit rights (hybrid tokens) should be preferred to utility tokens;

---

[6]In March 2021, a project was announced by the Spanish stock market operator (BME) to create a platform that facilitates the financing of SMEs through the issuance of digital tokens.

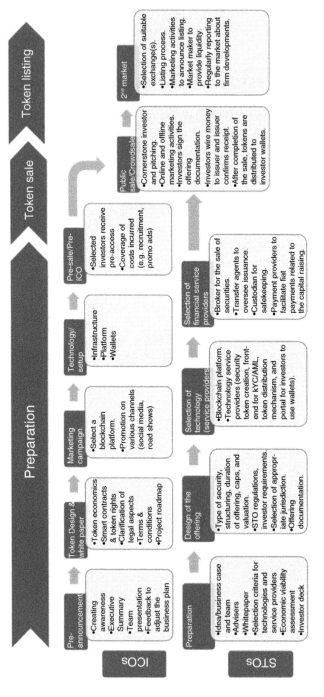

Fig. 4 ICO/STO launching process. (Ackermann et al., 2020; Lambert et al., 2021)

however, high market uncertainty exists. Miglo (2020) defends IEOs when there are large investment sizes and moral hazard problems.

4.2.1   Preparation

The first steps at this stage are related to forming the campaign management team (business development, marketing, legal, financial/accounting), clarifying the team's vision and the venture's business case/business plan (Adhami & Giudici, 2019; Momtaz, 2020; Lambert et al., 2021), and defining the technical, economic and legal aspects related to the tokens to be created. They mainly focus on the following:

- Rights attached to tokens and the monetary policy of tokens (*tokenomics*): the number of tokens to be issued[7]; pricing; thresholds and caps[8]; the proportion distributed to investors[9]; the setting of the timeline of the liquidity events and allocation mechanisms; the future supply of tokens; the sale model used[10] (e.g. sales at a fixed price, dynamic pricing, auctions); and the accepted methods of payment (Adhami & Giudici, 2019; OECD, 2019; Lynn & Rosati, 2021). In ICOs, a pre-sale or pre-ICO can be undertaken, offering tokens at a discounted price (often to insiders or cornerstone investors such as VC), enabling a pretest of market demand and the use of the funds raised to cover the costs of the main sale event (Adhami & Giudici, 2019; OECD, 2019; Momtaz, 2020). In STOs, the type of security (debt, equity) and the specific rights should be defined with the help of a financial advisor (Lambert et al., 2021).
- Target audience: developers, accredited or institutional investors, or the crowd. Regulatory issues can condition the target audience to be approached, and with their advisors, issuers can assess what the most appropriate jurisdictions are.
- Financial services: apart from the need to appoint transfer agents to oversee the offering and handle claims and to appoint payment providers to facilitate transfers in fiat currency, in STOs, brokers and custodians are singular agents supporting the process (Lambert et al., 2021), and the issuance platforms are expected to perform due diligence to ensure information completeness and accuracy (Deloitte et al., 2020b).

---

[7]Limiting the number of tokens has an important influence on the value of the tokens (Myalo, 2019) and can limit the risk of token inflation (OECD, 2019).

[8]A maximum amount of capital raised can be set as a hard cap to stop the sale of tokens when reached, and a minimum amount can be set as a soft cap to close the contract and return all funds raised to investors if it is not reached (Myalo, 2019). Additionally, maximum individual contributions can be set to diversify the investment base, limit the power of speculators and foster the development of the network, while minimum individual contributions could aim to limit access to institutional investors (OECD, 2019).

[9]Adhami and Giuduci (2019) explain that project promoters can retain some tokens to use them to reward future collaborators and advisors or to smooth down in the case of spikes in demand and shortage of available tokens to be spent on the platform.

[10]Howell et al. (2020) verify in their sample that most ICOs use a fixed pricing model and that auctions are very rare.

- Legal considerations: specially oriented to avoid non-compliance with securities laws (i.e. structuring the offering as an ICO but not verifying whether the tokens to be issued pass the Howey test).
- Technical structure, normally supported by a specialized platform and involving two main technological decisions (Stefanoski et al., 2020): the underlying blockchain to issue the tokens (e.g. Ethereum, Tezos, Stellar) and their technical representation (token standards such as ERC-20 or ERC-1400). Except for regulatory and strategic considerations, issuers will prefer a public and permissionless blockchain, with high user adoption, ease of use, and total value managed, although the choice could also be conditioned by the consensus algorithm (PoW or PoS), scalability, or privacy features (Stefanoski et al., 2020). The chosen blockchain will support the automatic execution of the offering *tokenomics* (e.g. through smart contracts). In STOs, it is particularly relevant that the platform chosen is enabled to fulfil all the tasks involved in a security lifecycle, such as vetting investors based on KYC/AML, the exercise of voting rights and the distribution of coupon or dividend payments (Lambert et al., 2021).
- Marketing campaign: as acknowledged by Momtaz (2020), marketing activity usually starts as early as the project itself and involves creating a website and employing a wide range of social media tools, including the coverage of online data aggregator sites (Adhami & Giudici, 2019). Roadshows are also used to approach potential investors (Momtaz, 2020). All the previous aspects are gathered and organized in the so-called white paper, which contains the technical details of the token offering, key data about the project and the team and a roadmap of the project development (Lynn & Rosati, 2021). The white paper is considered an important element of project marketing (Ackermann et al., 2020), but no best-practice standard exists to prepare it (Chamorro Domínguez, 2021). Its content and quality are considered the main determinants of the success of the offering (Fisch, 2019; Yen et al., 2021), in addition to the quality of the ICO team (Howell et al., 2018) or the development of a pre-sale (Ribeiro-Soriano et al., 2020). Other typical documents produced to provide information about the offering are an investor deck, a term sheet, a prospectus (in STOs), and purchase or subscription agreements (Lambert et al., 2021).

4.2.2   Token Sale

This stage involves the actual capital raising from investors, who send from their wallets the fiat or cryptocurrencies that have been paired with the tokens to the public digital wallet address of the offering and receive tokens in exchange, either immediately or after the sale is concluded. This usually happens when the hard cap is reached, but it can also be decided by the project promoters if demand is scarce or the soft cap is not reached (Adhami & Giudici, 2019). The duration of the sale depends on the effectiveness of the pre-sale communication, with some offerings concluded in just minutes or even seconds, while others last for weeks or months (Lynn & Rosati, 2021). Howell et al. (2020) report an average duration of 40 days in their sample of ICOs. IEOs show the shortest durations. Myalo (2019) reports the cases of Fetch.ai, which attracted $6 million in 22 s, and BitTorrent, which attracted more than \$7.2 million in 18 min. There are also 'ongoing' token sales that extend fund collection over a longer period (Adhami & Giudici, 2019).

4.2.3   Token Listing

Listing on a (normally unregulated) crypto exchange is essential to provide liquidity to token holders (Momtaz, 2020), but it is neither automatic nor guaranteed (OECD, 2019), except in IEOs, which are designed to minimize delays in listing (Miglo, 2020). Providing liquidity can rely on hiring the services of market makers and listing in more than one exchange (OECD, 2019; Lambert et al., 2021). Listing requirements are rather opaque and are not as rigorous as those of regulated exchanges (Momtaz, 2020). Token trading is sometimes locked up over a certain period. In the case of STOs, these lock-ups can be imposed by regulation (Lambert et al., 2021). For example SEC regulations impose on security tokens a lock-up period of 90 days, after which they can be sold only to other accredited investors for 1 year before being freely tradable (Mazzorana-Kremer, 2019). Not only is listing an indicator of the success of a token sale, but it can also have a relevant real effect on the project. For example Howell et al. (2020) find that listing causes higher future employment.

5   Concluding Remarks

As shown in this chapter, new fundraising models are constantly emerging in a rapidly evolving technological context. Reliance on digital platforms has enabled both crowdfunding schemes and token offerings. DeFi has opened the door for token offerings to become an effective instrument to ensure greater financial inclusion and the democratization of finance. Nevertheless, it seems more likely that traditional finance will assimilate DeFi rather than vice versa (Zetzsche et al., 2020). Regulations are also being updated to improve the protection of both issuers and investors, supporting DeFi with effective oversight and risk control (Zetzsche et al., 2020). The recent efforts of many traditional stock exchanges to integrate DLT within their platforms to facilitate the issuance and trading of tokens is a promising step forward. These developments can make token offerings an inclusive and flexible financing vehicle for start-ups and SMEs without forcing them to share ownership and granting access to an unlimited investor pool (OECD, 2019). ICOs, IEOs, STOs and other forthcoming variants should be considered complementary rather than substitutive of other financing instruments across the whole lifecycle of a start-up (Huang et al., 2020; Chew & Spiegl, 2021). Moreover, asset tokenization shows a remarkable potential to create new business opportunities and to transform the management and trade of traditionally illiquid assets (Stefanoski et al., 2020), with the tokenization of securities and the market for STOs showing greater potential for growth in the upcoming years (OECD, 2020).

Appendix 1: Examples of ICOs

	ICO			
	Filecoin[a]	EMCODEX[b]	Fanadise[c]	Teslafan[d]
Core business idea	Storage	Commodity exchange platform	A platform for NFTs	Decentralized crowdfunding platform
Background	Filecoin is a project of Protocol Labs, Inc. It enables the outsourcing of data storage	It aims to remove the current barriers to direct entry into the commodity market by producers	It aims to decentralize social media and tries to give content back to the creator and to the people	Teslafan is a sustainability-driven tokenized network. It builds a digital platform with the potential to add cognitive ability to businesses
How does it work?	Filecoin's POW function includes a proof-of-retrievability component that requires nodes to prove that they are storing a particular file	It is a true cross-chain token linking several independent ecosystems	Fanadise is a content platform for influencers to monetize their social presence and interact with followers	Teslafan is a combination of blockchain technology and artificial intelligence and their interactions in resolving the limitations and challenges of the industrial adaptation of machine learning
What blockchain technology is used?	Filecoin	Ethereum	Ethereum	Ethereum
What problems does it solve?	Filecoin aims to store data in a decentralized way	The project aims to democratize the commodity market through blockchain technology	The project aims to adequately reward internet content creators	The project aims to be a key protocol gathering machine learning with investors

[a]ICOholder (https://icoholder.com/en/filecoin), Coinmarketcap (https://coinmarketcap.com/es/currencies/filecoin/) and Howell et al. (2020)
[b]ICOholder (https://icoholder.com/en/emcodex-1001356), white paper of EMCODEX (2021)
[c]ICOholder (https://icoholder.com/en/fanadise-1000240), ICOmarks (https://icomarks.com/ico/fanadise) and Cryptototem (https://cryptototem.com/fanadise-fana/)
[d]ICOholder (https://icoholder.com/en/teslafan-1000504) and Coinmarketcap (https://coinmarketcap.com/es/currencies/teslafan/)

Appendix 2: Examples of IEOs

	IEO			
	BitTorrent[a]	Idealogy[b]	BitcoinAsia[c]	Quantocoin[d]
Core business idea	Decentralized P2P communications protocol	Business network platform	Travel package company	Virtual bank
Background	It is a peer-to-peer file sharing and torrent platform. The native cryptocurrency token was released in February 2019	It runs an open-source project on Ethereum to create a platform for cooperation	It is a decentralized peer-to-peer cryptocurrency for the travel and tourism industry	It is the first mobile blockchain bank
How does it work?	BitTorrent (BTT) tokens can be bid in exchange for faster downloads. Tokens will be stored in a built-in wallet and can be exchanged for TRON (TRX) tokens through a decentralized exchange	Innovators, developers and investors connected in one platform create an ecosystem that covers aspects from the idea to crowdfunding. Tokens combine payment and utility features	The token holders will be rewarded with various benefits in travel and tourism products. It can be used to book vacations with cryptocurrency	The QTC token is the core of all transactions made in the banking platform
What blockchain technology is used?	Tron	Ethereum	Ethereum	Waves
What problems does it solve?	BitTorrent's original goal was to disrupt the legacy entertainment industry and how consumers obtain content	It creates a productive environment for business cooperation	It can be used to book an entire vacation with cryptocurrency for Asia Continent	Slow transaction times, access to banking services for the unbanked, high processing fees and fraud and security

[a]Coinmarketcap (https://coinmarketcap.com/es/currencies/bittorrent/), ICOmarks (https://icomarks.com/ieo/bittorrent) and ICOholder (https://icoholder.com/en/bittorrent-28385)
[b]ICOholder (https://icoholder.com/es/ideaology-31790) and Coinmarketcap (https://coinmarketcap.com/es/currencies/ideaology/)
[c]ICOmarks (https://icomarks.com/ieo/bitcoin-asia) and Foundico (https://foundico.com/ico/bitcoin-asia.html)
[d]ICOmarks (https://icomarks.com/ieo/quantocoin), ICOholder (https://icoholder.com/es/quantocoin-17192), Foundico (https://foundico.com/ico/quantocoin.html) and white paper of Quantocoin (2020)

Appendix 3: Examples of STOs

	STO				
	St. Regis AspenCoin[a]	SPiCE Venture Capital[a]	Santander Digital Bonds[a]	Mt Pelerin[b]	tZero[c]
Asset class	Real estate	VC/PE fund	Bonds	Equity	Equity
Background	Luxury real estate project (Aspen, Colorado). First tokenized ownership of real estate	The first fully tokenized VC fund traded on Asian and US digital asset exchanges	The first end-to-end blockchain bond. The bank issued the bond directly onto the blockchain	Tokenized banking ecosystem: The core principle is the blockchain-based tokenization of the entire bank's balance sheet	tZERO's DLR platform provides its clients with a technological solution to automate the traditional REG SHO locate process to meet operational and regulatory requirements
How does it work?	The underlying asset is the fractional ownership in the resort. Investment in the tokens is equivalent to an economic interest equal to one common share of Aspen Digital, Inc. a single asset REIT, inclusive of non-voting rights and the REIT's income distribution	The underlying asset is the limited partner interest in a closed-end fund that invests in blockchain and tokenization companies	Santander securely tokenizes the bond and register it on the blockchain. Both the cash used to complete the investment, and the coupons are tokenized and represented digitally on the blockchain. The maturity of the bonds is 1 year	Assets (loans) and liabilities (customer deposits) are reflected on-chain through the issuance of tokens to be used and traded on Mt. Pelerin marketplaces	tZERO's DLR platform captures all inventory and audit trail information and stores that information permanently on a proprietary blockchain
What blockchain technology is used?	Ethereum/ Tezos	Ethereum	Ethereum	Ethereum	Ethereum

(continued)

STO				
St. Regis Aspencoin[a]	SPiCE Venture Capital[a]	Santander Digital Bonds[a]	Mt Pelerin[b]	tZero[c]
What problems does it solve?	It provides the opportunity to fractionalize a previously illiquid asset in real estate at a lower entry value for investors	It provides liquidity to VC funds	It reduces the number of intermediaries, improving the pace, efficiency and simplicity of the transaction. The counterparty risk is also reduced	It provides liquidity to the trading of financial instruments	It makes securities lending activities more transparent, and more efficient from both a cost and an operational perspective

[a]Source: Deloitte (2020b)
[b]Coinspeaker (https://www.coinspeaker.com/sto/mt-pelerin/) and STOscope (https://stoscope.com/sto/mt-pelerin)
[c]ICOholder https://icoholder.com/en/tzero), Stomarket https://stomarket.com/sto/tZERO) and STOscope (https://stoscope.com/sto/tzero)

References

Ackermann, E., Bock, C., & Bürger, R. (2020). Democratising entrepreneurial finance: The impact of crowdfunding and initial coin offerings (ICOs). In A. Moritz, J. H. Block, S. Golla, & A. Werner (Eds.), *Contemporary developments in entrepreneurial finance: An academic and policy lens on the status-quo, challenges and trends* (pp. 277–308). Springer International.

Adhami, S., & Giudici, G. (2019). Initial coin offerings: Tokens as innovative financial assets. In U. Hacioglu (Ed.), *Blockchain economics and financial market innovation: Financial innovations in the digital age* (pp. 61–81). Springer International.

Adhami, S., Giudici, G., & Martinazzi, S. (2018). Why do businesses go crypto? An empirical analysis of initial coin offerings. *Journal of Economics and Business, 100*, 64–75.

Anson, M. (2021). Initial exchange offerings: The next evolution in cryptocurrencies. *The Journal of Alternative Investments, 23*(4), 110–121.

Ante, L. (2021). Blockchain-based tokens as financing instruments: Capital market access for SMEs? In I. A. Boitan & K. Marchewka-Bartkowiak (Eds.), *Fostering innovation and competitiveness with FinTech, RegTech, and SupTech* (pp. 129–141). IGI Global.

Ante, L., & Fiedler, I. (2021). Cheap signals in security token offerings (STOs). *Quantitative Finance and Economics, 4*(4), 608–639.

Arner, D., Auer, R., & Frost, J. (2020). *Stablecoins: Risks, potential and regulation*. BIS Working Papers(905).

Bellavitis, C., Fisch, C., & Wiklund, J. (2021). A comprehensive review of the global development of initial coin offerings (ICOs) and their regulation. *Journal of Business Venturing Insights, 15*, e00213.

Benedetti, H., & Kostovetsky, L. (2021). Digital tulips? Returns to investors in initial coin offerings. *Journal of Corporate Finance, 66*, 101786.

Block, J. H., Groh, A., Hornuf, L., Vanacker, T., & Vismara, S. (2021). The entrepreneurial finance markets of the future: A comparison of crowdfunding and initial coin offerings. *Small Business Economics, 57*(2), 865–882.

Cermak, L., Rogers, M., & Hoffmann, L. (2021). *Stablecoins: Bridging the network gap between traditional money and digital value*. The Block Resesarch.

Chamorro Domínguez, M. C. (2021). Financing of start-ups via initial coin offerings and gender equality. In K. Miller & K. Wendt (Eds.), *The fourth industrial revolution and its impact on ethics: Solving the challenges of the agenda 2030* (pp. 183–197). Springer International Publishing.

Chen, Y. (2018). Blockchain tokens and the potential democratization of entrepreneurship and innovation. *Business Horizons, 61*(4), 567–575.

Chen, Y., & Bellavitis, C. (2020). Blockchain disruption and decentralized finance: The rise of decentralized business models. *Journal of Business Venturing Insights, 13*, e00151.

Chew, S. M., & Spiegl, F. (2021). Security token offering—New way of financing in the digital era. *Journal of Financial Transformation, 52*, 142–151.

Cointelegraph Research, CryptoResearch.Report. (2021). *The security token report 2021*.

Deloitte, HKbitEx and University of Hong Kong–Asian Institute of International Financial Law (AIIFL). (2020a). *Advantages of security token offerings*. Retrieved from https://www2.deloitte. com/content/dam/Deloitte/cn/Documents/audit/deloitte-cn-auditadvantages-of-security-token-offerings-report-en-210219.pdf

Deloitte, HKbitEX, King & Wood Mallesons and University of Hong Kong – Asian Institute of International Financial Law (AIIFL). (2020b). *Security token offerings: The next phase of financial market evolution?* Retrieved from https://www2.deloitte.com/content/dam/Deloitte/ cn/Documents/audit/deloitte-cn-audit-security-token-offering-en-201009.pdf

European Commission. (2020). *Proposal for a regulation of the European Parliament and of the council on markets in crypto-assets, and amending directive (EU) 2019/1937*.

European Parliament. (2020). *Digital finance: Markets in Crypto-assets (MiCA)*.

Fantacci, L., & Gobbi, L. (2021). Stablecoins, central bank digital currencies and US dollar hegemony. *Accounting, Economics, and Law: A Convivium*. https://doi.org/10.1515/ael-2020-0053

Fisch, C. (2019). Initial coin offerings (ICOs) to finance new ventures. *Journal of Business Venturing, 34*(1), 1–22.

FSB (Financial Stability Board). (2019). *Decentralised financial technologies: Report on financial stability, regulatory and governance implications*.

García-Rodríguez, A. (2021). Initial coin offerings: A new trend in the market, ch.8. In K. Thomas (Ed.), *The Routledge handbook of FinTech*. Routledge.

Gryglewicz, S., Mayer, S., & Morellec, E. (2021). Optimal financing with tokens. *Journal of Financial Economics, 142*(3), 1038–1067.

Holden, R., Malani, A. (2019). *The ICO paradox: Transactions costs, token velocity, and token value*. No. 26265.

Houben, R., & Snyers, A. (2020). *Crypto-assets. Key developments, regulatory concerns and responses. Study for the Committee on Economic and Monetary Affairs, Policy Department for Economic, Scientific and Quality of Life Policies*. European Parliament.

Howell, S. T., Niessner, M., & Yermack, D. (2018). *Initial coin offerings: Financing growth with cryptocurrency tokens sales*. Working Paper 24774, National Bureau of Economic Research.

Howell, S. T., Niessner, M., & Yermack, D. (2020). Initial coin offerings: Financing growth with cryptocurrency token sales. *The Review of Financial Studies, 33*(9), 3925–3974.

Huang, W., Meoli, M., & Vismara, S. (2020). The geography of initial coin offerings. *Small Business Economics, 55*(1), 77–102.

Kondova, G., & Simonella, G. (2019). Blockchain in startup financing: ICOs and STOs in Switzerland. *Journal of Strategic Innovation and Sustainability, 14*(6), 43–48.

Lambert, T., Liebau, D., & Roosenboom, P. (2021). Security token offerings. *Small Business Economics*. https://doi.org/10.1007/s11187-021-00539-9

Lynn, T., & Rosati, P. (2021). New sources of entrepreneurial finance. In M. Soltanifar, M. Hughes, & L. Göcke (Eds.), *Digital entrepreneurship: Impact on business and society* (pp. 209–231). Springer International Publishing.

Massey, R., Dalal, D., & Dakshinamoorthy, A. (2017). *Initial coin offering: A new paradigm*. Deloitte.

Mazzorana-Kremer, F. (2019). Blockchain-based equity and STOs: Towards a liquid market for SME financing? *Theoretical Economics Letters, 9*(5), 1534–1552.

Miglo, A. (2020). Choice between IEO and ICO: Speed vs liquidity vs risk. https://doi.org/10.2139/ssrn.3561439

Miglo, A. (2021). STO vs. ICO: A theory of token issues under moral Hazard and demand uncertainty. *Journal of Risk and Financial Management, 14*(6), 232.

Momtaz, P. P. (2020). Initial coin offerings. *PLoS One, 15*(5), e0233018.

Myalo, A. S. (2019). Comparative analysis of ICO, DAOICO, IEO and STO. *Finance: Theory and Practice, 23*(6), 6–25.

OECD. (2019). *Initial coin offerings (ICOs) for SME financing*. OECD.

OECD. (2020). *The tokenisation of assets and potential implications for financial markets* (OECD Blockchain Policy Series). OECD.

Piñeiro-Chousa, J., López-Cabarcos, M. Á., & Ribeiro-Soriano, D. (2021). The influence of financial features and country characteristics on B2B ICOs' website traffic. *International Journal of Information Management, 59*, 102332.

PwC/Strategy&. (2019). *5th ICO / STO report: A strategic perspective*. PwC/Strategy&.

PwC/Strategy&. (2020). *6th ICO / STO report: A strategic perspective*. PwC/Strategy&.

Ribeiro-Soriano, D., Piñeiro-Chousa, J., & López-Cabarcos, M. Á. (2020). What factors drive returns on initial coin offerings? *Technological Forecasting and Social Change, 153*, 119915.

Romero-Ugarte, J. L. (2018). Distributed ledger technology (DLT): Introduction. *Economic Bulletin, Banco de España(DEC), 19*, 1–11.

Schückes, M., & Gutmann, T. (2021). Why do startups pursue initial coin offerings (ICOs)? The role of economic drivers and social identity on funding choice. *Small Business Economics, 57*(2), 1027–1052.

Slyusarev, J. (2020). *Analytical report: IEOs in 2019-2020*.

Stefanoski, D., Sahin, O., Banusch, B., Fuchs, S., Andermatt, S., & Quertramp, A. (2020). *Tokenization of assets. Decentralized finance (DeFi). Volume 1. Spot on: Fundraising & StableCoins in Switzerland*. Ernst & Young.

Todd, R., & Rogers, M. (2020). *A global look at central bank digital currencies: From iteration to implementation*. The Block Research White Paper.

Wadsworth, A. (2018). Decrypting the role of distributed ledger technology in payments processes. *Reserve Bank of New Zealand Bulletin, 81*(5), 1–20.

Yen, J., Wang, T., & Chen, Y. (2021). Different is better: How unique initial coin offering language in white papers enhances success. *Accounting and Finance, 61*(4), 5309–5340.

Zetzsche, D. A., Arner, D. W., & Buckley, R. P. (2020). Decentralized finance. *Journal of Financial Regulation, 6*(2), 172–203.

Financing Start-Ups Through Artificial Intelligence

Ricardo Costa Climent and Darek M. Haftor

1   Artificial Intelligence in Start-Up Financing

To define the impact of artificial intelligence (AI) on the financing of start-ups, we must differentiate between two contexts. The first is the financing of technological start-ups based on AI, which is a priority for investors in financing because of both its innovative nature and the benefit it entails for organisations. The second context is the use of AI by investors and funders to support the most relevant start-ups, either through machine learning, which helps avoid financial failures, or by offering excellent tools for start-ups. Both contexts show the influence of the emergence of AI in all sectors and reflect how the versatility of AI has become an essential issue in any market.

Entrepreneurship is a key driver of economic development, employment and innovation (Schumpeter, 1942). However, new firm creation often requires external funding. Start-up financing has changed massively in recent years thanks to technological developments and the possibilities they offer.

The present era is witnessing a major revolution in the financial system. This revolution is driven by technology (FinTech) through tools such as crowdfunding, big data, blockchain, robo-advisors and digital payments (Arslanian & Fischer, 2019). Some claim that this automation of the financial markets is creating an assessment-based model using analytical, sophisticated and objective data. For

R. C. Climent (✉)
Uppsala University, Uppsala, Sweden
e-mail: ricardo.costacliment@im.uu.se

D. M. Haftor
Uppsala University, Uppsala, Sweden

University of Economics and Human Sciences in Warsaw, Warszawa, Poland
e-mail: darek.haftor@im.uu.se

© The Author(s), under exclusive license to Springer Nature Switzerland AG 2022
C. Lassala, S. Ribeiro-Navarrete (eds.), *Financing Startups*, Future of Business and Finance, https://doi.org/10.1007/978-3-030-94058-4_9

149

example, the creditworthiness of borrowers can be analysed without direct human assessment, which inevitably entails some degree of bias or error (OECD, 2018).

Recent years have witnessed the creation of new companies for which technology is a core part of their business models. This integration lets users optimise their resources and produces consumer satisfaction. For companies such as Facebook, Uber, WhatsApp and Airbnb, user finance is part of the business. For instance, Facebook users in the United States can transfer money through the Messenger app. Similarly, Amazon now offers U.S. students credit via its app. In China, WeChat and Alibaba have together created one of the largest money markets in the world. It is estimated that WeChat Pay and Alipay channelled around 58.8 trillion yuan (approximately US$8.8 trillion) in 2016 (Arslanian & Fischer, 2019; Chandler, 2017; Xie, 2018).

WeChat is one of the most common ways for Chinese users to transfer money to each other. It not only allows users to buy insurance products or invest in funds but also lets them schedule doctor's appointments, book a taxi, make donations or find dates. Presumably, therefore, the financial platforms of the future will not only offer financial products but also meet other consumer needs. Furthermore, this service will be provided by technology companies, not the traditional banking system (Arslanian & Fischer, 2019).

Technology companies such as Microsoft, Apple, Amazon and Facebook have digital platform business models. The technologies, products and services they offer provide value primarily by enabling interaction between users, who create strategic networks. This model can create direct network effects (i.e. where a user benefits directly from the participation of other users) or indirect network effects (i.e. where participation by a greater number of users enhances the service, product or technology for a given user). These network effects are directly linked to the creation and capture of value by the platform. The classical theory on network externalities states that the more users there are, the more value is created (Katz & Shapiro, 1985). However, other issues also condition network effects, such as network structure and behaviour (Afuah, 2013).

In this context, digital or technology-based platforms use AI to personalise their services or products and thus increase their installed base. The interactions of users with the platform provide information about their interests, tastes, needs, barriers and so on. Through data-driven learning, data are used to detect patterns more accurately to improve products or services, which keeps existing users interacting with the platform and even attracts new users. Gregory, Henfridsson, Kaganer and Kyriakou (2020) recently documented this phenomenon as a new form of network externality: the data network effect.

Through AI, the vast reserves of data amassed by certain technology companies give them a competitive advantage that is virtually impossible for rivals to match. Thanks to accumulated data and machine learning techniques, companies can race ahead of competitors and even enter other markets with a substantial advantage (Prufer & Schottmüller, 2017).

In summary, technology companies are creating both direct and indirect networks with users, which are affecting the value they provide (Haftor et al., 2021).

Technology companies such as Microsoft, Apple, Amazon and Facebook provide value depending on the size of their user network (Afuah, 2013). The more users there are, the more value is created. Technology companies now offer products that the traditional banking system does not. Peer-to-peer lending, for example, can provide the type of financing that previously came predominantly from banks (Arslanian & Fischer, 2019). Robo-advisory platforms use algorithms to offer financial planning services without human supervision. These platforms offer asset management solutions that are both more transparent and less expensive. The common thread of all these technology companies is the use of artificial intelligence (AI).

AI refers to technologies that enable machines to perform functions initially associated with the human mind, such as learning, interaction and problem solving (Nilsson, 1971). In the evolutionary process of AI, two major applications of AI can be highlighted: first, the automation of machines to replace routine human tasks, and second, the intensification of the use of machines to perform human tasks, thus improving performance and objectivity (Raisch & Krakowski, 2021). AI was initially applied to automation in production. With the development of learning algorithms and advances in data collection sensors, however, AI is now starting to be used to support, alter or augment the work of humans. AI is applied in decision support and management tasks, with some studies examining the advantages of combining these two applications instead of choosing one over the other. At present, there is a distinction between two major AI applications: first, the automation of machines to replace routine human tasks, and second, the intensification of the use of machines to perform human tasks, thereby enhancing performance and objectivity (Raisch & Krakowski, 2021).

With the rise of AI and its use, in this case in the FinTech and AI industries, new jobs are appearing. These jobs require different skills, such as creative design and programming. To engage with stakeholders, it is important to work with governments to develop policies, with regulators to establish laws and with the community to shape and adapt to the new ecosystem. A change of mindset is needed so that people choose to work in start-ups or create businesses instead of opting for the stable, traditional jobs that will be affected by this paradigm shift. This is the future that awaits the world, and some of these changes are already taking place. Therefore, it is crucial to educate younger generations to help them develop the skills they need to become designers, programmers or creative thinkers (Arslanian & Fischer, 2019).

As already explained, one of the new alternatives in the labour market is provided by start-ups. Start-ups are new or young companies that develop a product or service that provides value to consumers. They use cross-cutting innovation and create replicable and scalable business models (Baldridge & Curry, 2021). Such firms collaborate more informally than traditional firms. They create a disruptive develop-ment, which ultimately leads to rapid growth. According to Robehmed (2013), 'after about three years in business, most start-ups cease being start-ups. This often coincides with other factors that indicate a graduation from startup-dom: acquisition by a larger company, more than one office, revenues greater than $20 million, more than 80 employees, over five people on the board, and founders who have personally sold shares. Somewhat ironically, when a start-up becomes profitable it is likely moving away from startuphood. One thing we can all agree on: the key attribute of a start-up is its ability to grow'.

As already discussed, a feature of start-ups is their use of technology. By using technology and AI, they are more likely to receive funding, given the technology-based, cutting-edge nature of their business models. Initially, seed capital is the predominant form of funding, later being replaced by venture capital (Davila et al., 2003).

Start-ups generally initially require a small investment, usually from family, friends and fools (FFFs), as well as the founding partners. This investment is used to start the business. If it is successful and generates revenue, financial support is then sought from a business angel (Adler et al., 2019). The forms of start-up financing include accelerators, business angels, venture capital, crowdfunding and seed capital, which are described in detail in other chapters of this book.

From a theoretical viewpoint, a start-up can, by definition, be linked to business model theory (Amit & Zott, 2001). According to this theory, the creation and capture of value occurs through a system of activities that extend beyond the firm's boundaries and that are performed by a set of actors linked together through transaction mechanisms. Business model theory (Amit & Zott, 2001) was developed in 2001 in response to the emergence of new technology-based companies whose level of success could not be explained by traditional economic theories. This theory proposes four possible sources of value creation: novelty, efficiency, complementarity and lock-in. The essence of a start-up is the use of innovation and technology to offer a novel product or service that responds to an unmet demand.

Most start-ups focus their services or products on helping other companies with technology, AI or data management so that they can overcome a lack of capabilities and become more efficient. The start-up business model can be defined as an ecosystem in which the parties (employees, funders, partners, suppliers, etc.) establish a relationship based on complementarity. The network effect may be a value creation and capture initiative that triggers lock-in. However, for an early-stage start-up, rapidly building a network of users that allows it to take advantage of the positive network effect is a challenge. Therefore, they activate lock-in mechanisms to achieve maximum customer or user loyalty. Examples of these mechanisms include personalised customer service by small companies, offers and discounts and customised products or services.

Start-ups find it hard to establish a data network because it requires time, effort and huge amounts of data. However, the results and the potential benefits are extremely attractive. Start-ups are considering the use of machine learning to continue adding value and adapting to the changing environment, given that start-ups are currently receiving the most funding due to their potential. In terms of funding, the impact of the data network is also important and will continue to be so for years to come. As already explained, machine learning and artificial intelligence are essential to explore a company's foundations because they will have a direct impact on the nature of the company and the way it competes.

This chapter analyses AI as a key element for start-ups that can help new firms attract more funding than traditional companies with less potential. The chapter also analyses how AI has led to the creation of tools that support companies and entrepreneurs in their financing decisions, given the possibilities it offers in terms of big data analytics. This chapter continues by presenting the theory on AI. It then offers examples of start-ups and the use of AI to finance start-ups.

2   Theoretical Types of Artificial Intelligence

Today, vast sets of data are collected through computer applications, social media and internal company databases. This 'big data' must then be processed so that it can be useful and can support decisions that add value to companies and other stakeholders.

AI is used to process, interpret, learn and use the data and thus meet various aims (Kaplan & Haenlein, 2019). In AI, machine learning is employed to identify patterns that can lead to predictions and an understanding of business problems and their possible solutions (Vergne, 2020). In machine learning, machines sense data through users' interactions and facial or voice recognition. They are then able to programme using the information they have learned to offer recommendations or move and control objects (Kaplan & Haenlein, 2019). Narrow AI, which refers to performing a limited task, has short-term commercial potential. Focusing on this form of AI, Chui (2017) listed some business-related AI technologies, such as robotics and self-driving vehicles, computer vision, language, virtual agents and machine learning. All these technologies are based on or complemented by machine learning. Machine learning can be defined as the discipline concerned with using computational methods to recognise patterns in data and make predictions whose accuracy increases with the amount (and quality) of the data (Vergne, 2020). Advances in machine learning offer a novel approach to performing specific decision-making tasks and resolving business problems. In turn, machine learning is based on improving the price–performance ratio of computer processing technology, data storage, data management and networking technologies (Agrawal et al., 2018). When combined, these technologies make AI an important tool to enable platforms, products or services to generate value for users (Gregory et al., 2020).

Value creation is one of the fundamental goals for companies, which constantly strive to provide differentiated services or goods in either economic or qualitative terms. Value creation involves the activities that lead to a higher profit through novelty, innovation and the use of resources that are difficult to imitate (Lepak et al., 2007). Along with the creation of value, it is also necessary to consider the capture of value as two different but interdependent processes, equally important due to the need to guarantee the economic returns representing the company's total value. As mentioned earlier, through data entry flow, machine learning allows the development of prediction patterns that lead to more personalised offers and increase in precision as more data values are incorporated. This process creates value for users, who, therefore, continue to use the service and provide more data. Those pieces of data improve services, entering a virtuous cycle called data network effects. In this case, the value creation of the data network effects is obvious; the more people using the platform, the better the service. However, it is just as important to analyse the capture of this created value to ensure that these returns are distributed throughout the value creation network fairly and proportionately (Sjödin et al., 2020).

This design of the architecture formed by the parties involved in a company and their activities for the creation and capture of value is specified in the business model (Amit & Zott, 2001). The choice of business model is a strategic decision for digital companies because it forms the basis for decision making and price setting (Casadesus-Masanell Ricart, 2010). For example, digital businesses often employ two types of business models: *freemium* (i.e. free access to content in exchange for advertising) and *premium* (i.e. access to content through subscription or payments for use).

Free access can attract many users and therefore collect a lot of information about their interests and habits. This profile is attractive to advertisers who can personalise their ads and may, therefore, be willing to pay large fees. However, the advertising bombardment can anger users who then leave the platform. Hence, created value has not been balanced with the capture of said value. On the contrary, a premium model provides a secure base of users who are really interested in certain content and who are willing to pay for it. However, it scares away the doubtful who are unsure and are not willing to pay to try.

Combining some or all of the sources of value creation and capture proposed by Amit and Zott (2001), the business model themes (efficiency, complementarity, novelty and lock-in) can help start-ups design their business models in this sense, taking advantage of solid theoretical foundations and empirical demonstration.

3 Practical Examples of the Financing of Start-Ups Using Artificial Intelligence

This section presents examples of the use of AI for financial decision making through tools that directly provide information on the risks and profitability associated with investing in certain projects. This section also presents examples of technology companies that have adopted AI and have enjoyed massive growth after beginning as start-ups.

3.1 Artificial Intelligence as a Financial Tool for the Financing and Promotion of Start-Ups

3.1.1 Banks

The financing of start-ups through banks occurs in many locations. In Scandinavia, leading banks such as DNB Bank and SR-Bank offer 'corporate accelerators' for start-ups. These corporate accelerators are important because they maintain contact with the start-ups over a set period (Kohler, 2016).

Since the 2010s, these programmes have been in operation in numerous industries. This example shows that they are suitable for banks (Kanbach & Stubnet, 2016). Their goal is long-term collaboration, which ensures the renewal of profits and provides lasting value (Kohler, 2016).

In the traditional approach, the contribution is based on a partnership agreement where mentoring, education and specific corporate resources are sought in cooperation with start-ups. This system also applies to the Norwegian financial industry (Kohler, 2016). AI is used in financial institutions because it opens a world of possibilities. For example, it enables rapid analysis of both structured and unstructured data. It can also enhance the quality of the analysis by considering a larger number of variables, as well as providing more accurate results (Fernández, 2019). Consumers also benefit from a better service, such as the detection of credit card fraud, leading to lower transaction risk.

Norway's leading bank, DNB Bank, has created its own corporate accelerator programme: the 'DNB NXT Accelerator' (StartupLab, 2019). DNB developed this tool to provide start-ups with support from individual industry mentors who advise them on financial and consulting matters as part of the start-up partnership programme (StartupLab, 2019). The key for DNB is the reciprocity between the start-up and the financial institution itself. The goal is for the employees of the financial institution to learn from and work for and with the start-up (Hvamstad, 2019). Another example is SR-Bank (in collaboration with SpareBank 1 Nord-Norge), which has also developed a start-up accelerator programme (Eikeland, 2019). Based on AI, a chatbot service called 'Boost.ai' with an estimated value of 1 BNOK has had a positive outcome, to the detriment of other larger projects. The Boost.ai software uses data provided by the client company. It then learns through AI and develops a personalised virtual agent in just a few days. It is a clear example of customer service automation. In addition to DNB Bank, the telecommunications company Telenor has also adopted the technology of Boost.ai.

These examples show that the development of AI tools by Norwegian banks gives start-ups support from these banks. It also provides added value because employees can learn from the start-ups, thus growing personally and acquiring new knowledge.

3.1.2 Google

Email services such as the Gmail server (Google) use machine learning technology to filter the emails that users receive on a daily basis.

AI filters spam through machine learning. This task consists of absorbing the information and memorising steps to store information about types of emails and the way users send them. The server is able to filter emails and forward them to the corresponding mailbox based on information received previously.

The Gmail server learns from steps to protect users from malware. Based on experience with certain emails, this system can automatically mark emails as dangerous, preventing computers from becoming infected. This task is performed using experience built over time with AI and machine learning.

Google Cloud offers a series of AI and machine learning products through solutions that can be applied at the start-up level. This set-up supports their daily work because they can perform their projects with greater ease and agility, which is what these developers really need.

One example within the Google family is 'Vertex Al', an eagerly awaited machine learning platform. This platform enables the deployment and scaling of learning models through pre-tested tools and is one of the most influential AI platforms in the market. This application uses Google's established and automated platforms as a basis, favouring machine learning through Google Research. One of the aims of this platform is to reduce the operating use time, creating a method to reduce the lines of code needed to customise models (Google Cloud, 2021). Despite being more sophisticated, these tools are simpler to use, providing users with a degree of agility and ease of reproduction of the models without the need for previous sophisticated experience.

The Vertex Al learning tool provides a series of innovative machine learning solutions by eliminating the complexity of its predecessors. The optimisation of resources and the complexity of maintenance mean that, through AI, start-ups can monitor the development of their projects in a more agile and orderly manner. This capability is important because the projects of developing companies require knowledge and growth over time. Therefore, Vertex Al provides the previous, well-known AI service through the Google servers, just like the spam model of the Gmail server. In addition to having a low cost, this optimisation and simplicity of use allows start-ups to use it in a more optimal and agile manner to optimise the development of their projects.

One of the main features is the unification of several cutting-edge Google tools, such as Google Cloud. Accordingly, the AI models and learning tools can be used to create a single platform to make it easier to train and compare models with customised code training (Google Cloud, 2021). Integration is another key element of the tool because it combines different learning models, different languages and broad methods so that all the business needs can be met for a given type of start-up. The final feature is the compatibility of open-source frameworks (Google Cloud, 2021) and other open-source generators such as Tensor Flow, PyTorch and Scikit-Learn. Information can be shared in order to monitor and analyse the machine learning functions so that open-source models can be selected more quickly and efficiently, thereby simplifying the operational process of the tool.

Google receives all this information so that other users can continue to develop their projects. However, this information is stored on servers, and the steps that users take are memorised with the help of AI so that, in the future, these servers can automatically foresee and predict how users will behave.

3.2   Financing for Start-Ups Based on Artificial Intelligence

3.2.1   Vehicle Companies (Fig. 1)

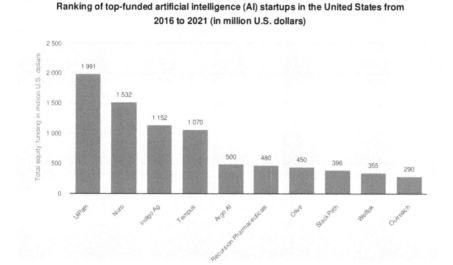

Fig. 1 Ranking of top-funded artificial intelligence (AI) start-ups in the United States from 2016 to 2021. (Statista, 2021)

According to Forbes, one of the leading companies in the use of AI is the American firm Nuro, which is valued at US$2.7 billion (Forbes, 2019). Using self-driven vehicles, Nuro aims to create a robotic delivery programme by delivering goods with its robot 'R2', which is fully self-driven and sustainable.

Nuro's vehicles are designed to be self-driven, albeit for short-range journeys. The safety of others is a priority, so they only transport material goods in controlled areas. The robot R2, which use 360° cameras, represents one of the biggest technological and commercial advances given its stage of maturity. The Lidar model consists of AI with long-range radars and ultrasonic sensors. It combines solid hardware with AI using tracking sensors, maps and geolocation.

The main feature of Nuro is safety, which is the top priority: 'The safest vehicle is the one that lets you stay at home without having to leave the house to collect your products' (Forbes, 2019). The Virginia Tech Transportation Institute has shown that the design of self-driven vehicles can reduce the likelihood of death by 60% in the event of an accident (Virginia Tech Transportation Institute, 2021). In general, smaller vehicles can provide greater overall benefits by being less noticeable by society, minimising their impact on the city. Also, in the event of an accident, pedestrians can dodge the vehicle more effectively, preventing fatalities (Nuro, 2021). Another notable feature of Nuro is that it only transports material goods from one location to another but does not transport people. The firm thus seeks to protect those on the outside. For Nuro, the priority is safety. People are placed before the business. In the event of an emergency, the R2 robot makes an emergency stop, with no regard for the goods it is transporting.

This AI application is designed to transport goods and not people, unlike other large companies such as Tesla (Nuro, 2021). The theory behind this system is to design the ideal vehicle for transporting these products. Thus, aspects such as external safety and other road users are prioritised. This type of vehicle is cheaper than other vehicles because its AI uses basic components. Therefore, the best possible system can be built efficiently without compromising other vehicles, ensuring that repairs are performed as quickly and efficiently as possible. In this sense, Nuro contributes to the development of autonomous AI through problem solving and the development of its own hardware and software. In the future, these elements could be applied to self-driven vehicles designed to transport people.

In terms of the legal considerations, the R2 model designed by Nuro is completely legal. It is registered and covered by the mandatory insurance required to use public roads under the National Highway Traffic Safety Administration. Nuro is the first company to obtain a permit to operate commercially in the state of California. It complies with all legal requirements to operate self-driven vehicles.

In terms of financing, the firm has partners from different sectors, including food, pharma and retail. These companies support Nuro in its core mission of changing regular deliveries through AI. In March 2021, new agreements were signed allowing new investors to participate further in Fidelity Management and Research Company programmes. There have also been capital injections from the banks SoftBank Fund 1 and Greylock. Thus, funding has come from a variety of markets, including private equity firms, companies that are interested in the product and automotive firms such as Woven Planet, a subsidiary of Toyota (Businesswire, 2021).

3.2.2   ByteDance (Fig. 2)

ByteDance is a Chinese technology company. It is the developer of the applications TikTok and Douyin. Both applications let users create and share short videos. Douyin is marketed exclusively in China.

ByteDance has invested heavily in AI and uses AI in all its processes. It also uses AI to improve the user experience through, for example, a recommendations algorithm that shows users which videos may be of interest.

The company has an AI factory that creates AI solutions for the firm on a large scale. It has four components: data pipeline, algorithm development, experimentation platform and software infrastructure.

ByteDance Data Pipeline

The data pipeline is concerned with how and where user data are collected, cleaned, processed and preserved. When ByteDance began to grow, it created a data portal platform to offer integrated data solutions to the different business units to ensure that they were connected.

ByteDance Algorithm Development

Algorithm development is related to the rules for machines to generate decisions, make predictions and solve problems without human assistance. ByteDance has always been one step ahead of its competitors in this regard. While the rest of the

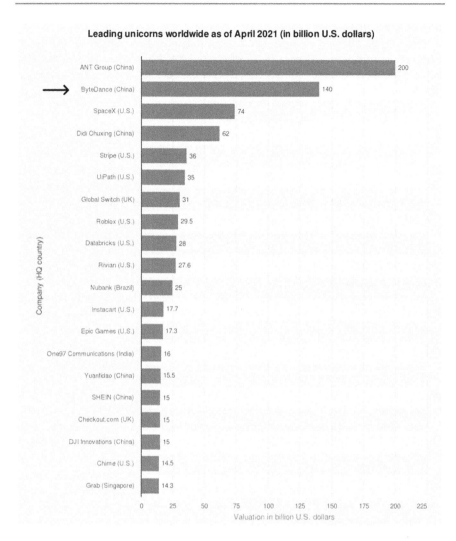

Fig. 2 Leading unicorns worldwide as of April 2021 (in billion U.S. dollars). (Statista, 2021)

industry was hiring IT professionals, ByteDance was hiring algorithm writers to develop AI algorithms.

ByteDance Experimentation
Predictions generated by AI algorithms are validated on the experimentation platforms of AI-powered firms such as LinkedIn. ByteDance uses experimentation to improve its algorithms. It has developed a platform for quick algorithm experiments.

ByteDance Software Infrastructure
To support the above-mentioned factory components, an effective software infra-structure is necessary. To ensure an effective software infrastructure, ByteDance developed 'Infrastructure 2.0' in 2018. This infrastructure enables the company to develop rapidly.

3.2.3 Graphcore

The start-up Graphcore is working on AI technology through its 'intelligence processing unit' (IPU), which consists of 59.4 billion transistors and 1500 processing units inside a silicon case. The aim of developing this artificial processing unit is to create linkages between different industries such as robotics, medicine and self-driving cars (Graphcore, 2021).

This new processor can be applied to all business areas. Accordingly, its unique architecture can be used by AI researchers to develop new types of applications. This start-up has major international partners such as the investment capital firm Amadeus, manufacturers such as BMW and Bosch and tech firms such as Dell (Graphcore, 2021). By investing in emerging companies, these large firms seek to outsource their research and development (R&D) processes by using machine learning tools to find innovative solutions to existing problems. This novel processor has a direct impact on the development of AI through machine learning by connecting multiple platforms in the development of machine learning tools.

The utility of this processor was recently exemplified by NVIDIA's application processor, which is up to 16 times faster and more efficient than NVIDIA's previous model. Graphcore seeks to compete with AI processors created by Google, although Google does not seek to commercialise them but uses them for its own platforms. Graphcore's aim is business oriented because it markets its processors for profit. Graphcore has specialised in the development of AI processors with numerous partners, some of which have already been mentioned. These partners have backed this start-up in its attempts to harness machine learning and AI to build an intelli-gence processing unit (IPU) capable of creating expansive machine learning models for use in different fields (Fortune, 2020).

3.2.4 Exabel

Exabel provides investment information on alternative data directly to investment teams. This information is delivered via Graphcore data processing, an online platform for AI analytics, data science and financial modelling. The business of these companies is based on AI, and they reflect the influence of the emergence of AI in all sectors. They also show the way in which the versatility of AI has become an essential issue on both sides of all markets in terms of both the financing of technological AI-based start-ups and the use of AI by investors and funders to support the most attractive start-ups.

References

Adler, P., Florida, R., King, K., & Mellander, C. (2019). The city and high-tech start-ups: The spatial organization of Schumpeterian entrepreneurship. *Cities, 87*, 121–130.

Afuah, A. (2013). Are network effects really all about size? The role of structure and conduct. *Strategic Management Journal, 34*(3), 257–273.

Agrawal, A., Gans, J., & Goldfarb, A. (2018). *Prediction, judgement, and uncertainty.* NBER Working Paper, 24243.

Amit, R., & Zott, C. (2001). Value creation in e-business. *Strategic Management Journal, 22*(6–7), 493–520.

Arslanian, H., & Fischer, F. (2019). *The future of finance: The impact of FinTech, AI, and crypto on financial services.* Springer.

Baldridge, R., & Curry, B. (2021). What is a start-up? *Forbes.* https://www.forbes.com/advisor/investing/what-is-a-startup/

Businesswire. (2021). *Toyota's $1.29 billion electric vehicle battery plant to create 1,750 jobs in North Carolina.* Link available at: https://www.businesswire.com/news/home/2021120700 5764/en/Toyota's-1.29-Billion-Electric-Vehicle-Battery-Plant-to-Create-1750-Jobs-in-North-Carolina

Casadesus-Masanell, R., & Ricart, J. E. (2010). From strategy to business models and onto tactics. *Long Range Planning, 43*(2–3), 195–215.

Chandler, C. (2017). Tencent and Alibaba are engaged in a massive battle in China play video. *Fortune.* http://fortune.com/2017/05/13/tencent-alibaba-china/

Chui, M. (2017). *Artificial intelligence the next digital frontier* (Vol. 47(3.6)). McKinsey and Company Global Institute.

Davila, A., Foster, G., & Gupta, M. (2003). Venture capital financing and the growth of start-up firms. *Journal of Business Venturing, 18*(6), 689–708.

Eikeland, M. (2019). *Innovationlab: Gründerhub accelerator.* Retrieved from https://innovationlab.net/case/grunderhub-accelerator/

Fernández, A. (2019). Artificial intelligence in financial services. *Banco de España Article, 3*, 19.

Forbes. (2019). *The promise of self-driving delivery vehicles: Insights from Nuro cofounder Dave Ferguson.* Lance Eliot. Link available at: https://www.forbes.com/sites/lanceeliot/2019/07/17/the-promise-of-self-drivingdelivery-vehicles-insights-from-nuro-cofounder-dave-ferguson/?sh=4fdd68067b44

Fortune. (2020). Link available at: https://fortune.com/best-companies/2020/nvidia/

Google Cloud. (2021). Link available at: https://cloud.google.com/blog/products/ai-machine-learning/google-cloudai-2021-highlights

Graphcore. (2021). Link available at: https://www.graphcore.ai

Gregory, R. W., Henfridsson, O., Kaganer, E., & Kyriakou, H. (2020). The role of artificial intelligence and data network effects for creating user value. *Academy of Management Review, 46*(3), 534–551.

Haftor, D. M., Climent, R. C., & Lundström, J. E. (2021). How machine learning activates data network effects in business models: Theory advancement through an industrial case of promoting ecological sustainability. *Journal of Business Research, 131*, 196–205.

Hvamstad, E., (2019). *Hegnar: Storbank sendte 24-åring til startup for å lære.* Retrieved from https://www.hegnar.no/Nyheter/Naeringsliv/2019/02/Storbank-sendte-24- aaring-til-startup-for-aa-laere?r=refresh

Kanbach, D. K., & Stubner, S. (2016). Corporate accelerators as recent form of start-up engagement: The what, the why, and the how. *Journal of Applied Business Research (JABR), 32*(6), 1761–1776.

Kaplan, A., & Haenlein, M. (2019). Siri, Siri, in my hand: Who's the fairest in the land? On the interpretations, illustrations, and implications of artificial intelligence. *Business Horizons, 62*(1), 15–25.

Katz, M. L., & Shapiro, C. (1985). Network externalities, competition, and compatibility. *The American Economic Review, 75*(3), 424–440.

Kohler, T. (2016). Corporate accelerators: Building bridges between corporations and start-ups. *Business Horizons, 59*(3), 347–357.

Lepak, D. P., Smith, K. G., & Taylor, M. S. (2007). Value creation and value capture: A multilevel perspective. *Academy of Management Review, 32*(1), 180–194.

Nilsson, N. J. (1971). *Problem-solving methods in artificial intelligence* (Vol. 5). McGraw-Hill.

Nuro, A. (Ed.). (2021). *Emerging contaminants*. BoD–Books on Demand.

OECD. (2018). *Financial markets, insurance and private pensions: Digitalisation and finance.* https://www.oecd.org/finance/Financial-markets-insurance-pensions-digitalisation-and-finance.pdf

Prufer, J., & Schottmüller, C. (2017). *Competing with big data*. Working paper. Tilburg University Department of Economics, Economics Research Group. Retrieved from https://research. tilburguniversity.edu/en/publications/competing-with-big-data

Raisch, S., & Krakowski, S. (2021). Artificial intelligence and management: The automation–augmentation paradox. *Academy of Management Review, 46*(1), 192–210.

Robehmed, N. (2013). What is a start-up? *Forbes.* https://www.forbes.com/sites/natalierobehmed/ %202013/12/16/what-is-a-startup/

Statista. (2021). *Ranking of top-funded artificial intelligence (AI) startups in the United States from 2016 to 2021.* Link available at: https://www.statista.com/statistics/621132/worldwide-highest-funded-ai-startups/

Schumpeter, J. (1942). Creative destruction. *Capitalism, Socialism and Democracy, 825,* 82–85.

Sjödin, D., Parida, V., Jovanovic, M., & Visnjic, I. (2020). Value creation and value capture alignment in business model innovation: A process view on outcome-based business models. *Journal of Product Innovation Management, 37*(2), 158–183.

StartupLab. (2019). *DnB NXT Accelerator.* Retrieved from https://startuplab.no/nxt/index. html#content3-1

Vergne, J. P. (2020). Decentralized vs. distributed organization: Blockchain, machine learning and the future of the digital platform. *Organization Theory, 1*(4), 2631787720977052.

Virginia Tech Transportation Institute. (2021). Link available at: https://www.vtti.vt.edu

Yifan Xie, S. (2018). Jack Ma's giant financial startup is shaking the Chinese banking system. *Wall Street Journal.* https://www.wsj.com/articles/jack-mas-giant-financial-startup-is-shaking-the-chinese-banking-system-1532885367

DeFi and Start-Ups: Revolution in Finance

Juan Piñeiro-Chousa, Ángeles López Cabarcos, and Isaac González

1 The Concept: Internet of Value

Transfer value over digital networks without a middleman is the main idea behind the expression 'the internet of value'. This also refers to the revolution that the internet has generated regarding information interchange and the potential revolution regarding value interchange.

This chapter will describe the key concepts that open new possibilities for finance and startups.

1.1 Decentralization

Removing the intermediary with open and trustworthy technology is probably the most crucial concept recognized in the cryptocurrency movement. The goal of Bitcoin was to create a currency without the need for central banks and commercial banks; in other words, the aim was the decentralization of digital currencies. Thus, Bitcoin started the movement that other projects have followed by applying this idea to new areas with different perspectives.

1.2 Permissionless

Physical money allows two parties to make a deal without asking for permission from a third party. Consider this an example: Person A exchanges $10 for 8 € with Person B. Nevertheless, digital money, as we know, is not so straightforward, especially in an international environment and with different currencies. First, both

J. Piñeiro-Chousa (✉) · Á. L. Cabarcos · I. González
Santiago de Compostela University, Santiago de Compostela, Spain
e-mail: j.pineiro@usc.es; angeles.lopez.cabarcos@usc.es; isaacjose.gonzalez.lopez@usc.gal

© The Author(s), under exclusive license to Springer Nature Switzerland AG 2022   163
C. Lassala, S. Ribeiro-Navarrete (eds.), *Financing Startups*, Future of Business and Finance, https://doi.org/10.1007/978-3-030-94058-4_10

persons would need to ask a bank for a digital account, which has several requirements, depending on the country. Then, there are several steps that need to be completed, such as international bank transfer slips and currency exchanges. In the best-case scenario, there is one-third party that helps make the exchange possible; in the worst-case scenario, there are several parties and many operations that help make it possible. In addition, one party can deny the operation for any reason, and then the transaction cannot take place. Decentralization also implies that no one party has the power to concede or deny access to the system.

1.3   'Don't Trust, Verify'!

If anyone can participate and there are no middlemen, then the only way to trust the system is by using glass walls. The open-source movement is critical in the software industry; it brings about transparency in publishing the code so that anyone, primarily specialists, can see how it works. In addition, when protocols need transparency, a committee releases documentation that describes the rules, details and anything related to the protocol. In this way, anyone can implement, use or interact with the protocol. Internet technology establishes an open protocol framework. The last requirement for trust is publicly available data, which collides with privacy. Most blockchains use anonymity to solve this matter; thus, everything is public, but there are no names, only account numbers.

In summary, with open-source, open protocols and anonymity, no one must trust technology or other parties; it is possible to verify everything. This idea has been condensed in the famous phrase in the crypto world: 'Don't trust, verify'!

2   The Technology: Blockchain and Smart Contracts

Technology that allows decentralized, permissionless and verifiable digital systems is a very impressive advancement. The turning point in history was the publication of the paper 'Bitcoin: A Peer-to-Peer Electronic Cash System' by Satoshi Nakamoto and the development of the subsequent open-source program. However, the technology came long before that, and the improvements were countless, which makes this one of the most significant new industries worldwide. This chapter will describe the key concepts and central ideas of this technology rather than following its history. Presenting the base technology that decentralized finance uses is the goal of this chapter.

2.1   Distributed Ledger Technologies

A digital ledger is essentially a database that lists the transactions between accounts and the current balance of those accounts. All modern banks have digital ledgers implemented on databases with high levels of security. Since the bank owns its ledger, the bank could change it; however, regulations, laws, and central banks monitor the behaviour of banks to prevent such behaviour. This scheme works very well if the top organization does its duty. However, if the top organization is corrupt, the whole system is compromised. Is there any alternative to this system?

Distributed ledger technologies (DLTs) are digital implementations of ledgers without a single owner (Romero-Ugarte, 2018). Instead of the traditional approach with one person or organization being in charge of the database, DLTs use cryptographic technology to run the database distributed in several nodes.

To align incentives, the typical way to run a DLT is to ask for fees from users to settle a transaction (example: Account A sent $10 to account B plus a $0.05 fee) and distribute that fee over the nodes to help to keep the DLT up and running. On the other hand, if a node engages in malicious behaviours such as trying to settle incorrect transactions or not helping to run the DLT, the node can be punished.

In this way, there are rules to maintain a digital ledger in which nobody can change the state of the database unless it controls more than 51% of the nodes to settle fake transactions. Thus, there is a broad decentralization of nodes and a good balance of incentives and punishments.

2.2   Blockchain

A blockchain is a concrete implementation of distributed ledger technology (Yaga et al., 2019). Therefore, it is similar to a database of transactions without an administrator.

The transactions that occur during a specific time frame are packeted in a block. In Bitcoin, for example these blocks have a duration of approximately 10 min. In real time, all the transactions go to the present block. When the block time is over, the block is closed, and a new block is opened for the transactions that occur in the next 10 min. Blocks can be compared to pages of a ledger book, and transactions can be seen as its lines.

To assure that blocks are immutable, each block stores a hash code of the precedent block, thereby creating a chain of blocks. In this way, if any node wants to maliciously change a settled transaction, it should change the block of the transaction, which will change the hash of the following block, which will thus change the hash of the next block and so on until the present block. Chaining the blocks in this way makes it exponentially difficult to change past transactions.

There are other implementations of the DLT, such as Hashgraph, which is led by the Hedera Hashgraph project. However, the large majority of cryptocurrencies are created on blockchains.

2.3   Consensus: PoW vs. PoS

The consensus mechanism is seen as the process of reaching an agreement on the exact form of the block (Bach et al., 2018). Since many nodes handle transactions, it is possible to have different blocks without bad intentions; additionally, malicious nodes could have untrue blocks. Therefore, when the block time ends and must be settled, all the nodes must agree on the actual block and settle it; that is the consensus. The alignment of incentives is the key to reaching the consensus and the good health of the blockchain. If the node collaborates, it will be rewarded; however, if the node acts maliciously, it will be punished. There are two main ways to do this, namely proof of work (PoW) or proof of stake (PoS).

In PoW, nodes must pay upfront for a costly computational effort (a tremendous amount of calculus). If they act maliciously, it is effortless to catch them because the block will be very different from the rest of the nodes. Punishment, not reward, is what awaits the effort made. If they collaborate with the network, then the network will reward the nodes using a random algorithm so that the reward will eventually occur. Nodes in PoW are called miners. Since computational work is very intensive in electricity and bitcoin mining is very profitable, miners use a significant share of world electricity consumption.

In PoS, nodes must deposit (stake) several tokens. If they act maliciously, then they lose part or all the tokens at stake; collaborating with the network means a reward for them. There are many variations of the PoS algorithm, such as delegated (DPos), bonded (BPoS), and hybrid (HPoS) algorithms. Indeed, there are many variations in the staked amount required, the rewards, and other details. Nodes in PoS are called validators, and they are much less intensive in electricity consumption. There are alternative consensus algorithms such as proof of authority, proof of location, proof of history, proof of burn, and more. Additionally, they can be hybrid solutions. However, all proofs have in common the necessity of reaching consensus in a decentralized system. These are ways to resolve the Byzantine general's problem that was proposed in 1982 as a logical dilemma.

The rewards received by miners and validators come from transaction fees collected in the blocks they help settle and, in some cases, newly minted tokens. Each blockchain defines the consensus mechanism in open-source code that anybody can check and in a more human-readable documents called white papers.

2.4   Smart Contract

A smart contract is an agreement that is made in code and executed in a blockchain. In this way, the two parties do not need to trust each other or a third party because the code is open-source, and the execution is unstoppable.

From arithmetic and computational perspectives, a ledger has a very restricted set of arithmetic operations. For example when Account A sends $10 to Account B, the operations involved are Account A balance minus ten and Account B balance plus ten. Ethereum and other blockchains were created to expand the operations allowed on a DLT to all the operations and structures of a computer code.

Nick Szabo coined the term smart contract, and Etherum was the first successful blockchain to implement the concept. The term came from the goal of providing a way to transform agreements into code executed on a neutral infrastructure.

However, the process should not hide its real essence, which is a computer code that runs over the nodes of a blockchain.

Before the arrival of smart contracts, the agreements should rely upon the trust of two parties or a trusted third party to assure that the agreement is fulfilled. For example if person A bets $10 with person B on the victory of the Lakers in their next match, either they trust each other, or they need a third party they both trust. With a smart contract, the agreement can be transformed into code and executed in a blockchain. Both conditions must be true; otherwise, if the computer in which the code is executed belongs to one party, if that party loses, the party could turn off the computer and thus make the code not be executed and the agreement not be fulfilled. Thus, smart contracts and blockchains remove the need to trust the other party in any agreement.

Example 10.1

```
send(A,BET,10) # Send 10 dollars From A account to BET account
send(B,BET,10) # Send 10 dollars From B account to BET account
if (lakers_win == true)
  send(BET,A,20) # If lakers win send 20 dollars to A
else
  send(BET,B,20) # If lakers not win send 20 dollars to B
```

2.5   Tokens

Some people use Bitcoin (capital B) as the name of the blockchain, bitcoin (lower-case b) for the cryptocurrency and BTC as the ticker. When Ethereum was created, Ethereum was used for the blockchain, Ether was used for the cryptocurrency, and ETH was used as the ticker. Until that moment, each blockchain had its own cryptocurrency. However, when Ethereum implemented the ERC20 feature, it allowed us to easily create new cryptocurrencies over the Ethereum blockchain, which are called tokens. Since their establishment, the creation of tokens has skyrocketed. Some authors use cryptocurrency for those running on their own blockchain and tokens for those running on other blockchains; however, in the literature, it is very common to see tokens as being synonymous with cryptocurrency.

Oxford dictionary defines a token as 'a round piece of metal or plastic used instead of money to operate some machines or as a form of payment'; we can apply this idea to the decentralized digital space. Cryptotokens, or simply tokens, bring an important novelty; i.e. everything is verifiable because it is created and traded on the blockchain.

3   Decentralized Finance

Decentralized finance, or DeFi, is the replication of financial services with smart contracts over blockchains, following the main features of crypto, i.e. the removal of intermediaries and permissionless use. Another vital feature of DeFi is composability. Since anybody can access any service without permission because of the open protocols, it is possible to create new services that use, improve or complement several services. This property is behind the famous phrase: DeFi functions as money Legos.

Cryptocurrencies are in essence a financial product. They are tradeable, they represent a digital asset, and they function as a digital form of money (Baur et al., 2018). In addition, of course, they are decentralized. Therefore, why is decentralized finance a subcategory in crypto? In short, DeFi tends to decentralize financial services prior to 2020 were in centralized crypto exchanges or traditional banks. Some authors share this financial services view (Gudgeon et al., 2020; Schär, 2020), while others have a wider categorization of DeFi (Chen & Bellavitis, 2020).

In the next sections, we will describe most of the DeFi categories and compare the centralized service with the decentralized version. It is important to note that this topic is very recent and is constantly changing. To support the definitions, we will refer to real projects that led the category at the time of the writing of this article. To describe the projects, we use whitepapers and official documentation, which is linked at the end of the chapter. This categorization is debatable and fuzzy; in fact, most sources have different categorizations, and some projects could be placed in several categories. However, our aim is to be educational in describing the roots but not formal in regard to categorization.

3.1   Stablecoins

Most cryptocurrencies are free trading, which means that they are priced by the market. In a very new technology with extremely fast adoption, the volatility is huge (Yin et al., 2021; López-Cabarcos et al., 2021), as shown in Fig. 1. The solution is the creation of a token that represents the price of an off-chain coin, which in most cases is linked to US dollars (USDs). This is called a stablecoin because its price is pegged to a real currency (Ante et al., 2021). Stablecoins are very useful when avoiding volatility and as a haven in crypto downturns. Therefore, they are a key part of the cryptocurrency ecosystem.

The first successful stable coin was USD Tether (USDT). As Fig. 2 shows, the price is most of the time very close to 1$. Tether is a company that mints one USDT token on-chain backed by one USD off-chain; in case of a reduction in supply, then they burn USDT tokens in the same amount of USD that they withdrew. Even on a blockchain, this is considered a centralized way to create a stablecoin because USDT users must trust in Tether's behaviour, audit behaviour or bank behaviour. Indeed, there have been concerns that USDT could not be fully backed. These concerns have attracted other players to create their own stablecoins, such as USDC (Coinbase), BUSD (Binance), HUSD (Huoby) and others.

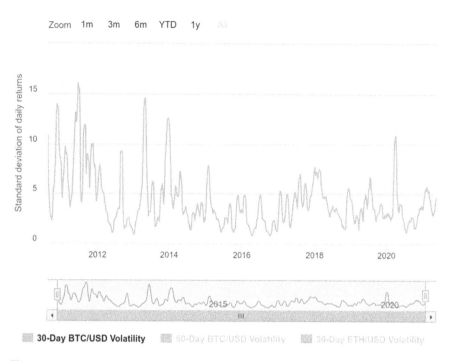

Fig. 1 BTC/USD volatility. Source: coinmarkecap.com

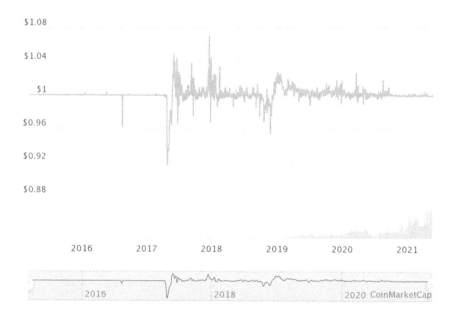

Fig. 2 USDT price chart. Source: coinmarkecap.com

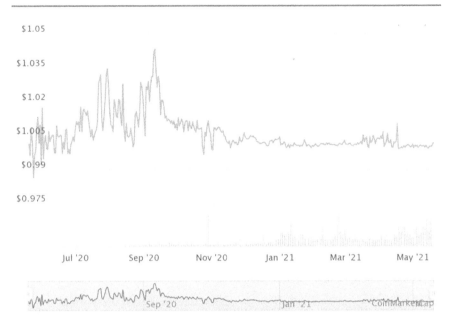

Fig. 3 DAI price chart. Source: coinmarkecap.com

Maker is a crypto project that creates a decentralized fully on-chain stablecoin called DAI, where 1 DAI is equal to 1 USD. Anybody can borrow DAIs by depositing ETH (or other cryptocurrencies) as collateral, such as a mortgage. The user can define the collateralization ratio starting at 150%. For example if the user chooses 200%, then he or she deposits 0.2 ETH ($200 at that moment) and he or she then receives 100 DAI. Overcollateralization is important to prevent the price falling of the deposit because if the price of the deposit falls under the collateralization ratio, then the position is automatically liquidated. For example if the 0.2 ETH that was deposited is now worth $120 under the 150% liquidation ratio, then the user loses the ETH and keeps the 100 DAI. This is called a collateral debt position (CDP) The Fig. 3 shows DAI is very close to 1$, particularly in recent times.

Ampleforth (AMPL) is another stablecoin that uses a less effective strategy. Instead of CDPs, Ampleforth has a smart contract that mints new AMPL when the price is higher than expected and burns AMPL when the price is less than expected. This idea is based more on supply reducing prices and less on supply increasing prices. Ampleforth is pegged to USD plus the Consumer Price Index to avoid inflation. As shown in the Fig. 4, the stability of the token remains questionable, but DAI or even USDT also had these stability problems in the beginning.

3.2   Lending and Borrowing

Lending and borrowing are key services in any financial system. Traditionally, banks offer loans, credits and mortgages to clients. Based on risk studies or backed

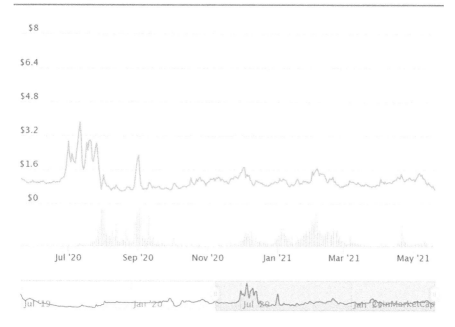

Fig. 4 Ampleforth price chart. Source: coinmarkecap.com

by collateral such as a real estate, the interest rate is adjusted to the situation. On the other hand, savers deposit money in banks and receive a yield. The bank acts as a central authority that makes decisions, and clients must trust these operations.

Of course, on a blockchain, two persons can agree on a relationship between the lender and borrower in their own terms. Indeed, there are centralized services that offer lending (deposit) and borrowing services (such as Nexo, Cello, Blockfi etc.). Additionally, centralized exchanges offer this kind of service. However, in this way, the client should trust the other party. This is centralized finance over blockchain.

When creating a lending and borrowing system in a decentralized way, the challenge is to create a decision-free mechanism of on-chain assets. The goal is to create a smart contract that allows users to lend and borrow without human intervention, such as risk studies. The assets must be on-chain, such as cryptocurrencies or nonfungible tokens. The problem with off-chain assets is the impossibility of assuring that they are transferred between the lender and borrower, as defined in the agreement. Therefore, to borrow one cryptocurrency, the user must deposit a collateral. Protocols like Aave or Compound are the actual leaders of this category.

The previous Fig. 5 is a screen capture from Aave, which shows for each token the market size (total deposits), the total borrowed, the annual percentage yield (APY) earned by depositors, and the annual percentage ratio (APR) borrowers pay in a fixed or variable way. The APR and APY depend on the market. If there are too many deposits and fee borrowers, such as WETH or WBTC, as seen in the image, then the APR/APY are very low; however, if the opposite is true, such as DAI, then the APR/APY are higher. The borrower must deposit a collateral to guarantee that it will return the principal plus interest. A typical use case is offering as a collateral a

Assets ▾	Market size ▾	Total borrowed ▾	Deposit APY ▾	Variable Borrow APR ▾	Stable Borrow APR ▾		
DAI	$ 1.14B	$ 905.74M	2.97% ⌾ 1.38 % APR	3.97% ⌾ 1.78 % APR	11.99 %	Deposit	Borrow
USD Coin (USDC)	$ 3.52B	$ 2.9B	2.83% ⌾ 1.38 % APR	3.66 % ⌾ 1.72 % APR	10.83 %	Deposit	Borrow
USDT Coin (USDT)	$ 703.24M	$ 521.93M	2.55% ⌾ 4.31 % APR	3.30% ⌾ 6.27 % APR	11.65 %	Deposit	Borrow
Gemini Dollar (GUSD)	$ 18.06M	$ 13.99M	2.70% ⌾ 4.74 % APR	3.87% ⌾ 6.12 % APR	–	Deposit	Borrow
Wrapped ETH (WETH)	$ 1.7B	$ 60.82M	0.02% ⌾ 1.33 % APR	0.44% ⌾ 2.00 % APR	3.55 %	Deposit	Borrow
WBTC Coin (WBTC)	$ 981.99M	$ 14.38M	0.01 % ⌾ 1.87 % APR	0.18 % ⌾ 7.36 % APR	3.23 %	Deposit	Borrow

Fig. 5 Screenshot of Aave user interface

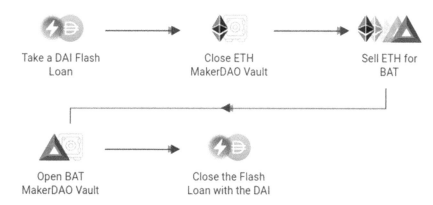

Fig. 6 Flash Loan use case: Collateral swap of a MakerDAO Vault. Source: Aave documentation

cryptocurrency that the user thinks is undervalued and receiving a loan in the form of a stablecoin, while not losing the cryptocurrency's rise in value.

Flash loans are a very specific loan in crypto. They are loans that are asked for and returned in the same smart contract. This is similar to asking a bank for a loan, using the money inside the building for trade in a very short period of time and then returning the money to the bank. The use case of flash loans is mainly for price arbitrage. For example if the same asset has a tiny different price in two different platforms, any expert could create a smart contract to ask for a huge amount of money to buy the asset in one platform and sell it on another. Fig. 6 is another use case in which a flash loan allows to close an ETH MakerDAO collateral debt position and create a new one in other cryptocurrency and then return de flash loan. The risk of these operations is very low because the smart contract is either fully executed (including asking for and returning the loan) or is not executed at all. In addition, they are very short-term loans (minutes). Therefore, fast and secure loans mean tiny interests with no collateral. Flash loans add huge liquidity to the system, which makes possible arbitrages that balance the whole DeFi ecosystem. Additionally, these loans can be used to stress and even hack some protocols (Qin et al., 2020), which makes them safer in the long run.

3.3 Decentralized Exchanges

The goal of centralized exchanges (CEXes) is to provide a way to trade and custody currencies and cryptocurrencies. Additionally, CEXes can offer other services, such as deposit yields, derivatives, credit cards and more. The problem with that perspective is that people must trust the company behind the exchange. Mt. Gox was the leader exchange in approximately 2014; however, the company was hacked and lost all of its funds, which totalled approximately 850,000 BTC ($450 million at the time, $42 billion at the time of writing). The critical risk is the custody of the funds, which crypto users can handle by themselves with a software called a wallet and a password. Therefore, the difficulty of fully decentralizing exchanges is the trading service.

A decentralized exchange (DEX) provides a way to trade cryptocurrencies (Fig. 7.b shows the interface to make a trade, also called swap) in a peer-to-peer manner using smart contracts. In addition, it aims to decrease default or scam risks, add privacy (avoiding the 'know your customer policy' that CEXes have), reduce the arbitrariness of the service conditions, and offer full transparency.

Of course, two parties can trade cryptocurrencies without a DEX, but a DEX offers the possibility to trade most cryptocurrencies at any time. Most DEXes use a form of automated market maker (AMM) (Wang, 2020) such that if one user wants to trade token A for token B, then that can be done because the DEX has a liquidity pool that contains those two tokens. The liquidity pool is filled with the deposits of many users (fig. 7.a shows the interface to provide liquidity to a pair of tokens). The trading user pays a fee for the trade, and the user that deposits tokens to the pool earns a proportional part of the total fees of the pool. The Fig. 8 below represent this process. For example in Uniswap, that fee is 0.3%; the deposits (total value lock) at the time of writing totalled $5 billion.

When a user provides liquidity with a pair of tokens (Fig. 7.a), the DEX gives back a receipt for the deposit. That receipt is in the form of an amount token, which are called liquidity provider tokens or simply LP tokens. LP tokens are a regular token, which means that they can be traded and used on the blockchain. At some point, some DEXes decided to incentivize people by giving rewards for specific pairs of tokens. The way to earn the reward is to stake the LP tokens after the deposit of that pair. This is called yield farming or just farming; it is a way to earn new tokens by simply staking some tokens on some specific DEXes.

3.4   Asset Management

The arrival of yield farming and a competition to attract liquidity providers to new platforms and their tokens brings about a new need, i.e. what would be the best way to stake the funds? Yearn Finance was created with that issue in mind. On the one hand, liquidity providers want to maximize their yield. On the other hand, experts propose strategies to maximize the yield earning fees if the strategy works well. In the middle is Yearn Finance; the platform was made with smart contracts to offer this possibility.

The Alpha Homora project brings about the possibility to earn yields with leverage. The combination of DeFi use cases such as farming and lending are good examples of how innovative this area can be based on openness and permissionlessness.

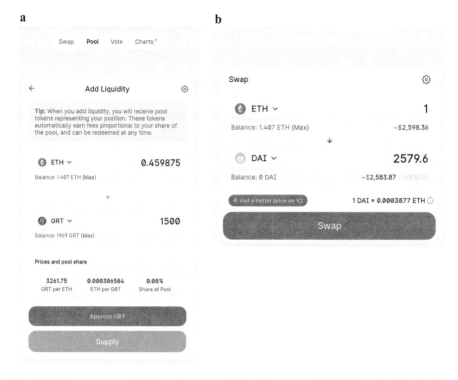

Fig. 7 (a) Screen capture of the interface to supply liquidity to a pool. (b) Uniswap interface for the traders

Fig. 8 Uniswap scheme of Uniswap pool, liquidity providers and traders. Source: Uniswap documentation

3.5   Funds

In traditional finance, funds are pools of money that have a specific purpose. For example a mutual fund is a pool made of investments by individuals managed by experts. They allocate funds to the assets they decide on according to the description of the fund. Another example is an ETF (exchange traded fund); in this case, instead of experts deciding on the investment, a basket of assets is made following the basket of assets in an index such as the S&P or Nasdaq to ensure that the fund follows the price of the index. An ETF can also follow the price of the basket of stocks from a category such as US small caps or European large caps, with defined the rules of picking the stocks.

The DeFi Pulse Index (DPI) is a token made with Set Protocol to represent the top DeFi protocols in Ethereum. It is like a DeFi ETF. It has clear rules that are coded in a smart contract to determine which assets to choose, and it weighs each asset depending on the capitalization. Each month, the tokens that compose the DPI are rebalanced following the rules. Set Protocol offers the possibility of anybody creating a basket of tokens similar to that of the DPI.

Enzyme Finance (formerly Melon) is an on-chain asset management protocol that enables anyone to set up and manage an on-chain fund or to invest in the funds. Enzyme, like Set Protocol, allows managers to create automatic strategies; however, unlike Set Protocol, Enzyme also allows manual decisions about the fund, thereby making the protocol closer to mutual funds than ETFs. The important part in both cases and in this category is that assets are staked on the protocol; thus, funds are fully backed. Indeed, managers can manage but cannot withdrawal to their own account during management because the funds are locked in the smart contract of the platform. Additionally, every action is traceable and public on the Ethereum blockchain.

3.6   Derivatives

A derivative is a contract whose value is derived from another underlying asset (commodity, currency, stock, index, bond etc.). Futures, options and swaps are some derivatives with very different use cases. Derivatives are very risky instruments that are mainly used to hedge or speculate.

Centralized exchanges provide derivatives in a centralized manner. Some derivatives need orderbooks that act extremely fast to handle orders and price variations. At this moment, most blockchains cannot offer this service at a reasonable speed. Therefore, either derivatives are not critically time-dependent, or the protocol uses a less decentralized strategy for orderbooks, which is usually a second layer or a parallel chain.

Hegic is an example of the first case. It offers an on-chain options trading protocol, which allows users to either buy ETH calls and place options as an individual holder (buyer) or sell ETH calls and place options as a liquidity provider (Fig. 9).

DYdX is an example of the second case. It is a DEX like Uniswap, but it also offers leverage trading (lending-borrowing) and perpetuals (similar to futures) on layer 2. There are many protocols that implement options in very different manners (Fig. 10).

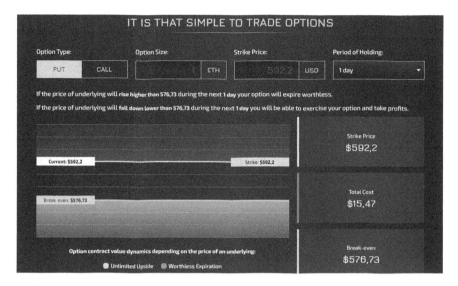

Fig. 9 Screen capture of the Hegic interface

Comparing Decentralized Options Platforms	American v. European	Cash v. Physical Settlement	Tokenized & Transferable	Liquidity: Order Book v. Pool	Protocol standardized v. User-customized	Collateralization/ Margin Requirement	Collateral Type
Opyn	American	Physical, Cash in V2	Yes	Uniswap Pool	Standardized	100%, less margin in V2	ETH + USDC
Hegic	American	Cash	No	Hegic Pool	Customized	100%	ETH + DAI
ACO	American	Physical and Cash	Yes	Order Book	Standardized	100%	ETH + USDC
Primitive	American	Physical	Yes	Primitive Pool	Standardized	100%	ETH + DAI
Opium	European	Cash	Yes	Order Book	Standardized	fixed	ETH + DAI + ERC-20s
Pods	American	Physical	Yes	Uniswap Pool	Standardized	100%	ETH + DAI + aUSDC
Synthetix	not released	Cash	Yes	Synthetix Debt Pool	Customized	100%	SNX
FinNexus	European	Cash	Yes	Order Book & Pool later	Standardized & Customized later	Dynamic margin, less than 100%	FNX + WAN + BTC + ERC-20s later

Fig. 10 'Coinmonks' comparison of Option protocols. Source: https://medium.com/coinmonks/a-comparison-of-decentralized-options-platforms-140b1421c71c

3.7   Synthetics

A synthetic asset is one that has the same price as another asset. It is widely considered a derivative asset. In crypto, synthetic assets play a key role because they allow us to represent off-chain assets inside the blockchain. For example to buy gold with Eth, people should sell Eth for fiat currency and then go to the market to

Fig. 11 Screen capture of the Synthetix interface

buy gold, thereby likely passing through centralized organizations such as banks and following KYC policies. If there is a synthetic token that represents gold, it is a simple on-chain transaction that becomes a fully decentralized transaction.

Synthetix is the main protocol on the Ethereum blockchain that allows the creation of synthetic assets called Synths. Synths examples are sXAU as a token that represents the gold price, sOIL representing the oil futures price, sNIKKEI tracking the price of Nikkei and sAAPL tracking the price of Apple stocks (see Fig. 11). There are also some inverse price tokens, such as iOIL, which represent the opposed behaviour of the price. To buy synthetic assets, first, the user must buy the Synthetix network token (SNX) and then stake it as a collateral with a 750% ratio (at the time of writing). Such a large ratio is important to keep the system healthy and avoid liquidations. Considering that all the synths are backed by the SNX token, when a user earns $1000 with a synth and another user loses $1000 with another Synth, then the system backing remains the same (Fig. 11).

3.8   Insurance

Insurance is a way to manage risks while hedging possible contingencies or losses. Typically, it is a contract called insurance policy between an insurer (mostly a company) and the insured (person or company) about the very well-defined circumstances in which compensation will be paid. Since the insurer and insured have opposite interests and the event covered could be debatable, both parties can use ordinary justice to solve a dispute.

Fig. 12 Screen capture of the Nexus Mutual interface

Decentralization over the blockchain of traditional insurance is a very difficult endeavour. Actually, most projects are partially decentralized, such as Nexus Mutual, the leading insurance project, which is a UK company that requires a KYC policy to use the service. Apart from that, the rest of the operations are decentralized. How? Anybody can request the coverage of an event from the available types, as seen in Fig. 12. Anybody can stake NXM (the protocol token) to earn yield, thus providing liquidity for the payments of the coverage. Anybody (under specific features such as expertise) can act as a judge of the protocol claims, thereby earning tokens for the job. These are the three parties involved in the service, and each party has its own incentives (Fig. 12).

As in traditional insurance, the most sensible part of the business is the resolution of insurer claims. In summary, Nexus Mutual randomly chooses several judges who see the on-chain data to decide whether the claim is legitimate or not. If the judges agree to either support or deny the claim, they are rewarded; if one or very few of them disagree, then they are punished. Since cover conditions are very clear and on-chain data are fully open, there are few possibilities of honest mistakes.

At the time of the writing of this article, there were three types of covers in Nexus Mutual, namely, the yield token, which covers the staked tokens in yield farming protocols if they are lost due to errors in the smart contract on the protocol; the protocol, which covers losses in any protocol if it is hacked or it has smart contract errors; and the custodian, who covers technical errors (not human errors) made by token custodians in exchanges or wallets. The limitations of coverage came from the need for unambiguity and the need for on-chain data. The company that is behind the Nexus Mutual claims that they are planning to release more types. Oracles, smart contract improvements, and ecosystem maturity will support these changes.

3.9 Oracles

Blockchain information is public, anonymous and related to transactions, addresses or protocols. It is possible to know how many tokens an address holds, how many transactions a smart contract has processed or when a transaction has been made. Etherscan.io is a website that easily watches all the on-chain information obtained by the Ethereum blockchain. However, what if we need real-world information? In the smart contract section, we offered the example of a bet made on a Lakers game. To execute the smart contract, we need to know if the Lakers won or lost. However, we cannot simply grab the result of the game from somewhere online and write it on the blockchain. Why not? Because we could have interests in faking the reality or simply make a mistake when writing the result. We need a way to insert out blockchain information (off-chain) into a smart contract inside blockchain (on-chain) in a truthful way. We need an oracle.

Oracles bring off-chain information to on-chain without the need to trust a single party. They use the typical scheme in a blockchain of reward/punishment on a random group of nodes that check information outside the blockchain (mainly on the internet). If all of them offer the same information to the blockchain, it is considered truthful information; in this case, they are rewarded, and the information is written on the blockchain. If they do not offer the same information, then the nodes trying to fake information are punished. The requester of the information is who pays the effort (rewards to validators) to bring the information on-chain. This is how Chainlink works, which is the main decentralized oracle network.

Oracles are not a financial service like the rest of DeFi. However, they are the door to the real world and are responsible for enlarging what a smart contract over blockchain can do. On the other hand, they are considered a weak spot if they work badly, as some cases have proven (Qin et al., 2020). In summary, the power and future growth of DeFi will rely on the solidity of the oracles used.

4   DeFi and Startups

DeFi is an open-source, open-platform and permissionless technology that aims to remove middlemen. Is there space for businesses and startups in the decentralized paradigm? Absolutely yes, but in a very different way.

Most of the projects cited in this chapter were created by startups or by people who developed a startup later, some of them with venture capital investments. According to explodingtopics.com, the following are some of the most prominent DeFi startups:

- Uniswap, 2018 Brookling (USA), $11 million (Series A).
- Compund, 2017 San Francisco (USA), $25 million (Series A).
- MakerDAO, 2014 California (USA), $27 million (Series Unknown).
- Aave, 2017 London (UK), $24 million (Initial Coin Offering).
- Synthetix, 2017 Sydney (Australia), $12 million (Venture Round).

Additionally, DeFi protocols are growing exponentially in terms of total value locked (deposits peak $80 billion, see Fig. 13), fees generated (only Uniswap generates more than $1 million a day), or the market cap of the DeFi tokens (at the time of writing: $100 billion).

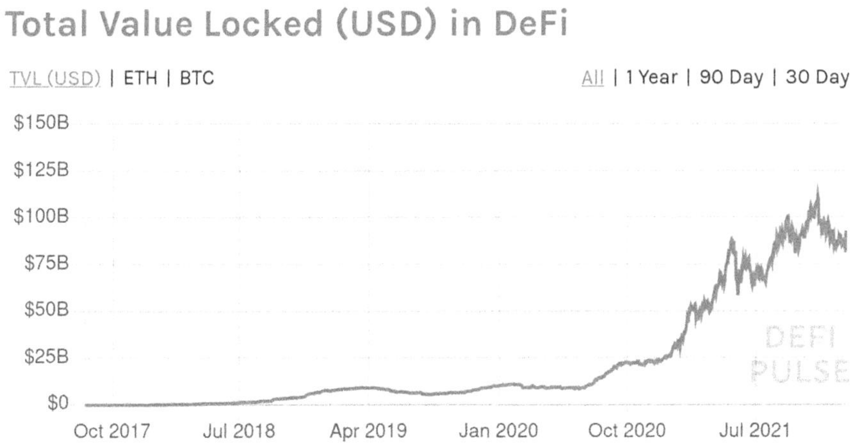

Total Value Locked (USD) in Defi

TVL (USD) | ETH | BTC   All | 1 Year | 90 Day | 30 Day

Fig. 13 Ethereum Defi Total Value Locked in USD. Source: Defi Pulse

Creating a leading project in Defi space is extremely difficult, not because of legal and capital entry barriers, as seen with traditional financial projects, but because of the need for very scarce and specialized talented people and new knowledge. Thus, the creation of a project from scratch will likely need capital to make a good team, at the bare minimum.

A typical way to create a software startup is to build and own the software and infrastructure (servers) and then sell the service to clients (SaaS model). In short, Defi removes the owning part or at least transforms it. The code is public, and once released, the code is unstoppable (there are some nuances here that we cannot cover), and the infrastructure is the blockchain, which is not controlled by the company.

Regarding Defi and startups, there is a dual reality, namely, the on-chain project and the off-chain company. The on-chain project is represented by a token or a smart contract that follows the rules of the blockchain and the contract. The off-chain company is a legal company that has some sort of influence in the community that created, impulsed, improved and expanded the on-chain project. The relation between the two is something that is unclear; in the roar of the Defi explosion, this lack of clarity is not yet a public debate. However, it very likely will become one.

One of the most rewarding parts of building a Defi project is token creation. Any project can create a new token or mint new tokens either before the launch of the project (ICO, IEO, IDO) (OECD, 2019) or after. Then, part of the allocation of the token goes to the team that built the project, the investors, the advisors or even the community. An example of Uniswap token allocation can be seen in Fig 14 and 15. For example Aave rises money selling tokens before a project launch, and Uniswap releases a token after several months of working without it. Again, avoiding many nuances, tokens can be seen as stocks of crypto projects. Traditional startups have a long journey to obtain a public IPO; however, in the Defi context, companies could be public from day one (Figs. 14 and 15).

Genesis UNI Allocation

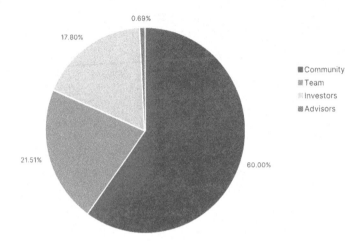

Fig. 14 UNI allocation. Source: Uniswap documentation

+10 Year Inflation UNI Allocation

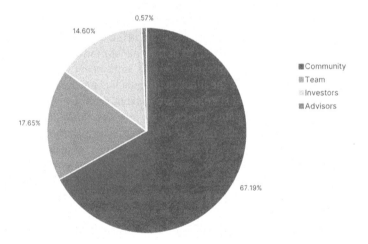

Fig. 15 UNI allocation. Source: Uniswap documentation

From a traditional business perspective, it seems very rare that the largest taxi company does not own a single car (Uber), that the largest accommodation provider does not own a single hotel (Airbnb) and that the largest media company does not generate content (Facebook). DeFi could be creating a paradigm in which financial software companies, instead of owning software and capital, manage communities of users that are ruled by public smart contracts on blockchains that align incentives to create markets of financial services, thereby reducing the need for trust.

References

Ante, L., Fiedler, I., & Strehle, E. (2021). The influence of stablecoin issuances on cryptocurrency markets. *Finance Research Letters, 41*, 101867.
Bach, L. M., Mihaljevic, B., & Zagar, M. (2018, May). *Comparative analysis of blockchain consensus algorithms*. In 2018 41st International Convention on Information and Communication Technology, Electronics and Microelectronics (MIPRO) (pp. 1545–1550). IEEE.
Baur, D. G., Hong, K., & Lee, A. D. (2018). Bitcoin: Medium of exchange or speculative assets? *Journal of International Financial Markets, Institutions and Money, 54*, 177–189. https://doi.org/10.1016/j.intfin.2017.12.004
Chen, Y., & Bellavitis, C. (2020). Blockchain disruption and decentralized finance: The rise of decentralized business models. *Journal of Business Venturing Insights, 13*, e00151. https://doi.org/10.1016/j.jbvi.2019.e00151
Gudgeon, L., Werner, S. M., Perez, D., & Knottenbelt, W. J. (2020). *DeFi protocols for loanable funds: Interest rates, liquidity and market efficiency*. Retrieved from https://arxiv.org/abs/200 6.13922
José Luis Romero Ugarte. (2018). *Distributed ledger technology (DLT): Introduction*. Economic Bulletin, Banco de España, issue DEC, pp. 1–11. Retrieved from https://www.bde.es/f/webbde/SES/Secciones/Publicaciones/InformesBoletinesRevistas/ArticulosAnaliticos/2018/T4/descargar/Files/beaa1804-art26e.pdf
López-Cabarcos, M. Á., Pérez-Pico, A. M., Piñeiro-Chousa, J., & Šević, A. (2021). Bitcoin volatility, stock market and investor sentiment. Are they connected? *Finance Rsesearch Letters, 38*, 101399. https://doi.org/10.1016/j.frl.2019.101399
OECD. (2019). *Initial Coin Offerings (ICOs) for SME Financing*. https://www.oecd.org/finance/ICOs-for-SME-Financing.pdf
Qin, K., Zhou, L., Livshits, B., & Gervais, A. (2020). Attacking the DeFi ecosystem with flash loans for fun and profit. *arXiv preprint arXiv:2003.03810*.
Schär, F. (2020). Decentralized finance: On blockchain- and smart contract-based financial markets. *SSRN Electronic Journal*. https://doi.org/10.2139/ssrn.3571335
Wang, Y. (2020). Automated market makers for decentralized finance (defi). *arXiv preprint arXiv:2009.01676*.
Yaga, D., Mell, P., Roby, N., & Scarfone, K. (2019). Blockchain technology overview. *arXiv preprint arXiv:1906.11078*.
Yin, L., Nie, J., & Han, L. (2021). Understanding cryptocurrency volatility: The role of oil market shocks. *International Review of Economics and Finance, 72*, 233–253. https://doi.org/10.1016/j.iref.2020.11.013

Whitepapers

Aave, https://github.com/aave/aave-protocol/blob/master/docs/Aave_Protocol_Whitepaper_v1_0.pdf
Alpha Homora, https://alphafinancelab.gitbook.io/alpha-homora-v2/
Ampleforth, https://www.ampleforth.org/paper/
Bitcoin, https://bitcoin.org/bitcoin.pdf
Compound, https://compound.finance/documents/Compound.Whitepaper.pdf
DeFI Pulse Index, https://docs.indexcoop.com/our-products/defi-pulse-index
Dydx, https://docs.dydx.exchange

Enzyme Finance, https://docs.enzyme.finance/
Ethereum, https://github.com/ethereum/wiki/wiki/White-Paper
Hegic, https://github.com/hegic/whitepaper
Maker, https://makerdao.com/en/whitepaper/#overview-of-the-dai-stablecoin-system
Synthetix, https://docs.synthetix.io/litepaper
Uniswap, https://uniswap.org/whitepaper-v3.pdf
Yearn Finance, https://docs.yearn.finance/

.

9 783030 94060